Lessons for the Young

ECONOMIST

The Ludwig von Mises Institute dedicates this volume
to all of its generous donors
and wishes to thank these Patrons, in particular:

Jeremy and Helen Davis
Scott Scharpen
Vijay Boyapati
David Atherton
Mary Diane Dolan

Lessons for the Young
ECONOMIST

ROBERT P. MURPHY

LvMI
MISES INSTITUTE

ISBN: 978-1-933550-88-6

For information write the Ludwig von Mises Institute, 518 West Magnolia Avenue, Auburn, Alabama 36832. Mises.org

Contents

PART II: CAPITALISM: THE MARKET ECONOMY

Acknowledgments

This book was launched in a meeting with Doug French and Jeff Tucker of the Mises Institute. At every step in its writing, I consulted with Zachariah Crossen, a history teacher who ran the sample chapters by his own (junior high) students to make sure the tone and language were correct.

Brian Shelley and Blake Stephenson provided useful feedback on an early draft. Tim Terrell went through the entire manuscript and provided many suggestions to improve it. Finally, I'd like to thank Sam Torode for the artwork, which was not only done excellently but also quickly (because I didn't give him much notice).

Part I

FOUNDATIONS

LESSON 1

Thinking Like an Economist

In this lesson you will learn:

- What it means to "think like an economist."
- The types of questions that economics can help explain.
- Why it is important for everyone to understand basic economics.

Thinking Like an Economist

This book is a manual for a new way of looking at the world. After you master the lessons contained within these pages, you will be able to understand events in ways that your untrained peers will miss. You will notice patterns that they will overlook. The ability to think like an economist is a crucial component of your education. Only with sound economic thinking will you be able to make sense of how the world works. To make responsible decisions regarding grand political ideas as well as your occupation and mundane household finances, you must first decide to learn basic economics.

Creative and careful thinkers throughout human history have developed various disciplines for studying the world. Each discipline (or subject) offers its own perspective as history unfolds before us. For a complete education, the student must become acquainted with some of the most important findings in each field. Economics has proven itself to be worthy of universal study. A well-rounded young adult will have studied not only algebra, Dante, and photosynthesis, but will also be able to explain why prices rise.

Every subject you study will contain a mixture of knowledge that is deemed important for its own sake, as well as practical applications that may prove useful in your daily life. For example, every student should have a basic understanding of astronomy, since it illustrates the grandeur of the universe; but basic astronomy can also come in handy when guiding a wayward yachtsman who has lost sight of land. For a different example, consider mathematics. The study of advanced calculus is rewarding for its sheer elegance (though some students might consider the reward inadequate for the effort required!). But everyone needs to know basic arithmetic in order to function in society.

We will see the same pattern holds in the subject of economics. It is, in a word, simply fascinating to learn that there are underlying principles or "laws" that explain the operation of any economy, whether in ancient Rome, the Soviet Union, or a county fair in Boise, Idaho. Yet economics also has much to offer in practical guidance of your daily life. Knowledge of economics, by itself, will not make you rich, but it's a good bet that *ignoring* the lessons of this book will keep you poor.

Economists look at the world in a unique way. Picture the crowds waiting to ride a popular amusement park roller coaster. A biologist surveying the scene might notice that people begin sweating as they approach their turn to get onto the ride. A physicist might notice that the first hill has to be the tallest. A sociologist might notice that the riders are arranged in groups of the same ethnicity. And an economist might notice that the first and last cars have much longer lines than the others, probably because people don't like waiting but they also prefer riding in the very front or the very rear.

The economic perspective is not useful in every situation. On the soccer field or at the prom, the lessons in this book will not prove as relevant. But in your life you will encounter many situations of critical importance when your decisions will need to be informed by sound economics. It is not necessary for everyone to *become* an economist. It is important for everyone to learn how to think like an economist.

Is Economics a Science?

In this book, we adopt the view that economics constitutes an independent *science*, just as surely as chemistry and biology are distinct fields of study. As we go through the lessons in this book, we will do so *scientifically*, meaning that we will use an objective set of "tools" for our analysis, that do not rely on particular ethical or cultural assumptions. The principles or laws of economics are the same, whether the economist is a Republican or a communist, and whether he lives in New Zealand or Somalia.

Warning! When we say economics is a science, we do *not* mean that we conduct experiments to test economic laws, the way a nuclear physicist studies the results of smashing atoms in a particle accelerator. There are important differences between a social science such as economics, versus a *natural* science such as physics. We will explain this in more detail in Lesson 2, but for now we simply want to caution you that basic economic principles can be discovered through mental reasoning. It wouldn't make sense to go out and "test" the laws of economics, just as it doesn't make sense to use a ruler to go out and "test" the various proofs that you might learn in a geometry class. The upshot of all this is that the lessons in this book will stand the test of time—there is no danger that a new experimental finding will overturn them tomorrow. In practice, professional economists make all sorts of conjectures, many of which turn out to be wrong. But the core body of economic theory—the types of laws and concepts contained in this book—is not testable; it's simply a way of viewing the world.

Despite the possible confusion of economic science with a natural science, nonetheless we use the term *science* because it's important to stress that there really are objective laws of economics. When politicians ignore the teachings of economics, their programs run into disaster—imagine the chaos if NASA ignored the laws of physics!

The Scope and Boundaries of Economic Science

It's a common misconception for people to think, "Economics is the study of money." Yes, economics obviously has a lot to say about money, and in fact one of the basic purposes of economics is to explain the different prices—which are quoted in units of money—of various goods and services being sold in the market place.

Contrary to this popular misconception, economics is broader than the mere study of money. In its widest scope, economics can be defined as the study of exchanges. This would include all of the exchanges in a normal market setting, where the seller hands over a physical object or provides a service, and in return the buyer hands over the appropriate amount of money. But economics also studies cases of **barter**, where the traders exchange goods or services directly with each other, without using money at all.

Pushing it to the extreme, economics even has a lot to say about cases where a *single, isolated person* takes actions to improve his or her situation. This is often called "Crusoe economics," after the fictional character Robinson Crusoe who was shipwrecked on an (apparently) deserted island. We will study Crusoe economics in Lesson 4. It will be clear that even an isolated person behaves "economically" because he takes what nature has given him and *exchanges* the status quo for an environment that he hopes will be more pleasant.

The common theme running throughout all of the examples of exchanges is the concept of **scarcity**. Scarcity can be succinctly explained by the observation that there are limited resources and unlimited desires. Even Bill Gates faces **tradeoffs**; he cannot literally do whatever he wants. If he takes his wife out to a fancy restaurant, he has reduced his options (ever so slightly) and has diminished his ability to buy other things in the future. We can describe the situation by saying, "Bill Gates needs to *economize* on his resources, because they are finite."

It is the universal fact of scarcity that gives rise to what people have termed the "economic problem": As a society, how should we decide which goods and services to produce, with the limited resources at our disposal? In Lesson 5, we will see how the institution of private property solves this problem. But it is *scarcity* that causes the problem in the first place.

Warning! Economics does *not* study a hypothetical "economic man," who cares only about acquiring material possessions or earning money. This is another common misunderstanding of what economics is all about. Unfortunately, there is some truth to this stereotype because many economists actually do build models of the economy that are filled with fictitious people who are very selfish and will only act altruistically if they are forced to do so. But in this book, you will not be learning any theories of that flavor. Instead, the lessons in this book do not depend on people being penny-pinchers; the laws we will develop in these pages apply to Mother Teresa as much as they apply to Donald Trump.

Economic science, as taught in this book, does *not* tell workers that they should take whatever job pays the most money, nor does it tell business owners that they must consider only financial issues when running their operations. These points will be made clearer during the subsequent lessons themselves, but we must stress up front that there is no "economic man" in the following pages; we are always discussing the principles that explain the choices of real people in the face of scarcity. The principles involve the fact that people *have* desires in the face of limited resources, but the principles are broad enough to cover people with any desires.

The Economics of Real People

Economics deals with the real actions of real men. Its [laws] refer neither to ideal nor to perfect men, neither to the phantom of a fabulous economic man (homo oeconomicus) nor to the statistical notion of an average man. . . . Man with all his weaknesses and limitations, every man as he lives and acts, is the subject matter of [economics].

—Ludwig von Mises, *Human Action*
(Auburn, Ala.: Ludwig von Mises Institute, 1998), pp. 646–47

Economics studies and tries to explain how people make exchanges. A shipwrecked sailor wants to "exchange" some sticks and two rocks for a crackling fire, while a missionary wants to "exchange" his leisure time for a grueling trip to a remote jungle where the residents have never seen a Bible. A complete theory of exchanges must cover these types of cases too, not just the more familiar example of a broker exchanging 100 stock shares for $2,000.

Why Study Economics?

One reason to study economics is that it's simply interesting. When you stop and think about what happens every day in a modern economy, it should take your breath away. Consider the bustling metropolis of Manhattan: Millions of people work on this tiny island that is less than 23 square miles in land area. Obviously there is not enough food produced on the island itself, to feed these hordes. At first some readers may not understand this claim—some of the finest restaurants in the world are in Manhattan! But these exquisite restaurants rely on vendors to give them the raw materials to produce their very expensive dishes. If invading Martians placed an impenetrable plastic bubble around Manhattan (with small holes in the plastic to allow for ventilation), within two months hundreds of thousands of New Yorkers would be dead from starvation.

Yet in the real world—where no Martian bubble obstructs trade—farm produce, refined gasoline, and other items are shipped into Manhattan on a daily basis, allowing the inhabitants to not only eke out a bare survival, but actually to thrive. The workers on the tiny island of Manhattan transform the materials at their disposal into some of the most highly valued goods and services on the planet—think of the expensive jewelry, clothing, financial services, legal work, and Broadway performances "produced" in Manhattan. When you consider the incredible complexity of these processes, it is a wonder that its operation is normally so flawless that we take it for granted. The lessons in this book will shed some light on how the market economy achieves such feats, day in and day out.

Another reason to study economics is that it will help you make decisions in your personal and professional life. Of course, the lessons in this book will not *by themselves* make you rich. Rather, they will give you a framework to help analyze your plans so that you are more likely to achieve your objectives. For an analogy, studying geometry alone will not allow you to become a professional engineer, designing four-lane bridges. But nobody would want to drive on a bridge designed by someone who is ignorant of geometry.

Beyond its intrinsic beauty and practical applications to your own life, economics is a crucial topic because we live in a society plagued by an activist government. Unlike other scientific disciplines, the basic truths of economics must be taught to enough people in order to preserve society itself. It really doesn't matter if the man on the street thinks quantum mechanics is a hoax; the physicists can go on with their research without the approval of the average Joe. But if most people believe that minimum wage laws help the poor, or that low interest rates cure a recession, then the trained economists are helpless to avert the damage that these policies will inflict on society.

For this reason, it is the young adult's duty to learn basic economics. The lessons in this book will show you how.

Lesson Recap . . .

- This book will teach you to think like an economist. Different subjects (chemistry, biology, etc.) offer different perspectives on the world. Some perspectives are more useful in certain situations than others. Economics is a distinct field, or science, and it has important insights on how the social world works.

- Economics is the study of exchanges. In a modern economy, the most familiar exchanges involve money, but economic principles apply to any type of exchange.

- Every citizen should understand basic economics because of the danger of destructive government policies that ignore the lessons in this book.

NEW TERMS

Barter: A situation where people exchange goods and services directly, rather than using money in an intermediary transaction.

Scarcity: The condition of desires exceeding the available resources to satisfy them. Scarcity is a universal fact requiring people to make exchanges.

Tradeoffs: The unfortunate fact (caused by scarcity) that making one choice means that other choices become unavailable.

STUDY QUESTIONS

1. Can economics make you rich?

2. Is economics a science? Why or why not?

3. Does scarcity affect everyone?

4. Do the laws of economics still work inside a maximum security prison?

5. *Isn't it just as important for the average person to understand particle physics, since much of the funding for this research comes from government grants?

*Difficult material.

**More challenging material.

LESSON 2

How We Develop Economic Principles

In this lesson you will learn:

- The difference between a purposeful action versus mindless behavior.
- The difference between a social science and a natural science.
- Why the methods used to develop basic economics are different from those used in physics or chemistry.

Purposeful Action versus Mindless Behavior

When we look at the world and try to make some sense of it, one of the most basic and crucial distinctions we all make—usually without even realizing it—is the difference between purposeful action versus mindless behavior. When describing the trajectory of a baseball, we might mention things like mass, velocity, and air friction. We *don't* say that the baseball "wants to move in a parabola," or that the ball "gets bored with flying and eventually decides to land." This would be nonsense talk to modern ears, and would strike us as very unscientific. But suppose that instead of a baseball, we are describing the motions of a jet aircraft. In that case, we would have no problem saying that the pilot "wants to avoid the turbulence" or that he "is running low on fuel and decides to land."

This difference in how we describe the two events reflects a fundamental decision we make when interpreting the world around us. When we observe events, we can either attribute them to natural laws, *or* we can explain them (at least in part) by reference to the *intentions* of a conscious being. In short, we can choose whether to believe that another *mind* is at work.

We are here touching on some very deep philosophical questions, and obviously we are not going to give you "the final word" in this short lesson. But in order to make sense of economic theory, to give it a solid foundation, we need to be aware of the distinction between **purposeful action** versus mindless behavior. The laws of economics apply to the former, not to the latter. As we will see in Lesson 3, economics always involves the operation of at least one mind, meaning an intelligence that has conscious goals and will take steps to influence the material world in order to achieve those goals.

The difference between purposeful action versus mindless behavior is not simply the difference between human beings and "inanimate" matter. Various movements of a human being's physical body can be examples of mindless behavior, too. For example, if I tell you, "I'll give you $20 if you raise your right leg," then we would interpret your subsequent behavior as an intentional response, where you *purposely* moved your leg because you *wanted* the money. But if your doctor whacks your right knee with a hammer to test your reflexes, the resulting movement in your leg would not be an example of purposeful action. Although your nervous system and brain were involved, we wouldn't really say that your *mind* was involved. (Note that *brain* and *mind* are very different things, and that difference is crucial to this lesson.)

The lessons in this book apply to purposeful actions performed by conscious people who have goals in mind. Sometimes the boundary line between what is "conscious action" and "reflexive behavior" can be blurry, but that won't really detract from the principles in this book. It's true, a baseball outfielder might not be fully aware of the mental operations he performs when throwing the ball to second base. But he is very definitely trying to throw out the runner, because he wants his team to win the game.

Even if he "miscalculates" and overthrows the base, all the lessons in this book apply to his intentional action, because he is a conscious being trying to exchange one situation for a different one that he thinks will be more desirable.

The economic principles in this book are not confined to "perfectly rational people." The lessons in these pages apply to real people who use their minds to make exchanges in the real world every day.

The Social versus the Natural Sciences

Economics is a "social science," meaning that it studies people and aspects of society. Other social sciences include psychology, sociology, and anthropology. The natural sciences, on the other hand, study aspects of the natural world. The natural sciences include physics, chemistry, biology, astronomy, and meteorology.

Because of their different subject matter, the social sciences focus on purposeful action, as described in the preceding section, while the natural sciences focus on mindless behavior. Even though he might not even be aware that he is doing it, the social scientist's explanations and theories at least implicitly rely on the hypothesis that there are other minds at work, influencing events. In sharp contrast, with the notable exception of biology, the natural scientist typically doesn't refer to a conscious intelligence when explaining events in his field of expertise.

This awareness of other minds, and the fact that other thinking humans have their individual motivations, pervades the social sciences. It's not confined to the formation of theories to explain events, either: Even the raw "facts" of the social sciences are themselves mental things, and not purely natural or physical. For example, a sociologist might come up with a theory relating an increase in the crime rate with the increase in the rate of divorce. But in order for the sociologist to even collect data to test this theory, she needs to "get inside other people's minds" in order to know which events should be *classified* as crimes and divorces in the first place; these are not mere brute facts of nature.

Even the "Facts" of the Social Sciences Are Related to the Mind

Take such things as tools, food, medicine, weapons, words, sentences, communications, and acts of production. . . . I believe these to be fair samples of the kind of objects of human activity which constantly occur in the social sciences. It is easily seen that all these concepts . . . refer not to some objective properties possessed by the things, or which the observer can find out about them, but to views which some other person holds about the things. These objects cannot even be defined in physical terms, because there is no single physical property which any one member of a class must possess. . . . [T]hey can be defined only by indicating relations between three terms: a purpose, somebody who holds that purpose, and an object which that person thinks to be a suitable means for that purpose.

—Friedrich A. Hayek, *Individualism and Economic Order* (Chicago: University of Chicago Press, 1948), pp. 59–60

For example, if Sally runs her car over Joe and he dies, this may or may not count as a homicide. If Sally had a heart attack five seconds before the crash, it was probably not a crime, but rather just an accident. On the other hand, if the cops arrive at the scene to hear Sally yelling, "That's the last time you'll cheat on me!" then it's time to read Sally her rights. Notice that ultimately it is Sally's *mind* that makes the difference; the sociologist needs to make guesses about *what Sally consciously intended* in order to know if a crime occurred. No amount of physical description per se can decide the matter, except insofar as the description sheds light on *what Sally was thinking* when the car struck Joe. Her mental will has the power to transform a regular car into a *murder weapon*. To stress the point one last time: Nothing physical changes in the composition of the car during this transformation; the physicist and chemist wouldn't notice anything happening to the molecules forming the car. On the contrary, when we say that Sally "turned the vehicle into a murder weapon," we are rendering a judgment concerning the intangible, directly unobservable state of Sally's mind. The physical movements of Sally's hands and feet as she controlled the car are not the crucial issue; it is her conscious *intentions* that determine whether we need to add one more homicide to the running total.

As the example of Sally hitting Joe with her car illustrates, even the "raw facts" of the social sciences are tinged with our understanding of other people's minds. In contrast, typically in the natural sciences neither the raw facts, nor the theories developed to explain them, rely on an appreciation of the intentions of other thinking beings. The natural scientist can look out upon the physical world and try to come up with explanations of its "mindless" behavior.

The Success of the Natural Sciences versus the Social Sciences

There is a sharp difference between sciences such as physics, chemistry, and biology on the one hand, versus sciences such as psychology, sociology, and anthropology on the other. People refer to the former as "hard" and the latter as "soft," and—especially among the hard scientists!—there is a general feeling that the so-called hard sciences are more rigorous and indeed "scientific" than the so-called soft sciences. Generally speaking, the smartest and most celebrated scientists in the world are found in the hard sciences; besides the obvious icon of Einstein, the physicists Richard Feynman and Stephen Hawking have also captured the popular imagination. In contrast, it is not nearly as prestigious to win awards in psychology, and few people could even *name* the top sociologists of the last century. While some people might condemn the particular physicists who helped create atomic weapons, even so the overwhelming majority support *physics* itself. Yet in another sharp contrast, many people are skeptical and even hostile to some of the social sciences, particularly economics and psychiatry.

What is going on here? If we hadn't known the answer already, we might have expected things to be the reverse, where public opinion revered the scientists who studied *people* and not mindless particles.

One possible answer is that the social sciences have justified some pretty awful things, such as electroshock therapy for people incarcerated against their will, and the government-sponsored slaughter of millions of pigs during the Great Depression while Americans starved. So maybe these types of episodes are the reason many people distrust psychiatrists and economists. But again, why don't people also tend to blame physicists for Hiroshima, or the chemists for gunpowder?

We suggest the reason is that the physics and chemistry behind powerful weapons are *right*. The physicists said to the military, "If you drop this object from an airplane, it will induce a fission reaction that will release an incredible amount of heat." And the physicists were perfectly accurate in their predictions. In sharp contrast, the psychiatrists told the courts, "Give us authority to imprison people we think are mentally ill, and allow us to inject them with drugs and perform other experiments on them. This will make them well, and yield a society with adjusted people who do not exhibit aberrant, anti-social behavior." Many of the supposedly top-notch economists too told governments during the 20th and 21st centuries: "Give us control of the printing press, and we will spare the world any more ravaging depressions and rampant price inflation." Obviously, the track record of the psychiatrists and most influential economists is not nearly as laudable as that of the natural scientists.

For some reason, it seems that even the most accomplished geniuses in the social sciences can lead their disciplines down dead-ends, where more and more of the experts in the field (as well as the general public) begin to suspect that the "state of the art" is a waste of time. Many people would agree that "psychiatry was doing all right . . . until Sigmund Freud," or that, "Economics took a major wrong turn when John Maynard Keynes came on the scene." Yet almost nobody would say, "Isaac Newton did a lot of great work in physics, until that nutjob Einstein came along and ruined it."

One important reason for this gulf between the success and prestige of the natural sciences on the one hand, versus the mediocre results and hostility to the social sciences on the other, is that the objects of study in the natural sciences are fairly simple, and their behavior seems to be governed by a concise set of rules. Consequently, the hard sciences can (typically) rely on *controlled experiments* to evaluate their theories. This is why it's much less likely that physics will go down a cul-de-sac the way many people think Freudian psychology or Keynesian economics did. Physical theories make predictions about objects in the material world. It would be very difficult for a newfangled yet ultimately inferior theory to sweep the profession in a hard science (such as physics), because its inferiority would be demonstrated repeatedly in experiments. Einstein famously resisted some of the philosophical implications of quantum theory, but no physicist (including him) could argue with the accuracy of the theory's predictions about experimental measurements made on subatomic particles.

Since subatomic particles don't (as far as we know) have minds, in order to understand their behavior—in order to "explain" subatomic particles—a theory in physics can't be asked to do anything more than to predict, with greater and greater precision and accuracy, what these particles will do in various circumstances. Now we should point out that in actual practice, things are not so simple in day-to-day physics. One theory may yield better predictions in a few experiments, while another theory may be simpler and more elegant. Some physicists may "believe in" the more elegant theory, and search for possible flaws in the experiments that cast doubts on their preferred theory. Even so, in the long run a theory in the hard sciences that systematically and unambiguously yields better predictions will eventually displace its rivals.

Most professionals in the social sciences think that the same method—the "scientific method"—should be used in their fields as well. However, the problem is that, quite literally, the objects of their study have minds of their own. It has proved fiendishly difficult to come up with a set of concise laws that accurately predict the behavior of people in various circumstances. In the social sciences, especially economics, things are so much more complicated that in many cases it is simply impossible to perform a truly controlled experiment.

To illustrate this important difference between the natural sciences and economics, first suppose two groups of physicists are arguing about the strength of the electric charge on a certain particle. After conducting an experiment using a clever new technique, one group in Australia announces that the previous estimate needs to be revised. However, the rival group of physicists argues that the Australian experiment is flawed, because the laboratory's proximity to the South Pole distorted the measurements. They settle the dispute by conducting the same experiment at several different latitudes, to see if the measured results move closer to the previous estimate as the laboratory gets closer to the equator. The crucial assumptions behind all of this research are that the underlying laws governing the particles are the same, and that the experimenters can hold every other (relevant) factor constant while isolating the effects of the magnetic charge emanating from the earth's poles. The story we just told gives an idea of why physics seems to "work" so well; there really is good reason to suppose that over the years, the physicists will develop theories with greater and greater accuracy in predicting how the physical world works.

Things are not nearly as straightforward when two groups of *economists* argue over rival theories. For example, one group of economists—the **Keynesians**—believe that the Great Depression was caused by a collapse in "aggregate demand," and that President Herbert Hoover and then Franklin D. Roosevelt should have pushed through massive government **deficits**—spending borrowed money—to counteract the slump. A different group of economists—the **Austrians**—disagree strongly, and instead think that the initial crash in 1929 was caused by a preceding "boom" engineered by the Federal Reserve, which is the U.S. central bank established by the government. According to the Austrians, Hoover and Roosevelt made the Depression drag on for more than a decade with their misguided interventionist policies. The Austrians dispute the Keynesian deficit theory, pointing out that Hoover and FDR ran what were at the time *record high* (peacetime) budget deficits during their administrations, which coincided with the slowest and most agonizing recovery in U.S. economic history. The Keynesians counter that, large as the deficits were, the government "obviously" didn't borrow and spend *enough*, as proved by the lingering unemployment.

At this early stage of the book, we have not yet mastered the concepts to proceed further with this actual dispute. (In subsequent lessons, you will learn the tools you need to better appreciate the two sides of the argument.) For now, the point is that the *dispute remains unresolved*, even though professional economists have been arguing about the causes of the Great Depression for more than seventy years. The controversy won't die, because the exact conditions of the world economy in the late 1920s were unique. Economists can't test the Keynesian theory by, say, holding everything else constant except doubling the U.S. federal budget deficit in 1932, in order to observe the effect on the unemployment rate.

Federal Budget Deficits vs. Unemployment, 1930 – 1939

	1930	1931	1932	1933	1934	1935	1936	1937	1938	1939
Budget Deficit (% of GDP)	-0.8% (surplus)	0.6	4.0	4.5	5.9	4.0	5.5	2.5	0.1	3.2
Unemployment Rate	8.9%	15.9	23.6	24.9	21.7	20.1	17.0	14.3	19.0	17.2

Sources: The American Presidency Project (http://www.presidency.ucsb.edu/data/budget.php) and the Bureau of Labor Statistics

Economists Can't Agree on the Right Medicine

[T]he proper injunction to government in a depression is cut the budget and leave the economy strictly alone.

– Austrian School economist Murray Rothbard

Just as we saved our way into depression, we must squander our way out of it.

– *Business Week* economist Virgil Jordan, writing in 1932

Quoted in Robert P. Murphy, *The Politically Incorrect Guide to the Great Depression and the New Deal* (Washington, D.C.: Regnery, 2009), pp. 52,57

It is no doubt true that economists who, for moral or political reasons, endorse larger government spending, will tend to subscribe to the Keynesian arguments about the causes of the Great Depression. It is also true that opponents of "Big Government" will tend to be attracted to economic doctrines that stress the benefits of low taxation and slim government budgets.

But it is the inability to perform controlled experiments that allows the persistence of such diametrically opposed economic theories, with both camps firmly convinced that they are right and their opponents are either dishonest or sloppy. These passions are on a much tighter leash in the hard natural sciences, because in those disciplines the facts "speak for themselves" to a much greater degree than in the social sciences.

Fortunately, all is not lost. Even though the methods of the natural sciences are of limited use in economics, there are other ways of discovering economic principles or laws, relying on techniques that are not available to the physicist or chemist. As you master the lessons in this book, you will gradually develop a new framework for interpreting the world. Things that seemed incoherent before will make perfect sense to you. And as you will see, the lessons in this book will *not* appeal to experimental or even historical results to prove their validity. Once you have grasped the essential points of each lesson, they will be yours forever. You may decide that the concepts are more or less useful to you, but you will never need worry that newly published economic research will render them *false*. How is this possible? We explain in the next section.

How We Develop Basic Economics

As we discussed above, economic theorists face two huge problems: the objects of their study have minds of their own and it is much harder to perform a controlled experiment in economics than in a natural science such as chemistry. These differences partly explain why the so-called hard sciences enjoy a much better reputation for objectivity and success than the soft sciences, including economics.

However, the economist does have one enormous advantage over the natural scientist: the economic theorist is himself a thinking being, with conscious goals. Because he has an insider's view of acting in the economy, the economist can more easily understand the motivations and constraints faced by other actors in the economy. In contrast, the particle physicist doesn't have any idea "what it's like to be a quark," and so the physicist must rely exclusively on the familiar empirical techniques to gain insight into the behavior of quarks.

Earlier in this lesson we focused on the important distinction between purposeful action versus mindless behavior, because this difference is key to developing useful economic principles. The economic principles we will develop in this book are all *logical implications* of the fact that there are other people with minds who try to achieve their own goals. In other words, if we as social scientists decide to commit to the "theory" that there are other minds operating in the world—just as each of us can directly experience his or her *own* mental awareness—then that "theory" starts spitting out other pieces of knowledge that are consequences of it. You will probably be surprised in Lesson 3 when we show just how much of economics is packed into the simple observation that, "John Doe is acting with a purpose in mind." Right now we won't list any of these results, because you should first understand exactly what it is you'll be *doing* as you work through Lesson 3.

Rather than looking to physics or chemistry for guidance on how to develop good economic principles, a much better role model is geometry. In standard (i.e., "Euclidean") geometry, we start with some basic definitions and assumptions that seem reasonable enough. For example, we define what we mean by a *point* and a *line*, we explain what we mean by the *angle* formed at the intersection of two lines, and so forth.

Once we have our starting definitions and assumptions in hand, we can use them to start building "theorems," which is a fancy word for the logical **deduction** of the consequences of our original definitions and assumptions. A geometry textbook will start with the most basic theorems, and then use each new result to deduce something even more complicated. For example, early on a simple theorem may run like this: "*If* we start out with four lines that form a rectangle, *then* we can draw a new, fifth line that divides the rectangle into two identical triangles." Once that (very simple) theorem is proved, it can be added to the toolbox, and subsequent, more difficult theorems can invoke this earlier theorem in one of their steps.

The procedure or method of geometry is quite similar to what we'll do in this book to build up basic economic principles. In the next lesson we'll define some concepts (such as profit and cost) and show their relation to our basic assumption that events in the social world are driven by purposeful actions. As we go through the lessons, we will continue to add new insights, by building on the previous lessons and by introducing new scenarios where we can apply our earlier results.

At this stage, there are two important observations you should make about the example of geometry. First, notice that it doesn't make sense to ask a mathematician to go out and "test" the theorems in a geometry textbook. For example, consider the Pythagorean Theorem, which is probably the most famous of all geometrical results. The Pythagorean Theorem says that if you have a triangle with a 90-degree angle, and you label each side with a letter, then the following equation will hold:

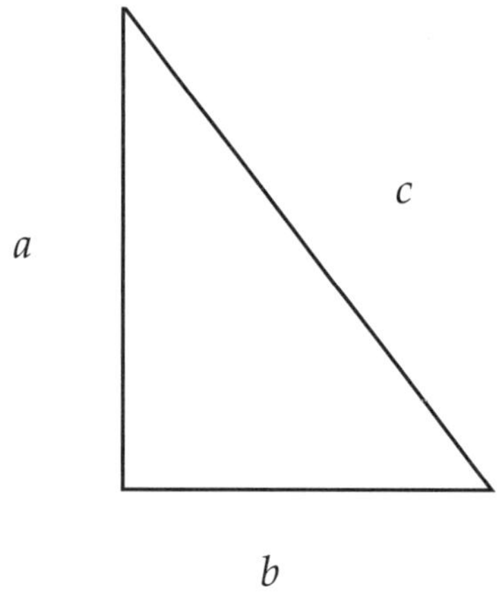

$$a^2 + b^2 = c^2$$

Once you have seen an actual *proof* of the Pythagorean Theorem, you understand that it *must* be true. To amuse yourself, you can take a ruler and a compass (used to measure angles) and "test" the theorem out on triangles that you draw on a piece of paper. However, you'll find that in practice the theorem won't appear to be exactly true; you might find that the left-hand side of the equation adds up to 10.2 inches while the right-hand side comes out at 10.1 inches. Yet if you get such "falsifications" of the theorem, and point them out to a mathematician, he will explain that the triangle you were measuring did not really have an exactly 90-degree angle after all (maybe it was 89.9 degrees), and the ruler you used to measure the lines was an imprecise tool, since it only has so many notches on it and in practice you were "eyeballing" how long each line was to some extent.

The important point is that the mathematician knows that the Pythagorean Theorem *is* true, because he can *prove it* using indisputable, step-by-step, logical deductions from the initial assumptions.

This is a good analogy for how we derive economic principles or laws. We start with some definitions and the assumption that there is a mind at work, and then we begin *logically deducing* further results. Once we have proved a particular economic principle or law, we can put it in our back pocket and use it in the future to help in proving a more difficult result. And if someone asks us whether the data "confirm or reject" our economic principle, we can respond that the question is nonsense. An apparent "falsification" of the economic law would really just mean that the initial assumptions weren't satisfied. For example, we will learn in Lesson 11 the Law of Demand, which states that "other things equal, a rise in price will lead to a drop in the quantity demanded of a product or service." Now if we try to "test" the Law of Demand, we will certainly be able to come up with historical episodes where the price of something rose, even though people bought more units of the good. This finding doesn't blow up the Law of Demand; the economist simply concludes, "Well, 'other things' must not have been equal."

We now move on to the second important observation you should take away from our discussion of geometry: Just because something is logically deduced from earlier definitions and assumptions (sometimes called **axioms**), the resulting proposition might still contain important and useful information about the real world. We stress this point because many people think that a field of study can be "scientific" and provide "information about the real world" only if its propositions can, at least in principle, be refuted by experiments or measurements. This requirement is obviously not fulfilled in the case of geometry, and yet everyone would agree that studying geometry is certainly *useful*. An engineer who sets out to build a bridge will have a much better shot if he has previously studied the logical, deductive proofs in a geometry class, even though (in a sense) all the theorems in the textbook are "merely" transformations of the information that was already contained in the initial assumptions.

The same is true (we hope!) for the economic principles and laws contained in this book. You will not need to go out and test the propositions to see if they're true, because any apparent falsification would simply mean that the particular assumptions used in the proof were lacking at the time of the "test." However, you will find that gaining this "armchair knowledge" through careful introspection and logical reasoning, will actually allow you to make sense of the real world in all its complexity. You will do much better navigating the economy, and making sense of its outcomes, once you have mastered the logical (yet un-testable) lessons in this book.

Lesson Recap . . .

- A purposeful action is performed by a conscious being with a mind, who is trying to achieve a goal. Mindless behavior refers to motions in the physical world that are the result of "mere nature" and not the intentions of another thinking being.

- The natural sciences include fields such as physics, chemistry, and meteorology. They study the natural world and try to deduce the "laws of nature." The social sciences include such fields as sociology, psychology, and economics. They study different aspects of human behavior, including our interactions with each other in society.

- The natural sciences develop theories that try to predict the behavior of mindless objects with better and better accuracy. They enjoy success because these objects seem to obey a constant set of fairly simple rules, and because in many settings they can perform controlled experiments. In the social sciences, including economics, the objects of study have minds of their own, and controlled experiments are much more difficult to perform. To develop economic principles, the economist relies on his own experience of purposeful action, and deduces the logical implications from it. In this respect economics is closer to geometry than to physics.

NEW TERMS

Purposeful action: An activity undertaken for a conscious reason; behavior that has a goal.

Keynesian economics: A school of thought (inspired by John Maynard Keynes) that prescribes government budget deficits as a way to lift the economy out of recession and restore full employment.

Budget deficit: The amount the government must borrow when it spends more than it collects in taxes and other sources of revenue.

Austrian economics: A school of thought (inspired by Carl Menger and others who happened to be Austrian) that blames recessions on government interference with the economy, and recommends tax and spending cuts to help the economy during a recession.

Logical deduction: A form of reasoning that starts from one or more axioms and moves step-by-step to reach a conclusion.

Axioms: The starting assumptions or foundations in a deductive system. For example, the method of constructing a straight line between two points could be an axiom in a geometry textbook. Axioms are not proved, but are assumed to be true in order to prove other, less obvious, statements.

STUDY QUESTIONS

1. If someone sneezes when pepper is thrown in his face, is that a purposeful action?

2. Does "purposeful action" include mistakes?

3. *Are *brain* and *mind* interchangeable terms?

4. Can we perform controlled experiments to test economic theories?

5. **Would you classify Intelligent Design theory as a natural or social science?

LESSON 3

Economic Concepts Implied By Action

In this lesson you will learn:

- Why only individuals, not collectives, can make choices.
- How economists use *preferences* to explain individual choices.
- The proper way to think about preferences.

Introduction

In the previous lesson we stressed the distinction between purposeful action versus mindless behavior. Economics studies the former; everything in economics is ultimately connected to the fact that we, as outside analysts, are imputing *conscious motives* behind the events we are trying to describe. We can't even classify a physical object as "money"—let alone give an explanation of its purchasing power—unless we "get inside the heads" of the people who are passing around various pieces of this object. (After all, people pass germs around too, but we don't classify them as money!)

Economics is the methodical, or scientific, study of exchanges. An exchange—in the sense that we use it in this book—is very definitely a purposeful action. In this lesson, we are going to spin out some of the logical implications of our decision to study exchanges. To repeat the message from the previous lesson: Note that we are not going to make a bunch of predictions from our "theory" that people engage in conscious exchanges, and then go test these predictions against our observations of the world.

No, you'll see that all we're really doing in this lesson is unpacking the knowledge that was already contained in the very notion of "purposeful action" in the first place. If you buy into the claim that we can usefully describe other people as engaging in goal-seeking behavior, then you will naturally understand our elaborations of that idea in the present lesson. On the other hand, if you tried to apply the concepts in this lesson to a purely mechanical process, such as a rock falling off a cliff, then it would be nonsense—because it just doesn't seem helpful to explain a rock's behavior as due to purposeful action.

Only Individuals Act

If we as economists are going to explain an event by referring to a purposeful action, this obviously implies that there is *some individual* performing the action. After all, to say that a conscious intelligence influenced events, implies that there must be some intelligent being to whom the consciousness *belongs*.

Now we don't have to actually know the precise identity of the individual, in order to conclude that an individual has taken a purposeful action. A detective can look at a blood-soaked kitchen and say, "Somebody killed this poor woman—that butcher knife didn't stab her through some freak accident." The detective can thus explain the physical arrangement of the kitchen, by supposing that some other, intelligent individual consciously chose to act to kill the victim. This is a perfectly good hypothesis, even though the detective (as yet) doesn't know anything else about the actual killer. But he *does* know that the killer had a goal in mind—no matter what the extenuating circumstances may be, nobody is going to believe him if he says, "Sure I was holding the knife when this happened, but believe me it was an accident."

Just to make sure you really understand the concept, we note that the "individual" behind an action doesn't necessarily need to be a human being. There are plenty of people who claim that their best explanation for what happened to them was that they were abducted by aliens and subjected to all sorts of unpleasant sensory experiences. Again, our rule holds: These people aren't blaming "nature" for what happened, they are instead saying that intelligent beings influenced events. For whatever reason, the aliens had the goal of probing Billy Bob as he drove his pickup truck home one dark night, and the aliens acted on that desire. For a different example, a religious person might interpret the sudden remission of her cancer as due to the intervention of God. In this case, she too is explaining events in the physical world by reference to the purposeful action of an intelligent individual—one who in this case doesn't possess a physical body.

When we decide to interpret an event as a purposeful action, we are necessarily supposing that there must be an intelligent individual carrying out the action. (There can't be an action without an actor.) So the connection between an action and an actor is a logical one, flowing out of the very concept of "purposeful action" itself. Now in practice, our attempt to *link up* a specific action with a specific actor is based on more than simple logic. For example, when the detective decides "this is a homicide," he is logically implying that there must have been (at least one) killer. But he might use faulty DNA tests to end up arresting the wrong guy. So we see, there is more than a logical deduction involved, when trying to arrest the actual killer. But the important point for our purposes is that the detective's decision to classify a bloody kitchen *as a crime scene* necessarily means that there must be a killer (or killers). But going from this logical conclusion to the next step of identifying a particular person as the killer, requires more than mere logic.

To drive home the subtle interconnections of logical and empirical reasoning, we can consider a more fanciful example. Suppose a psychiatrist can see the left hand belonging to one of his patients as it grabs a pen and begins spreading ink onto a check. The psychiatrist classifies this as a purposeful action, and thus *logically* he must also believe that there is some conscious individual performing this action. However, the psychiatrist might think, "That's my sweet patient Sally paying me for this week's services as I help her with her split personality syndrome," when in reality it is Sally's alter-ego, Snippy, who isn't filling out the check at all but instead is writing "YOU ARE TOO NOSY!!" on the paper before handing it over to him. In this example, we again have to keep in mind the limits of logical deduction. Once the psychiatrist decides to interpret the movements of the hand and pen as *purposeful action*—as opposed to a mere reflex—then he logically must conclude that there is an intelligent being with a motive who is moving the pen in order to achieve some goal. However, if the psychiatrist jumps to the conclusion that the intelligent being is the personality he knows as "Sally," and that she is moving the pen in order to give him payment for his services, then the psychiatrist is going beyond the range of logical deduction, and he might be wrong.

As these examples illustrate, in everyday life we do a lot more than simply rely on logical deductions once we decide to interpret an event as a purposeful action. We use all sorts of empirical evidence to refine our understanding of what we observed. But economic theory focuses on the knowledge we can deduce merely from the fact of purposeful action itself, without the other empirical evidence in a given case that may or may not lead us to a fuller explanation.

Barring odd cases such as multiple personalities or hypnotic control, generally speaking we associate each human body with one specific mind (and vice versa). So when we see the physical body associated with "Bill" pouring a can of soda down its throat, we naturally describe this by saying, "Bill was thirsty so he decided to drink something." Although we don't usually stop to think about it, when we talk like this we are referring to an intangible, conscious will called "Bill" that tries to get its way by influencing the components of the glob of cells that we label, "Bill's body."

We are brushing up against deep philosophical issues once again, which go far beyond the scope of a book on economics principles. In this section, we only need to make one more point: Because a purposeful action is associated with a single individual (namely, the actor), it means that when an economist tries to explain an event by reference to purposeful actions, he ultimately must break it down into the motivations or goals of the individuals involved. This statement sounds obvious, but it is surprising how casually people—even respected social scientists—ignore the rule.

For example, an historian might write, "In 1941 Japan attacked the United States." Strictly speaking, this is nonsense. "Japan" isn't an individual and so can't take purposeful actions (such as bombing Pearl Harbor). Individual *Japanese pilots* flew planes and attacked ships belonging to the U.S. Navy. The statement "Stalin occupied East Germany" is at least sensible (since Stalin is an individual), but it's nonetheless misleading if interpreted literally. *Really* what happened is that Joseph Stalin gave orders to his subordinates, who in turn relayed them to *their* subordinates and so on, such that many many soldiers *chose to obey* those orders and carried out *purposeful* actions that resulted in a new (and scary) political situation for the people living in East Germany.

In many cases this sloppy use of language is fine; there is no danger of confusion when a sports fan yells out from his office cubicle, "Chicago just kicked a field goal to tie the game!" Everyone knows what he means by that statement; no one will be misled into believing that somehow a lifeless geographical location managed to block burly men long enough to propel a pigskin between two posts.

Only Individuals Act

The first truth to be discovered about human action is that *it can be undertaken only by individual "actors."* Only individuals have ends and can act to attain them. There are no such things as ends of or actions by "groups," "collectives," or "States," which do not take place as actions by various specific individuals. "Societies" or "groups" have no independent existence aside from the actions of their individual members. Thus, to say that "governments" act is merely a metaphor; actually, certain individuals are in a certain relationship with other individuals and act in a way that they and the other individuals recognize as "governmental."

—Murray Rothbard, *Man, Economy, and State* (Auburn, Ala.: Ludwig von Mises Institute, 2004), pp. 2–3

However, in many cases this sloppy use of language is very dangerous, leading people to reach the wrong conclusions about the world. For example, many people would endorse the following statement: "Man our government is so incompetent and dumb! On the one hand it pays farmers to grow tobacco, while on the other hand it pays ad agencies to develop anti-smoking campaigns. Make up your mind!"

In reality, there is no such thing as "the government" that has a mind of its own and can perform purposeful actions. Instead, there are *individuals*—politicians, judges, bureaucrats, etc.—belonging to the government who enjoy special privileges because of their status. Different combinations of (some of) these individuals make conscious decisions to steer tax dollars toward tobacco farmers and anti-smoking campaigns. The simplistic approach to viewing these programs as actions taken by "the government" is not only technically inaccurate, but it is actually dangerously misleading. After reading the lessons in this book, you will realize that there are perfectly sensible reasons for the actions of government officials. Their actions often don't make any sense *when compared to the official justifications given for the actions*, but there's a simple explanation for that too: government officials routinely lie. (Notice that lying is itself a purposeful action.)

Individuals Have Preferences

Besides the (obvious) point that an action requires an actor, we can draw further deductions. When we say that an individual performs a *purposeful* action, we mean that he has a purpose or a goal in mind. Remember, we don't say that the baseball "wants to fall back to the ground." But we *would* say, "The pilot landed the helicopter because he wanted to use the bathroom."

So we see that when we discuss purposeful, intentional actions by others, we are implicitly saying that they have opinions or desires about how the world should unfold. In economics, we use the word **preferences** to describe these feelings; people act the way they do because they *prefer* the world to unfold one way, rather than another. For example, when we say, "Bill drank the soda because he was thirsty," we are automatically *also* saying (even if we don't speak the words), ". . . and Bill *prefers* to not be thirsty." After all, it wouldn't make much sense to say, "Bill drank the soda because 2+2=4." The reason it *does* make sense to say, "Bill drank the soda because he was thirsty," is that we can read between the lines, as it were, and fill in the unspoken claim that Bill is unhappy with his condition of being thirsty.

As you may have noticed, there is another unspoken truth that is packed into our simple statement about Bill's chugging of the soda. When we decide to classify his behavior as a purposeful action, we are also deciding that *Bill himself must believe* that drinking soda can relieve thirst. After all, if a case of soda fell out of an airplane into a primitive village, the people who discovered it might have no idea that puncturing the hard shells and pouring the dark liquid into their mouths would relieve the unpleasant feelings of thirst. (And they certainly wouldn't realize how much it would rot their teeth.) Instead, they might consider the cans sacred (since they fell from a giant flying object that they had never seen before), or their musicians might incorporate them into other forms of purposeful action, having nothing to do with thirst.

It's important to realize that a person's beliefs can be *wrong*, and yet still motivate a purposeful action. For example, if we went back in time and observed doctors in the 1800s placing leeches on patients, we would say, "They are doing that on purpose, because they *prefer* the patients to be healthy rather than sick, and because they *believe* that blood-letting is an effective treatment." (On the other hand, someone armed with more accurate medical knowledge might place leeches on his enemy because he *prefers* him to be weak and he believes that drawing away blood will achieve this goal.)[1]

We will develop the point more fully in the next lesson, but here we mention that people use parts of the world in order to achieve their goals. Philosophers describe this by saying people use *means* to achieve their *ends*. Economists describe this by saying people use **goods** and **services** to satisfy their preferences.

Preferences Are Subjective

Because preferences are tied to specific individuals, we say that preferences are **subjective**. Loosely speaking, the difference between a subjective versus an objective statement, is akin to the difference between an opinion versus a fact. It makes sense to say, "Mary prefers vanilla ice cream to chocolate, but John prefers chocolate ice cream to vanilla." These two statements are perfectly compatible, because preferences (in this case, preferences for ice cream flavors) are subjective and can differ from person to person.

In contrast, it does *not* make sense to say, "The ice cream has 300 calories for Mary, but 280 calories for John." The number of calories in a serving of ice cream is an objective fact; it can't differ from person to person. Mary and John might *disagree* with each other about how many calories the ice

[1]There are apparently rare cases in which even modern doctors would recommend blood-letting as an effective treatment, but clearly the earlier practice was not, in general, good for the patient.

cream has, but in that case at least one of them is simply *mistaken*. Yet both of them could be simultaneously "correct" when Mary says, "Vanilla tastes better than chocolate," while John says the opposite. To repeat, Mary and John can disagree with each other about which flavor of ice cream tastes better—with neither one nor the other being wrong—because preferences are subjective. There is no "fact of the matter" concerning which ice cream tastes better, the way there definitely is an objective way to demonstrate how many calories are in a serving.

Warning! Many critics of economics—both from the progressive "left wing" as well as the religious "right wing"—totally misunderstand what economists mean by saying that preferences are subjective. These critics think that economists are somehow endorsing moral relativism, or that they are saying no one can judge the actions of anyone else. But these complaints are without merit, because economists aren't saying those things at all!

Remember, we are simply tracing out the logical implications of our decision to classify observed behavior as purposeful action. If we see Mary go up to the counter and choose vanilla ice cream, while we see John go up to the counter and order chocolate, we won't get anywhere in our understanding unless we realize that Mary and John have *different tastes* when it comes to ice cream flavors. As we will see more clearly in Lesson 6, the only satisfactory way to explain market prices is to first recognize that preferences are subjective. This recognition in no way *condones* the preferences of particular individuals.

For example, an economist can't possibly explain the price of tobacco without acknowledging that some people prefer to spend their money on cigarettes, rather than on other products. After the economist states this fact, he can—with perfect consistency—then ground his teenage son when he catches him smoking in the garage with his hooligan friends. If you're still not seeing the distinction between professional analysis versus personal beliefs, forget about economics and consider an FBI profiler. To track down a serial killer, the profiler needs to "think like the killer," and try to understand what desires are causing the killer to act the way he is. Obviously this analysis doesn't mean that the profiler is neutral with regard to the actions the killer takes, or that murder "is a personal choice."

To sum up: When people engage in purposeful actions, they are motivated by desires that are not necessarily identical from person to person. In order to explain exchanges, economists must recognize that preferences are subjective.

Preferences Are a Ranking, Not a Measurement Using Numbers

Because preferences are tied to a person's exchanges, the preferences can only reveal a *ranking* of goals. When Mary chooses vanilla over chocolate ice cream, this purposeful action only indicates that she prefers vanilla. We *can't* determine "how much" Mary prefers vanilla over chocolate; indeed, that statement doesn't even make sense in terms of strict economic logic.

In everyday conversation, we all know what it means to say that "Mary *really* prefers vanilla over chocolate but her sister Jane only *slightly* prefers vanilla to chocolate." But it's important for you to see that this type of talk makes no sense in terms of the *preferences* that we use in economic reasoning.[2]

After all, what does it really mean—from the standpoint of pure economic logic—to say that Mary has a preference for vanilla over chocolate? All it means is that, faced with a choice between the two flavors, Mary would pick vanilla. But that is the same thing we can say about her sister Jane, whose friends would testify that she has only a "slight" preference for vanilla. Jane too, when faced with a choice, would pick vanilla over chocolate. So in terms of logical deductions that we can make based on a person's purposeful actions, all we can say as economists is that both girls exhibit a preference for vanilla over chocolate.

We can take this train of thought further to drive home the lesson. Even if Jane announces, "I just *barely* prefer vanilla to chocolate!" that wouldn't give an economist the ability to conclude that her preference for vanilla is "less

---

[2]We're not saying people are using language in a sloppy manner in everyday conversation, we're merely pointing out that the term *preferences* has a very precise meaning in economics. By analogy, in physics the term *work* has a very precise, scientific meaning as well, and it doesn't overlap perfectly with the everyday use of the term *work* in conversations.

intense" than Mary's. No, it would merely allow the economist to conclude that Jane preferred to yell that particular sentence, versus yelling something else or keeping her mouth shut. Remember, we are using the notion of a person's subjective preferences to explain the concrete *actions* that the person takes. If someone utters a statement, that informs economists about the person's preferences all right, but only because the utterance itself is a purposeful action![3]

To help you remember the points of this lesson, consider the analogy of *friendship*. For example, Sally might have three friends, and so we could say that in her mind she holds feelings of friendship for each of them. We can push it further and ask Sally to *rank* her friends. She might say that Bill is her best friend, that Mary is her second-best friend, and that Joe is her third-best friend. Such talk is perfectly meaningful.

But what if we then asked Sally *how much better* a friend Bill was than Mary? Now things start to sound a little strange. And if we asked her, "Does Bill possess at least 30% more friendship than Joe?" we would have entered the realm of the absurd. The moral of this story is that it makes sense to rank friends, but even so there's still no such thing as an objective "unit of friendship" behind the scenes, driving our ranking.

The same is true with preferences in general, at least as we use them in economics. As you will learn in upcoming lessons, to understand and describe exchanges, we need to assume that people have a *ranking* of goals or ends. People take actions to satisfy their most important preferences, or to achieve their highest goals. We do *not* have to say that people have a mathematical "utility function" that they seek to maximize, even though such talk is commonplace in other economics textbooks. This alternate approach is only useful in coming up with specific answers to contrived numerical problems; it doesn't actually shed more understanding on the process of exchange. In fact, the use of mathematical utility functions is very harmful when learning basic economic principles, because it often causes the student to forget where the notion of *preference* comes from in the first place.

---

[3]At this stage of the book, these examples may seem tedious, but it's important for you to grasp the point now, before we explain how prices are formed in later lessons.

An Alternate View

Even professional economists do not always heed the principle that preferences are a ranking, not a measurement. For example, economists often use the term **utility** to describe how much pleasure or satisfaction a person gets from a particular situation. Therefore they might describe our scenario by saying, "Mary chose vanilla ice cream because it gave her *more utility* than the chocolate ice cream would have given her."

So far, so good. But then many economics textbooks push it further and start assigning numbers to measure *how much* utility, so that (say) Mary gets "55 utils" from vanilla but only "34 utils" from chocolate, and so in order to "maximize utility" she obviously chooses the vanilla. If you are taking a Ph.D.-level class, the textbook will explain that "utils" don't *really* exist, the way "kilograms" are an objective unit of weight and "meters" are an objective unit of height. Instead, the Ph.D.-level textbook will explain, economists can use mathematical utility functions just as a convenient shortcut to describing preference rankings. So when the function assigns "55 utils" to a bowl of vanilla ice cream but only "34 utils" to the chocolate, all that really means is that Mary would choose the former over the latter. The utility function could just as well have assigned "18.7 utils" to the vanilla and "2.3 utils" to the chocolate; the important thing is that Mary acts "as if" she is maximizing this arbitrary mathematical function.

In this book, we will *not* be using the confusing terminology of "utils," and we won't be performing calculus on "utility functions" the way other economics textbooks do. These practices, though common, are dangerous because they can mislead you into thinking that we are measuring the amount of psychic satisfaction an individual derives from particular actions.

It may be that one day neuroscientists come up with an objective way to quantify various degrees of happiness, such that they can coherently talk about Mary being "three times more satisfied" than Bill. But even if this happens, our point here remains the same: *In the field of economics*, such talk is meaningless. In economics, we use terms like "preferences" as a way to explain or describe the purposeful actions of individuals. When someone chooses one thing over another, all we can conclude is that the person preferred the chosen item over the discarded item. Psychologists or neuroscientists (or even common sense) might shed more light on the event, but economic logic *per se* can go no further. The economist isn't claiming to have all the answers; far from it! The economist is actually being humble here by admitting the *limits* of what economic reasoning can say about a given event. In Lesson 6, we will see how subjective preference rankings interact to yield objective market prices. At that time, you will understand better why we are stressing these points in this lesson.

Different Individuals' Preferences Can't Be Combined

If preferences are subjective to each individual, and cannot even be measured or quantified for each individual, then obviously it would make no sense at all to try to combine or aggregate individual preferences into "social" preferences. Unfortunately, even professional economists often engage in just this type of reasoning. Many people (try to) justify **progressive income taxation**, for example, by claiming that "a dollar means more to a poor man than to a rich man." The idea is that taking $1 million from Bill Gates won't lower his utility very much, whereas handing out $1,000 to a thousand different homeless people will greatly boost each of their utilities. Therefore, the typical argument goes, total or "social" utility has been increased by the redistribution of some of Bill Gates's wealth.

In Lesson 18 we will examine the consequences of progressive income taxation. For now, we point out that the typical justification for it is absurd. You can't add up different amounts of utility from various people. In fact, if you use the alternate term *preferences* it will be more apparent why combining them from different people is an impossible task. It makes sense to ask, "What is the total weight of the population?" or "What is the average age of the population?" It does *not* make sense to ask, "What is the total preferences of the population?" or "What is the average amount of utility per person?"

To make sure you understand just how nonsensical it is to (attempt to) perform arithmetical operations on different people's preference rankings, once again let's switch to the analogy of friendship. Suppose that Sally and Larry have the following "friendship rankings":

Friendship Rankings

Sally	Larry
1st (best): Bill	1st (best): Joe
2nd: Mary	2nd: Bill
3rd: Joe	3rd: (none)
4th: Tom	4th: (none)
5th: Adrian	5th: (none)

Before continuing, make sure you understand the table: Sally has five friends total. Her best friend is Bill, her second-best friend is Mary, and so on. Larry, on the other hand, only has two friends. His best friend is Joe, and Bill is his second-best friend. Notice that even among their shared friends, Sally and Larry don't have the same ranking order. Sally thinks Bill is a better friend than Joe, while Larry thinks that Joe is a better friend than Bill. There is nothing strange about this, because preferences are subjective.[4]

Now suppose a busybody school administrator comes along and says, "This is terrible! Poor Larry doesn't have as many friends as popular Sally! I have a great idea to make things fairer. I'll write a note in Sally's handwriting that says, 'You smell!' and put it in Adrian's lunch bag. This will cause a big fight between Adrian and Sally, so he won't be her friend anymore. Then I'll arrange it so that Adrian sits near Larry on the school bus. They will eventually become friends. I can't predict whether Adrian will become Larry's 1st, 2nd, or 3rd-best friend, but no matter what, he will be ranked

[4]To explain the difference in friendship rankings, we don't even have to assume that Joe and Bill act differently depending on whether they are with Sally or Larry. Even if Joe and Bill are each "the same person" whether hanging out with Sally or Larry, it's still perfectly sensible for them to be ranked differently because—you guessed it—preferences are subjective. Maybe Joe is always making gross noises with his armpit, and Sally thinks it's disgusting while Larry thinks it's hilarious.

higher as a friend of Larry than he was as a friend of Sally. Through my benevolent intervention, I will have increased the total amount of friendship among the children."

Obviously the above story is quite silly. But we have used a silly story to demonstrate the silliness of trying to add up subjective, individual preferences. Hopefully you can now see that trying to increase "social utility" by taking money from a rich man and giving it to a poor man, is simply nonsensical. Perhaps proponents of progressive taxation can justify it on other grounds, but appealing to the economic concept of preferences (or utility) doesn't get the job done.

Lesson Recap . . .

- Once we decide to classify certain events as purposeful actions, we can make further logical deductions. For example, for every action there must be an *actor*, an intelligent person who performed the action. Although people can act in combination with each other, any particular action is performed only by one person.

- We interpret someone's action by saying he or she has preferences. These are the goals that a person tries to achieve through actions.

- Economists say that preferences are subjective, meaning that they are unique to each person. To call preferences subjective doesn't condone or applaud them, it simply recognizes that people have different tastes.

NEW TERMS

Preferences: An individual's goals or desires. Economists interpret a person's actions as attempts to satisfy his or her preferences.

Goods: Scarce physical items that an individual values because they can help to satisfy his preferences.

Service: A person's performance of a task that another person values because it helps to satisfy preferences. Services are the "goods" that people create through their labor power.

Subjective: Unique to each individual; "in the eye of the beholder."

Utility: A term common in economics textbooks to describe how much value a person gets from a good or service.

Progressive income taxation: A system that taxes individuals or corporations at higher rates based on the level of income.

STUDY QUESTIONS

1. Why is it questionable to say, "Germany attacked France"?

2. Why do statements about a man's actions (implicitly) involve his beliefs as well?

3. Can purposeful action be based on a faulty belief? Give examples.

4. What does it mean when economists say preferences are subjective?

5. *Does economics say you shouldn't give money to charity?

LESSON 4

"Robinson Crusoe" Economics

In this lesson you will learn:

- How even a one-man economy illustrates economic concepts and categories.
- The importance of saving and investment.
- How economists explain individual choices.

Introduction

In the first three lessons you learned that economics is the study of exchanges, and you also learned that the apparently simple decision to classify human behavior as "purposeful action" leads to many insights that will help us explain how modern market economies operate. In Part II of this book, we will begin our full-blown analysis of a market economy with buyers and sellers using money in their transactions. This is what most people probably think that a book on economics is supposed to do!

Yet before we dive into the deep end, in the present lesson—the last of our "Foundations" section—we will sketch out some of the basic economic truths that apply even in the very simple case of a single person on a remote island. There are a surprising number of conclusions we can draw even in this extremely limited case.

Over the years, many critics have derided this so-called "Robinson Crusoe" economics, named after the shipwrecked mariner in Daniel Defoe's famous novel.[1] Obviously, we are not saying that an isolated person is an accurate description of a modern economy. Rather, we are saying that *before we can analyze an economy composed of billions of interacting people*, we should start with just *one* person and make sure we understand what makes *him* tick.

As you will see, in this lesson we are developing *general* principles about an individual's purposeful actions in the face of scarcity. These general principles will still hold true, even when Crusoe is rescued and returned to civilization. But to avoid overwhelming students at step one, we are here starting out with the simpler case in which Crusoe is (initially) all by himself and must act to improve his situation, given his circumstances.

Crusoe Creates Goods With His Mind Powers

All alone on his tropical island, Crusoe quickly realizes that he doesn't like the way things are developing. His stomach is starting to rumble, his throat is dry and itchy, and he doesn't see any natural shelter from the horrific rainstorms that must occasionally strike the island. Rather than resign himself to his fate, Crusoe decides to *take action* to alter the unfolding of history, so that events transpire in a manner more to his liking.

Before he can make a sensible decision on how to proceed, Crusoe first needs to see what he has to work with. He climbs to the top of a hill and surveys the island. Crusoe notes that there are plenty of coconut trees, as well as some small streams of running water in the distance. There are several rocks of varying sizes, as well as strong vines. Crusoe's mind begins whirring as he decides what to do first.

At this point we can stop and describe the situation in terms of economic concepts. You probably realized, with Crusoe, why the particular items mentioned in the previous paragraph were *relevant* to his situation, and would be among the facts that you would consider if you found yourself in

---

[1]Modern readers might identify more with Tom Hanks's character in the 2000 movie *Cast Away*.

Crusoe's place. In economic jargon, Crusoe took an inventory of the *goods* at his disposal. That is, he appraised himself of the stockpile of physical items available for his use that exhibited *scarcity*.

After all, Crusoe could have truthfully said, "Hmm, this island is subject to the earth's gravitational pull, meaning I won't drift off into outer space and freeze to death. There is a plentiful supply of oxygen here, meaning I won't suffocate. And the presence of an atmosphere is very good for transmitting sound waves, so that I can hear a storm approaching." These attributes of the island are also extremely useful to Crusoe, and contribute to the achievement of his goals. But Crusoe wouldn't focus on them when formulating his plans, because they aren't *scarce*. Crusoe doesn't need to **economize** these general, background conditions the way he needs to exercise stewardship over the coconuts, vines, etc.

The distinctive mark of scarcity is that there are *tradeoffs* involved. Until he finds another source of food (such as fish after he constructs some tools), Crusoe needs to make sure he doesn't eat his coconuts too quickly. (He also wouldn't burn down a bunch of coconut trees just for kicks.) If he decides to use certain rocks in order to make a shelter, Crusoe can't simultaneously use those same rocks when building a fire. And even if the supply of vines is ubiquitous, even so Crusoe must be considerate when cutting them down to make a fishing net, because it takes him *time* to walk deeper into the jungle and get more vines.

As these examples all demonstrate, Crusoe needs to *think through the consequences of his actions* whenever his plans involve the rocks, vines, coconuts, and so on. Because these items are scarce, Crusoe might later *regret* the influence on them, because this will impair his ability to satisfy goals in the future. Items that can help a person achieve his or her goals, and could help the person achieve even more goals if there were more of these items available, are called *goods*. In contrast, background conditions like gravity and oxygen are not (typically) goods in the economic sense, because no action Crusoe takes will render them less useful to the achievement of his goals. Crusoe doesn't need to worry about sprinting too fast and thereby "using up all the oxygen," and he doesn't face any tradeoffs in relying on gravity when knocking down coconuts with a long stick.[2] Further, there

---

[2]If Crusoe burns the stick as kindling, then he can't knock down coconuts with it. But gravity will still operate just the same, regardless of his actions.

aren't any goals that Crusoe could accomplish, if only he had "more oxygen" or "more gravity." So although oxygen and gravity are necessary for his very life, Crusoe doesn't have to economize on their use, and hence they are not classified as economic goods.

It's important to realize that an object becomes a good when a person incorporates it into his plans. A coconut on the tropical island is not a good because of its physical characteristics per se, but rather because (a) it can serve to alleviate hunger, (b) Crusoe would prefer to not feel hungry, and (c) Crusoe is *aware* of point (a). If Crusoe were ignorant of the fact that coconuts are edible, then he might not consider them as goods. For a different example, certain plants on the island might have medicinal properties, but if Crusoe doesn't know it, then those plants will not attain the status of economic goods.

Consumer Goods versus Producer Goods

Now that we understand what goods are in general, we can begin to make some distinctions. On the one hand, Crusoe recognizes that there are scarce items that can help him to directly achieve his goals. For example, the running water in the stream can directly quench his thirst, and the coconuts can directly satisfy Crusoe's hunger. Economists call these **consumer goods**.

On the other hand, there are items that are certainly useful, and which would allow Crusoe to achieve more of his goals if he had more of such items—hence they are goods—but they are not *directly* useful to him. They are only indirectly useful because they help Crusoe to obtain more *consumer* goods. For example, a long stick, in and of itself, doesn't do anything for Crusoe, and if it were the only object on the island, Crusoe would not consider it a good at all. But because there are coconuts hanging on trees—some of which are out of Crusoe's reach—suddenly the stick acquires value *indirectly*. Crusoe now considers the stick to be a good, even though it doesn't directly satisfy hunger, because it indirectly helps him to achieve his goal. Economists call items such as the hypothetical stick **producer goods** or **factors of production** or **means of production**.

As with goods in general, the distinction between consumer versus producer goods is in the mind of the acting individual. For example, if the Incredible Hulk should wash up on Crusoe's island, he might consider the stick a great device for scratching that hard-to-reach spot between his shoulder blades. To the Hulk, the same physical stick would be a consumer good.

Land, Labor, and Capital Goods

Even within the class of producer goods, we can make more distinctions. Those producer goods that are the direct gifts of nature are typically called **land** or **natural resources**. These include somewhat permanent items such as a flowing stream, or a tree that will yield a flow of coconuts indefinitely; but also included are depletable resources such as a small deposit of tin that Crusoe can use to make cooking pans and fish hooks.

The single most important and versatile producer good is Crusoe's own **labor**, which is the flow of productive services Crusoe performs with his body. In terms of the logic of economic principles, it would be perfectly sensible to group labor along with other natural resources that provided an indefinite flow of services (with adequate maintenance). However, economists have historically accorded labor special treatment, because labor is the one factor of production that every individual possesses, and also because labor is the one producer good that is required for every production process. When Crusoe devotes his physical efforts toward the *indirect* satisfaction of goals, he is engaged in labor. On the other hand, if he achieves direct satisfaction of goals through control of his hands, brain, etc., then economists call this **leisure**. Crusoe will allocate his "body power" among labor and leisure activities, in order to satisfy the goals he considers most important. Historically, economists have referred to the **disutility of labor** to underscore the fact that individuals directly enjoy leisure, and will only devote some of their scarce time to labor if it allows the achievement (indirectly) of more important ends than the leisure being sacrificed.[3]

Finally, **capital goods** are those factors of production that were created by people.[4] Every capital good is produced from the combination of (at least one) natural resource and labor. Most capital goods are also produced with the help of (pre-existing) capital goods.[5] For Crusoe on his island, examples of capital goods would be a fishing net that he constructs out of vines and his labor, and a shelter that he creates out of rocks, branches, mud, leaves, and his labor.

---

[3]Notice that *leisure* doesn't necessarily imply lounging around on the beach, and *labor* (or *work*) doesn't necessarily imply physical exertion. Crusoe might love swimming in the ocean, which gives quite a good workout and can even leave his muscles sore the next day. But before he can enjoy himself in this activity, he first engages in the extremely boring—but physically undemanding—task of gathering small twigs for the night's fire.

[4]Both components of this definition are important. If Crusoe created goods that were *not* factors of production, they wouldn't be capital goods—they would be consumer goods. And if Crusoe had goods that were factors of production, but which he hadn't created, then they wouldn't be capital goods either—instead they would be natural resources.

[5]Logically speaking, the very *first* capital good ever produced in human history, must have been made when someone used his labor to transform the raw gifts of nature into a factor of production.

Income, Saving, and Investment

We now know that Crusoe can separate his world into various types of scarce objects, in the categories of natural resources, labor, capital goods, and consumer goods (which include leisure). Connecting all of these is the flow of *time*, and Crusoe's understanding of how his actions *now* can alter his happiness in *the future*. Specifically, Crusoe can choose to save and invest today, in order to raise his future income.

Income refers to the flow of new consumer goods (and services) that an individual has the potential to acquire during a period of time.[6] **Saving** occurs when someone consumes less than his income; it is "living below one's means." **Investment** occurs when ingredients of production are devoted to future income, rather than immediate consumption.

In Lesson 10 we will discuss in much greater detail the relationship between income, saving, and investment in a modern market economy, in which most exchanges involve money. For now, we quickly illustrate that these advanced concepts have their analogs even in the simple Crusoe economy.

It's easiest to explain with a numerical example. Obviously the following numbers are chosen for simplicity, and serve only to make the scenario concrete enough so that you can really think through the types of tradeoffs Crusoe faces. In that light, suppose that with his bare hands, Crusoe can find an appropriate tree to climb and knock down 1 coconut per hour. If Crusoe devotes 10 hours per day to work, while leaving the rest for leisure (which includes sleep), that means his raw labor can extract 10 coconuts per day from the natural resources available to him on the island. Fortunately, eating 10 coconuts per day provides enough nourishment to maintain Crusoe in decent health. But working 10 hours per day, with no weekend, is hardly an ideal lifestyle. Besides the grueling schedule, Crusoe knows that if he should ever become sick or injured, he could easily die because of the vulnerability of his hand-to-mouth existence.

---

[6]Technically, *gross income* refers to the maximum amount of consumption during a specified time interval, whereas *net income* is the maximum amount of consumption possible, after sufficient investment has been made to maintain next period's gross income at the same level.

There is a solution. Crusoe is a disciplined and resourceful man, and realizes that the ability to save and invest can greatly improve his standard of living. Soon after assessing his situation on the island, Crusoe begins saving 20% of his income every day. In other words, Crusoe continues to work 10 hours per day, day in and day out, gathering (earning) 10 coconuts per day. But he only *eats* (consumes) 8 coconuts each day, and sets aside (saves) 2 coconuts out of each day's income.

After living below his means in this fashion for 25 days, Crusoe has accumulated a stockpile of 50 coconuts. From that point on, he once again resumes eating 10 coconuts per day—he consumes his full paycheck every day, as it were. The main reason Crusoe stopped accumulating additional coconuts is that he discovered their taste begins to suffer five days after being knocked down from the tree. Therefore, Crusoe has settled into a comfortable routine: Every day he picks a fresh batch of 10 coconuts and adds them to one side of his stockpile. During the day, he eats the *oldest* 10 coconuts from the other side of his stockpile. With this rotation, Crusoe still enjoys a full 10 coconuts (which still taste pretty good) per day, but he also has a savings fund of 50 coconuts that he can draw down in case of emergency. For example, if Crusoe should come down with a tropical illness that makes him unable to work, he has enough saved up to eat for ten days on half-rations.[7] Because of his willingness to put in hard work and save its (literal) fruits, Crusoe has greatly enhanced his material position compared to his original situation. Rather than living on the edge of starvation, Crusoe now has a buffer of ten days.

The simple act of saving and accumulating consumption goods is very useful, but Crusoe realizes he can do much better. After surveying the materials at his disposal, Crusoe sets out to *invest* his savings in a long-range venture, which he expects will permanently increase his future flow of daily income. Relying on his stockpile of 50 coconuts, Crusoe decides to take two days off from climbing trees to knock down new coconuts for the stockpile.

But our hero isn't taking a much needed vacation! On the contrary, Crusoe spends the first day—all 10 hours—wandering the island, gathering

[7]We can assume that the coconuts don't taste nearly as good, but are still edible, by the tenth day after being knocked down from the tree.

branches of the appropriate length and thickness. The process is slow-going, because when Crusoe spies a good candidate, he needs to use a sharp rock to saw away at the branch, before he can safely snap it off the tree without ruining it.[8] During this day, Crusoe eats 10 coconuts, reducing his stockpile down to 40. Even though he has worked all day, he has no new coconuts to show for it. Instead, he has only a collection of sturdy and long branches, which he has transformed from their original shape and location.

During the second day, Crusoe spends another 5 hours using sharp rocks to further prepare the branches. Then he spends 2 hours cutting down vines and bringing them back to camp. Finally, in the remaining 3 hours of the second workday, Crusoe lays the branches on the ground, end-to-end but with a large degree of overlap. Then he uses the vines to tie the branches snugly to each other. At the end of the second day, Crusoe's stockpile has dwindled to 30 coconuts. But in addition to this (shrinking) stockpile of savings, Crusoe has a new capital good: A long and sturdy pole.

The next day Crusoe takes his capital good out for a spin. He discovers with great satisfaction that in a single hour, his labor power—aided by the new capital good—can yield 5 coconuts. This is such a tremendous boon to his **productivity** that Crusoe now decides he's been working too much! Rather than working 10 hours per day gathering food, Crusoe now spends only 4 hours per day knocking them down. This brings in a daily flow of 20 coconuts per day, twice what he was "earning" with his bare hands. Wanting to replenish his stockpile to the fullest amount that still allows for tasty coconuts, Crusoe saves some of his new earnings for a few weeks, until his stockpile has grown to 100 coconuts.[9] He once again has five days' worth of full-rations, except *now* a "full-ration" means 20 coconuts per day. In the new **equilibrium**, Crusoe spends 4 hours per day knocking down 20 new coconuts, which he adds to the stockpile. During that same day, he eats the 20 oldest (ripest) coconuts in the stockpile.

---

[8]Notice that the sharp rock is a natural resource that Crusoe uses with his labor in order to produce a capital good, the sawed-off branch.

[9]Starting on his first day of using the pole, Crusoe has 30 coconuts in the stockpile. If he only consumes 15 out of his daily income of 20 coconuts, it will take him two full weeks to accumulate a stockpile of 100 coconuts. After that point—i.e., on the fifteenth day after he has constructed the pole—Crusoe can begin consuming the full 20 coconuts of his income per day.

Things are obviously looking up for Mr. Crusoe. Before, he had to put in 10 hours per day of fairly intensive work; it's hard to climb trees all day. In exchange for all that toil, Crusoe enjoyed 10 coconuts each day. But after his wise investment in the construction of a capital good, Crusoe finds that he only needs to spend 4 hours per day knocking down coconuts with the pole—a much easier task than climbing a tree and grabbing them with his bare hands. He also gets to enjoy twice as many coconuts per day as before, which is frankly the upper limit of how many coconuts he would *want* to eat.

There is one more important detail. If Crusoe wants to permanently *maintain* his new, higher standard of living, he can't enjoy 20 hours of leisure per day. No, in addition to spending 4 hours per day laboring in the collection of new coconuts, Crusoe must also devote some of his scarce time to the maintenance of his pole. For example, suppose that after using the pole for a full week, the component branches wriggle out of their tight knots, and each end of the pole is quite battered. What this means is that after the seventh day of using his brand new capital good, Crusoe will need to devote some time to replacing the two end branches, as well as re-wrapping the entire pole with new vines.

Now if Crusoe only works the minimum 4 hours per day, collecting coconuts, he can only get away with this slacking for seven days. On the morning of the eighth day, Crusoe would find himself with a useless pole, and he would have to spend (let's say) 7 hours on that day, working to collect new vines and two new branches, and to assemble the new pole. Moreover, in addition to working so many hours, Crusoe would have to draw down on his coconut stockpile, since he wouldn't be able to gather any new coconuts that day.

Rather than engage in this volatile schedule—seven days of light work with many coconuts, with an eighth day of intense work and no coconuts—Crusoe can smooth things out. In a typical day in the new equilibrium, he can spend 4 hours knocking down 20 new coconuts to add to his stockpile (while of course eating the ripest 20 from the same stockpile of 100). But then he also spends a fifth hour each day working on the preservation of his capital good. This way, after seven days have passed in a typical week,

Crusoe will have performed the 7 hours' worth of labor necessary to restore the pole after it has been worn down from a week of usage.[10]

In the jargon of economics, we can step back and describe what Crusoe has done. By consuming less than his daily income—by living below his means—Crusoe saved coconuts in order to build up a fund to guard against sudden disruptions in his future income. Moreover, Crusoe then invested his resources into the creation of a capital good that greatly augmented his labor productivity. After the completion of the pole, Crusoe only consumed his *net* income each day, because he invested enough of his *gross* income to just balance the **depreciation** of his capital good.

Goods Are Valued Unit by Unit

One of the most important advances in economic theory was the realization that people valued goods unit by unit, rather than comparing entire classes of goods against each other. Using their jargon, economists now say that people evaluate goods based on **marginal utility**.

The classic illustration of this new way of thinking is the so-called "water-diamond paradox." At first glance, it seems odd that the price of water should be so low—restaurants will serve it for free!—while the price of diamonds should be so high. (Try asking your waiter for a complimentary glass

[10]To make the story work out, technically Crusoe would have to use the fifth working hour of the seventh day, as well as the first working hour of (the next week's) first day, in order to swap out the two battered end branches and retie the whole pole with the new vines. This complication comes from the fact that even though Crusoe takes 7 hours to repair a broken pole, he can't spread that work out evenly as the last hour of each day for the course of a week, because the last tasks—swapping out the end branches and retying it all together—take more than an hour, according to the description we gave earlier. If you are a purist and really want to plot out exactly what Crusoe would do with his time for each day of the cycle, keep in mind that Crusoe has the option of devoting more than 4 hours of a given day to coconut collection (while still only consuming 20 that day), so that the stockpile temporarily exceeds 100. Then, on a later day when Crusoe needs to devote more than the fifth hour to pole maintenance, he can draw down on the stockpile. With proper planning, all the numbers work out: the stockpile never falls below 100, and Crusoe never needs to eat a coconut older than five days.

filled with diamonds.) If economists think that the value of goods is ultimately related to humans trying to satisfy their subjective goals, how can diamonds possibly be more valuable than water? After all, you can't satisfy too many goals if you die of thirst.

In the early 1870s, three different economists independently worked out the solution to this problem: Yes, it's true that the way to explain the value of an object, is to get inside the head of the person who values it and understand his goals. But when this person makes actual choices in the real world, he never faces the tradeoff of "all the water" versus "all the diamonds." If that really *were* the choice, then the person would most probably pick the water. But in normal life, there is so much water available that any *particular* gallon of it, has a very low value. In contrast, there aren't enough diamonds to go around to satisfy all the uses people have for diamonds. That's why any particular diamond is still quite valuable. Economists would say that diamonds are scarcer than water.

This principle of valuing goods by individual units applies in Robinson Crusoe's world. For example, suppose one night Crusoe is careless and falls asleep while his campfire is still sending out embers. The wind carries one right onto Crusoe's humble shelter (constructed out of vines, branches, and leaves). By the time Crusoe wakes up, the whole building is ablaze.

Crusoe realizes he has to hurry outside before the shelter collapses on him, and he has time to grab just one thing to rescue from the inferno. The only objects in the shelter are a fresh coconut and a watch that he was wearing at the time of his original shipwreck. What object should he choose to grab as he runs from the fire?

A superficial guess would say, "Crusoe should take the coconut, assuming that the goal of avoiding starvation is more important to him than keeping a useless memento from civilization."

But that answer is wrong. *That particular coconut* will not mean the difference between starvation and nourishment. Indeed, Crusoe still has a stockpile of 99 more coconuts that are not near the fire. At the very worst, all the sacrifice means is that Crusoe will have to settle for eating only 19 coconuts on some particular day (not even necessarily the next day), rather than his normal 20. In fact, Crusoe may simply decide to work an extra 12 minutes at some point[11] to knock down 21 coconuts and replace the one lost to the fire.

The general principle is that Crusoe will evaluate goods *unit by unit*. When he is deciding how valuable a particular coconut is, compared to a particular watch, he considers how his goals will be affected by those particular items. It is completely irrelevant to Crusoe that 100 coconuts are more valuable to him than 100 watches; that's not the decision he faces as he runs out of the burning hut. No, he has to decide if *one* coconut is more valuable than *one* watch. And as we've seen, the loss of one particular coconut isn't devastating at all. It simply means that Crusoe will have to eat a little less at some point, or that he'll have to work a little more. Economists would say that *on the margin* the loss of a coconut is fairly insignificant. That's why it's perfectly sensible for Crusoe to grab the watch, which he values for sentimental reasons.

Pulling It All Together: What Should Crusoe *Do* With Himself?

We're finally ready to explain how Crusoe actually conducts himself. To put it simply, Crusoe will make decisions in order to achieve his most important goals. In the language of economics, Crusoe will act to achieve his highest-ranked preferences; some economists would say Crusoe will "maximize his utility."

However there is an important caveat. When Crusoe makes a choice, he can't simply consider the **benefits**, as he subjectively perceives them. He must also consider the **costs**. The cost of a particular decision is the value that Crusoe places on the most important goal that he *won't* be able to achieve, because of the decision. Economists often drive home the point by using the longer term **opportunity cost,** which they define as *the subjective value placed on the next-best alternative* that must be sacrificed because of a choice.

[11]Remember that with his pole, Crusoe can gather 5 coconuts per hour, which means he gathers 1 coconut every 12 minutes.

Up till now in this lesson, we have been explaining the nature of the tradeoffs Crusoe faces in his daily decisions. Without realizing the connections between his choices, we wouldn't be able to make much sense of Crusoe's actual decisions. For example, let's reconsider Crusoe's actions as he ran out of the burning hut. We said that he faced a choice, between grabbing a coconut or grabbing a watch. But actually, we cheated a bit; we zoomed ahead to what we knew the real tradeoff was. In reality, Crusoe had all sorts of options at his disposal. Rather than grabbing the coconut or watch, he could have decided to use his hands to punch himself in the face. Or he could have picked up the coconut, but then hurled it at the burning roof. In fact, we just took it for granted that Crusoe would *leave* the hut in the first place. He certainly had the option to calmly eat his last coconut before passing out from smoke inhalation.

When we discussed Crusoe's actions after he foolishly let his hut catch on fire, we didn't bother considering all of the silly possibilities just mentioned. We knew that Crusoe would first and foremost choose to save his life by running out of the hut, because (we assume) he placed self-preservation very high on his list of preferred outcomes. (It was much much higher than, say, "getting a few minutes more sleep.") And in that context, we knew that he faced the subsequent decision of grabbing just one item on his way out. We didn't bother comparing the benefits of rescuing the watch, versus the cost of not being able to punch himself in the face with two free hands. *That* wouldn't have been an accurate description of the true cost of his action, because "the joy of face pummeling" is presumably not high on Crusoe's list of preferences.

Instead, when trying to understand the decision Crusoe really faced, we looked at what the *best* option was, that he would thereby have to sacrifice because of his decision to grab the watch. In our story, we assumed that Crusoe's next-best alternative was grabbing the coconut.[12] The economist would explain Crusoe's action in this way: Crusoe decided that the benefits of having the watch outweighed the cost of having one fewer coconut. This is simply using different words to say: The goals Crusoe could achieve with

[12]In other words, if the watch had already been outside, Crusoe would have chosen to rescue the coconut.

a watch and 99 coconuts, were more important to him than the goals he could achieve with no watch and 100 coconuts.

The other decisions Crusoe makes are more complicated, but the basic principle is the same: Crusoe always chooses the option for which the benefits exceed the costs. For example, when Crusoe decides to work a fifth hour on a particular day, in order to gather more vines, it's because he considers the benefits to outweigh the costs. In this case, the benefits are (ultimately) the extra pleasure he will get from consuming more coconuts in the future. (Remember that he needs the vines to maintain his pole in good condition, in order to knock down coconuts.) The cost is the value Crusoe places on the most important goal that he now *won't* be able to achieve. For example, suppose on his way to cut down more vines, Crusoe sees a pile of perfectly cut vines lying on the ground, the result of a freak lightning strike. In that case, Crusoe might decide to enjoy an extra hour of leisure. That means the cost of his original decision (to spend an hour cutting vines) was the value to Crusoe of having 20 hours of leisure that day, instead of 19.[13]

The last point in this lesson is that all of Crusoe's actions are guided by his **expectations**, which is to say his *predictions about the future*. When Crusoe makes a particular decision, he is really choosing the outcome that he *expects* will give him more benefits than costs. He very well could be mistaken. For example, Crusoe might spend several weeks collecting branches and other materials, in order to construct a raft. He thinks he will be able to use it to escape to the high sea, where he hopes someone will rescue him. The benefits of this small chance of escape are more important to Crusoe than the leisure he is giving up during the construction of the raft.

However, after many attempts, Crusoe realizes that the ocean won't let him escape the island on his raft. Unfortunately, he can't find anything on his island that would serve as a large sail. He realizes with great regret that his efforts on the raft were a complete waste of time. Or more accurately, a complete waste of *leisure*.

---

[13]Remember that Crusoe works the first four hours of the day gathering coconuts. At that point, he has 20 hours remaining in his day. If he works a fifth hour gathering vines, than he only has 19 hours remaining for leisure—and that includes sleep.

Despite Crusoe's mistake, as economists we still explain his original choices by saying that Crusoe considered the benefits of getting out to sea to be greater than the cost of many hours of leisure. Even though this wasn't the true tradeoff involved, Crusoe *believed* that it was, and it is ultimately Crusoe's beliefs (and preferences) that guide his decisions.

Lesson Recap . . .

- We can learn many basic economic concepts and principles by studying an imaginary "economy" consisting of just one person. After mastering the tools in a simplified setting, we can apply them to more complicated (and realistic) scenarios involving many people.

- One of the most important decisions a person makes is whether to devote time and other resources to the present or to the future. Through saving and investment, people sacrifice current enjoyments but achieve much greater enjoyments in the future.

- Economists say that an individual will engage in more and more "units" of an activity so long as the subjective benefits outweigh the costs.

NEW TERMS

Economize: The act of treating a resource with care because it is scarce and can only satisfy a limited number of goals or preferences.

Consumer goods and services: Scarce physical items or services that directly satisfy a person's preferences.

Producer goods / factors of production / means of production: Scarce physical items or services that *indirectly* satisfy preferences, because they can be used to produce consumer goods and services.

Land / natural resources: Factors of production that are gifts of nature.

Labor: The contribution to production flowing from a person's body.

Leisure: A special type of consumer good that results from using one's body (and time) to directly satisfy preferences, as opposed to engaging in labor.

Disutility of labor: Economists' term to describe the fact that people prefer leisure to labor. People only engage in labor because of its indirect rewards.

Capital goods: Producer goods that are produced by human beings; they are not direct gifts from nature.

Income: The flow of consumer goods and services that a person has the potential to enjoy during a specific period of time.

Saving: Consuming less than one's income would allow; living below one's means.

Investment: Diverting resources into projects that are expected to increase future income.

Productivity: The amount of output produced by a factor of production in a period of time, often used in reference to labor.

Equilibrium: A stable situation after all disturbances or changes have worked themselves out.

Depreciation: The wearing away or "using up" of capital goods during the course of production.

Marginal utility: A technical economics term referring to the subjective enjoyments of one additional unit of a good or service.

Benefits: The subjective enjoyments flowing from a course of action.

(Opportunity) cost: The benefits of the *next-best alternative* to a given action.

Expectations: An individual's forecasts of the future, which involve his or her understanding of "how the world works" and therefore guide current actions.

STUDY QUESTIONS

1. Does economics assume that people act in isolation from the rest of society?

2. What does it mean to say Crusoe creates goods with his "mind powers"?

3. Can leisure be more physically demanding than work?

4. Why does Crusoe need to worry about depreciation of his capital goods?

5. How do expectations affect someone's decisions?

Part II

CAPITALISM: THE MARKET ECONOMY

LESSON 5

The Institution of Private Property

In this lesson you will learn:

- The reason society requires institutions to deal with scarcity.
- The three main institutional settings in which this book will apply economic analysis.
- The essential features of a capitalist system, also known as a market economy.

Society Requires Rules

So far in this book, we've explained that economics studies exchanges, and that basic economics simply spins out the logical implications of purposeful actions. In Lesson 4, we defined some of the basic concepts of economics, and applied them to a hypothetical man stranded on a tropical island. The laws or principles that we developed for our Robinson Crusoe are valid for everyone else, and are just as applicable in a bustling metropolis as on Crusoe's island. But in these more complicated settings, economics will show us patterns that we could not have noticed in the simple Crusoe scenario.

However, once we move from an isolated person into a world of two or more people, there's a new wrinkle in our analysis: What happens when two people want to use the same unit of a good in incompatible ways? In the case of Crusoe, we could say that in a sense, he was "exchanging with" Nature herself. For example, Crusoe would give up five hours of his leisure every day, and in return Nature would give him a daily stream of 20 coconuts. Given the physical realities of the island, those were the "terms of employment" offered to Crusoe.

At an abstract level, the situation is the same when Crusoe gets rescued and returns to civilization. He looks around his environment, discovers the various exchanges that are available to him, and proceeds to make those choices that give him the highest benefits relative to their costs. Yet at the same time, economics says that *everybody else is doing the same thing*. All alone on his island, Crusoe had the only intelligent mind, so only Crusoe was evaluating the value of various units of coconuts, rocks, vines, and so forth.

In a large city, all of the physical items that can satisfy human goals are being appraised by millions of different minds. If a man sees a coconut, it's not simply a question of whether it's worth his effort to go grab it. For if that coconut is already part of someone else's stockpile of savings, the two people's goals can't *both* be achieved.

In society, the economic problem of scarcity leads to conflict. There aren't enough units of goods to go around and satisfy everyone's goals or preferences. In addition to the tradeoffs and constraints imposed by Nature, in society there are the additional constraints imposed by everyone on each other.

In this book we will focus on three different **institutions** that humans have historically used to deal with the social conflict caused by economic scarcity. In this Part II of the book, we will apply the insights of economics in the realm of **capitalism**, or what is called a market economy. In Part III, we will briefly explore the attempt to handle scarcity through **socialism**, a system in which the government owns all goods or at least all the producer goods. And finally in Part IV, we will use economics to analyze what happens in a so-called **mixed economy**, where the government actively interferes with a background market economy, in order to improve its alleged shortcomings.

Capitalism: This Is Private Property

The term *capitalism* was originally a smear used by Karl Marx, who wanted to convey the idea that it was a system serving the narrow interests of the **capitalists**. However, as we'll see in later lessons, the capitalist system showers wealth on all of its members, whereas the socialist system concentrates incredible power in the hands of the privileged elites.

A capitalist system is based on **private property**. In this institutional arrangement, goods and services are owned by individual private citizens, or by groups of such citizens. In a pure capitalist system, not only every house and car, but every tractor, acre of farmland, and assembly line are all respectively owned by private citizens, sometimes organized in groups. A good's **owner** is the person with the legal authority to decide how that good shall be used. So in a capitalist system, when a man spots a coconut, he isn't (legally) allowed to consume it, unless he is the owner, or unless he gets permission from the owner.[1]

Property Is Fundamental

Property does not exist because there are laws, but laws exist because there is property.

—Frédéric Bastiat, "Property and Law" (1848), http://bastiat.org/en/property_law.html

[1]At least in the United States, the term "private property" sometimes means, "Stay away!" For example, if you and your friends are wandering through the woods and come across a barbed wire fence with a sign saying , "Keep out! Private Property," you probably don't want to mess with the guy who posted the sign. But in terms of capitalism versus socialism, even the parking lot of a mall is "private property." The owner(s) of the mall are simply giving blanket permission for all potential customers to use their property while they browse. Of course, if you and your friends are loitering in the parking lot and harassing customers as they park, the owners of the mall have the legal right to boot you from *their property*.

Don't Take Our Word For It

"Thou shalt not steal."

—The Lord God, quoted in Exodus 20:15

In practice, there are no real-world examples of a pure capitalist system. In addition to its **private sector**, every major economy today has a **public (government) sector**. At the same time, since the fall of the Soviet Union, there are no major economies today that even claim to operate under pure socialism. Instead there is a spectrum of the relative scope of the government versus the private sector.

Political theorists and economists have argued extensively about the ideal position on this spectrum—including its two end points of pure capitalism versus pure socialism. Because this book is an introduction to basic economics, rather than political philosophy, we will simply present sketches of three points on the spectrum: the two ends and the midpoint.

In this section of the book (Part II), we will sketch the operation of a pure capitalist system, one in which all goods and services are privately owned and exchanged in the marketplace. We will simply assume that the participants in the market respect these property boundaries. Other books can provide economic analysis to help you form an opinion as to the proper role for government to play in the provision of judicial, police, and military services that might be necessary to sustain widespread respect for private property.

The Market Economy and Free Enterprise

Economists often refer to "the market" as if it were a being with an independent mind. For example, economists who are suspicious of political interference might say, "The bureaucrats should mind their own business and leave these decisions to the market!"

However, the **market** or the **market economy** simply refers to the whole web of exchanges that individuals make with their private property. When economists say things like, "The market channeled more teachers into the town as its school-age population grew," this is just shorthand for saying that the incentives in a society based on private property led *individual teachers to choose* to relocate to the particular town. In subsequent lessons you will learn how these incentives operate in a market economy, but for now we should just be clear that "the market" is not a person or even a place, but refers to interactions between owners of private property.

People often describe a capitalist system as having **free enterprise**. This means that individuals (or groups of individuals) are free to enter any line of work they so choose. In medieval times, entry into the various professions was strictly regulated by **guilds**. For example, someone couldn't simply announce that he was a better tailor or carpenter than the other workers in town, and try to outcompete them. But in a market economy, anyone who wants to enter a certain profession can do so. Of course, he needs to respect the private property rights of others: If he wants to operate out of a store, he needs to rent the space or buy it himself. And if he is to be a *successful* tailor, he will need to convince potential customers to voluntarily trade away their money in exchange for his products and services. The crucial element of free enterprise is that there is no *additional* hurdle that the would-be tailor needs to jump over; all he needs to do is convince other private owners that they can all mutually benefit from dealing with him in his capacity as a tailor.

Finally, we note that the most significant piece of property is your own body. Whether we are dealing with Crusoe on his island, or brain surgeons in a major city, the services performed by human beings are some of the most valuable items in the economy. In a capitalist system, these items too must be assigned private owners. **Slavery** occurs when some individuals have the legal right to the bodies (and the services they perform) of other individuals. Both for moral and practical reasons, slavery forms no part of a pure capitalist system. In a market economy, workers are free to choose their employers—or to go into business for themselves—as a natural consequence of their ownership of their bodies.

Lesson Recap . . .

- Society requires institutions to establish rules and procedures so that people can interact with each other peacefully, and avoid conflict over scarce resources.

- This book will study the three institutional settings of capitalism, socialism, and a mixed economy.

- A capitalist system, also known as a market economy, features private ownership in resources. People are free to choose their own occupations and start whatever business they want, but any resources the business uses must be purchased or rented from the owners.

NEW TERMS

Institutions: Social relationships and practices that allow people to interact with each other. Institutions provide a framework of predictability in society.

Capitalism: A economic system relying on private property and free enterprise. No single person or group controls the system as a whole.

Socialism: An economic system in which government officials decide how society's resources shall be used to produce particular goods and services.

Mixed economy: A system that allows private citizens to legally own resources, but in which government officials lay down rules that limit the choices the legal owners can make with their property.

Capitalists: The people in a capitalist society who control (large amounts of) financial wealth. The very wealthy capitalists exercise a large degree of control over businesses.

Private property: A system in which resources are owned by people outside of the government.

Owner: The person who has legal authority to decide how a particular unit of a resource or good shall be used. The owner can usually transfer ownership to another person.

Private sector: The portion of an economy that is controlled by people outside of the government. (For example, a grocery store is in the private sector.)

Public sector: The portion of an economy that is controlled by the government. (For example, the local police station is in the public sector.)

Market / Market economy: Can be a synonym for *capitalism*. It also refers to the collection of voluntary exchanges that occur in a capitalist system.

Free enterprise: A system in which individuals can choose their own occupations and are free to start whatever business they wish. They don't need special permission from anyone to enter an industry.

Guilds: The organization of occupations in the medieval period, before the capitalist era. A person who wanted to become a blacksmith or a carpenter would first need to be accepted by other members of the guild.

Slavery: A system in which some human beings are considered the legal property of others.

STUDY QUESTIONS

1. Did Crusoe need an institution of private property?

2. Why does economic scarcity lead to potential conflict in society?

3. What are the three main institutional settings we will study in this course?

4. Is the sketch of a pure market economy a realistic depiction of the United States?

5. What does it mean when an economist says, "We should let the market decide"?

LESSON 6

Direct Exchange and Barter Prices

In this lesson you will learn:

- Why people trade with each other.
- The definitions of *direct exchange* and *barter*.
- How prices are formed in barter.

Why Do People Trade With Each Other?

In Lesson 4 we learned a lot about economics just from studying Robinson Crusoe and his "exchanges" with Nature. However, the true meat of economics comes from studying trades involving more than one person. To understand a market economy, we need to first understand individual trades between two people, because individual trades are the building blocks of the entire market economy.

For Robinson Crusoe, every "exchange" that he made with Nature was designed to benefit himself. Crusoe only chose those alternatives where he judged that the benefits outweighed the costs.

The same is true when a person exchanges, not with Nature, but with another person. Since we are assuming (in Part II of this book) a market economy with secure property rights, we know that *both* people in a voluntary exchange expect the benefits of the trade to outweigh the costs. In other words, both parties expect to walk away from the trade better off than they were before the trade.

How can this be possible? Some critics of capitalism think that if one person gains from a trade, it must be at the expense of the other party; they believe that one man's gain translates into another man's loss. But these critics are wrong! Remember that *preferences are subjective*. Suppose Tina comes to school with an orange in her lunch, and Sam comes to school with an apple. It wouldn't be strange if Tina would prefer an apple to her orange, while *at the same time* Sam would prefer an orange to his apple. If Sam and Tina become aware of each other's predicament, they can *both be happier* by trading.

Very often people make mistakes in their forecasts of what will make them happy. For example, maybe Sam has too much acid in his system and eating the orange causes a burning sensation, so that he ends up throwing it out after two bites. In that case, Sam will regret that he made the earlier trade with Tina. Even so, the important point for now is that *at the moment of exchange*, both parties in a voluntary trade (expect to) benefit from it. So long as the exchanges are voluntary and honest—in other words, so long as the exchanges aren't forced or based on deception—people can achieve more of their goals by having the option of trading their property with each other.

Direct Exchange / Barter

Ultimately we want to explain exchanges involving **money**. For most readers, this will mean explaining the prices of goods and services as they are traded against dollars, euros, yen, and so forth. We will actually explain these principles in the next lesson. For the remainder of this lesson, we will explain the principles behind exchanges that do not involve money. Specifically, we will focus on (what economists call) **direct exchange**, or what is also called **barter**.

In a direct exchange, both parties have a "direct" use for the object that they are receiving in the trade. Our story of Tina and Sam involved direct exchange, because each student wanted the other's fruit in order to consume it.

Direct exchange (or barter) can involve not only consumption goods, but also producer goods. (Refer back to Lesson 4 if you don't remember the difference.) For example, Farmer Brown might give a pound of bacon to Farmer Jones, in exchange for a bag of tomato seeds. Farmer Jones values the bacon as a consumption good; he will fry it and eat it that morning for breakfast. But Farmer Brown doesn't want to eat the tomato seeds he got in exchange! No, they are a producer good for him, because he will mix them with other items (such as soil and fertilizer) in order to produce tomatoes in the future. Don't be confused: Even though you might say that Farmer Brown doesn't "directly" benefit from the tomato seeds, the trade still counts as "direct exchange" (or barter) because both farmers want to personally use the items they receive in the transaction.

We only leave a state of barter and enter the realm of **indirect exchange** when people receive an item during a trade that they don't plan on using themselves, whether for consumption or production. What happens in this case is that they plan on *trading the item away to somebody else* in the future. This is actually what happens in every trade involving money. When you sell a few hours of your leisure cutting your neighbor's lawn for $20, you are engaged in indirect exchange. You don't plan on eating the $20 bill, and you don't intend to combine it with other materials in order to build something. The reason you value it, is that you expect to be able to find somebody else (in the future) who will sell you something you *do* directly value, in exchange for the money. We will develop the theory of indirect exchange in the next lesson. Here, we are explaining direct exchange (or barter), where both parties intend to use the traded objects for consumption or production (but not for a subsequent exchange).

Prices

In any market exchange, units of one good (or service) are traded for units of another good (or service). The **price** is the ratio of those units. For example, if the price of a DVD is $20, that means the buyer must give up 20 units of dollars while the seller gives up one unit of the DVD.

In barter, the familiar distinction between buyer and seller disappears, because there is no money. For example, when Farmer Brown gives a pound of bacon to Farmer Jones in exchange for (say) 100 tomato seeds, Brown is simultaneously a *buyer* of seeds and a *seller* of bacon. (Of course, Jones is the opposite: a buyer of bacon and a seller of seeds.) We can also say that the price of a pound of bacon is 100 tomato seeds, and that the price of a tomato seed is 1/100 of a pound of bacon.

As we will see in the next lesson, part of the beauty of a monetary economy is that we don't need to use barter prices, with every good (and service) having an entire list of exchange rates with every other good (and service) in the economy. For example, if there are 20 different types of goods that all trade against each other, then a trader in a pure barter economy would (in principle) need to keep track of (20x19)/2=190 different exchange ratios, or barter prices. But if there is one type of good involved in *every* trade—and that's precisely what money does—then the trader only needs to keep track of 20 prices: the exchange rate of each of the 20 goods against units of money. But before we can explore (in the next lesson) the special case of how prices are formed when money is involved in every transaction, we need to first understand the more general case of barter. We explore this topic in the next section.

How Prices Are Formed in Barter

For the remainder of this lesson, we will work with a specific numerical example to illustrate why specific prices occur in barter exchanges. Of course there is nothing magical about the numbers we will choose; the idea is simply to give you a concrete example to make sure you can visualize the more general principles.[1]

Our example revolves around three siblings—Alice, Billy, and Christy—who arrive home on Halloween after an evening of Trick or Treating. They each start with different amounts of Snickers and Milky Way candy bars. As we will see, because of their different holdings, and because of their different tastes, the children will be able to reap **gains from trade**. In other words,

[1]You may find some of the material in this section too difficult to fully understand. If that is the case, just read it and absorb as much as possible. The important take-away message is not for you to know exactly *how* economists can explain actual barter prices, but just to know that they *can* do so, if they know the preference rankings of the potential traders (and make a few assumptions).

through voluntary exchanges, the children will all walk away from their small "market" happier than they entered it. In our hypothetical example, we want to ultimately show why a specific exchange rate between Snickers and Milky Ways emerges. In other words, we want to understand how the children's initial holdings and their preferences will lead to a specific "Snickers-price" of Milky Ways, or (equivalently) a specific "Milky-Way-price" of Snickers.

In order to work through the example, we'll first need to come up with a convenient way to represent the information. The following table represents Alice's preferences, or rankings, of various combinations of Snickers and Milky Way bars. To keep things manageable, we will only consider cases where the children can have at most four of each type of candy bar. That means there are 25 possible combinations each child could have, in our example. (One possibility is having 4 Snickers and 4 Milky Ways. A second possibility is having 3 Snickers and 0 Milky Ways. A third possibility is having 1 Snickers and 2 Milky Ways. And so on, for all 25 possibilities.)

Before proceeding, let's make sure you understand the information in the table on the next page. We have chosen the numbers so that there is a definite sense in which Alice "likes Snickers more than Milky Ways." For example, if Alice initially has *no* Snickers or Milky Ways, and if she has to choose just one, she will pick a Snickers. The table below tells us this, because the combination (0 Snickers , 0 Milky Ways) has the lowest ranking, while the combination (1 Snickers , 0 Milky Ways) is ranked at 23rd, above the combination (0 Snickers , 1 Milky Ways) which is ranked in second-last place.

However, it's important for you to remember that people value goods *unit by unit* (or "on the margin"). It's true that if Alice initially has zero of each candy bar, she would prefer to receive a Snickers over a Milky Way. However, suppose that Alice already starts out with 1 Snickers bar. *Now* if someone offers her a choice between an (additional) Snickers versus a Milky Way, she will choose the Milky Way. This is because Alice ranks the combination (1 Snickers , 1 Milky Way) in 17th place, which is well above the combination (2 Snickers , 0 Milky Way) coming in at a lowly 21st place.

We have constructed Alice's ranking to be systematic; she basically likes Snickers more than Milky Ways, and she also prefers to have more candy rather than less. But notice that Alice also prefers variety. For example, she

Alice's Preference Ranking for Various Combos of Snickers (S) and Milky Ways (M)		
	1	4S , 4M
	2	4S , 3M
	3	3S , 4M
	4	3S , 3M
	5	4S , 2M
	6	2S , 4M
	7	3S , 2M
	8	2S , 3M
	9	4S , 1M
	10	1S , 4M
	11	2S , 2M
↑ Preferred Combos ↑	12	3S , 1M
	13	1S , 3M
	14	2S , 1M
	15	1S , 2M
	16	4S , 0M
	17	1S , 1M
	18	0S , 4M
	19	3S , 0M
	20	0S , 3M
	21	2S , 0M
	22	0S , 2M
	23	1S , 0M
	24	0S , 1M
	25	0S , 0M

would rather have 1 Snickers and 1 Milky Way—ranked in 17th place—than 3 Snickers and 0 Milky Ways (ranked in 19th place). In this specific comparison, at first glance it seems that Alice is violating two of the "rules" of her tastes—she is opting for *fewer* candy bars and *fewer* Snickers bars! But there is nothing strange going on here at all. The 17th-ranked combination gives her an even mixture of Snickers and Milky Ways, whereas the 19th-place combination, even though it has an extra candy bar, is loaded up with all Snickers. So there is nothing odd or "irrational" about Alice preferring the combination of 1 bar of each. Just as we can't say that people value water more than diamonds, by the same token we can't really say that Alice values Snickers (or more candy bars) more than she values Milky Ways (or fewer candy bars). It all depends on how many units of each good Alice starts out with when she is faced with a specific decision.

If you spend a few moments studying the table above, you will see the patterns in her preferences. In the real world, people's preferences don't mechanically obey a simple set of "rules," but we picked the commonsense ranking above to make it easier for you to follow the example.

Now that we understand Alice and her preferences, we can add her brother Billy to the mix. We'll suppose that his tastes are identical to Alice's. However, because the children start out with different combinations, there are still gains from trade. This information (and more) is summarized in the following table.

To repeat, we have purposely chosen Billy's preference rankings to be identical to Alice's, in order for you to see the effects of the children starting with different combinations of candy bars. In the real world, of course, people aren't identical copies of each other, especially when their preferences can encompass not merely 25 different scenarios, but an enormous number of combinations of many different goods and services.

Although the children have the same tastes for various combinations of Snickers and Milky Way bars, they come home from Trick or Treating with different collections. Alice comes to the bargaining table with 4 Snickers and 0 Milky Ways, while her brother shows up with 0 Snickers and 4 Milky Ways. A simple inspection of their rankings reveals that there are gains from trade. In other words, by rearranging their property, Alice and Billy can *both* end up with a Snicker-Milky Way combination that each subjectively prefers to the combination he or she started with.

However, economic logic alone can't tell us the exact terms on which Alice and Billy will agree to their exchange. To keep things simple, let's assume that they won't be splitting candy bars, so that they can only trade whole bars. Given the information in the table, what can we say about their trading?

Alice and Billy's Possible Trades of Snickers and Milky Ways

Preference Rank	Alice	Key	Billy
1	4S , 4M		4S , 4M
2	4S , 3M		4S , 3M
3	3S , 4M		3S , 4M
4	**3S , 3M**		3S , 3M
5	4S , 2M		4S , 2M
6	2S , 4M		2S , 4M
7	**3S , 2M**		3S , 2M
8	2S , 3M		**2S , 3M**
9	4S , 1M		4S , 1M
10	1S , 4M	**Initial Combo**	1S , 4M
11	**2S , 2M**	**Price: 1S for 1M**	**2S , 2M**
12	3S , 1M	**Price: 2S for 1M**	3S , 1M
13	1S , 3M	**Price: 1S for 2M**	1S , 3M
14	**2S , 1M**	**Price: 1S for 3M**	2S , 1M
15	1S , 2M		**1S , 2M**
16	**4S , 0M**		4S , 0M
17	1S , 1M		**1S , 1M**
18	0S , 4M		**0S , 4M**
19	3S , 0M		3S , 0M
20	0S , 3M		0S , 3M
21	2S , 0M		2S , 0M
22	0S , 2M		0S , 2M
23	1S , 0M		1S , 0M
24	0S , 1M		0S , 1M
25	0S , 0M		0S , 0M

The first principle to remember is that in a voluntary trade, both parties benefit. If we assume—and this might be an unrealistic assumption!—that the siblings don't steal each other's candy, then we know that any exchange must make Alice *and* Billy better off. That means we can rule out

Alice ending up with any of the combinations ranked 17th through 25th on her preferences, and we can rule out Billy ending up with a candy combination ranked 19th through 25th on his preferences. It is always an option to refrain from trading and just eat the candy they personally acquired from Trick or Treating, and so each sibling will end up at least as happy *after* trading as he or she was *before* trading.

Because our example is so simple, we can pretty quickly run through the possible trading outcomes by experimenting with various "prices." Suppose that Alice and Billy trade Snickers for Milky Ways at the ratio of 1:1. Are there mutually advantageous trades at this price?

Let's look at Alice's preferences first. She starts in the 16th-ranked cell, with (4 Snickers , 0 Milky Ways). So the question is: Would Alice be willing to trade away one or more Snickers bars, in exchange for an equal number of Milky Ways? We can see that the answer is yes. She could trade away 1 Snickers for 1 Milky Way, and end up with the (3S , 1M) combination ranked in 12th place. But she could do even better still by trading another unit, and moving up to the 11th ranked combination of two of each candy bar.

A similar analysis holds for Billy. He could move from the 18th ranked combination up to the 13th by trading away 1 Milky Way for 1 Snickers. But he could do better still by trading an additional unit, and moving up to the 11th ranked outcome on his own preferences.

For our current lesson, we will not delve too deeply into the exact procedure Alice and Billy use when bartering. You can imagine Alice first giving Billy 1 Snickers in exchange for 1 of his Milky Ways, and then they pause to reevaluate. Or you can imagine Alice offering 2 Snickers right off the bat, in exchange for Billy's 2 Milky Ways. The important point is that *if we set the price at 1:1*, then the only stable stopping point—the only **equilibrium position**—occurs when Alice and Billy have rearranged their candy bars so that they both end up holding 2 of each kind. Alice wouldn't give up a third Snickers to acquire yet another Milky Way, because that would move her back down to the 13th ranked combination (1S , 3M).

Be careful! It may seem as if we just "proved" that Alice and Billy will each end up with 2 of each candy bar, but we've only showed that this is the logical stopping point *if* they trade Snickers for Milky Ways at a 1:1 ratio (price). There are other prices that would still allow them to make mutually beneficial trades.

For example, suppose Alice says to Billy, "I will give you 1 of my Snickers bars if you give me 2 of your Milky Ways. That's the only trade I am willing to make. Take it or leave it." Is this a good deal? It's certainly a good deal for Alice. It would allow her to end up with 3 Snickers and 2 Milky Ways, the 7th most valuable combination on her ranking.[2]

The trade would also make Billy better off. He would end up with 1 Snickers and 2 Milky Ways, an outcome that is ranked three slots higher than if he doesn't trade at all. But he wouldn't engage in the same trade a second time, because then he would be left with (2S , 0M), a movement back down his preference ranking.

On the other hand, Billy could have issued a comparable ultimatum to Alice, saying that he would give up 1 of his Milky Ways in exchange for 2 of her Snickers, or else he would take his Halloween loot to his room and slam the door. If Alice believed his threat, she could improve her position by accepting the deal. The dark gray cells in the table above indicate the final combinations at a price of 2:1.

There is yet a fourth possibility. Suppose Alice is particularly cutthroat and demands 3 Milky Ways in exchange for just 1 of her Snickers. As the white cells indicate, this too is a possibility—if Billy really believed this to be the "going price," he would improve his lot by moving from the initial 18th position to the 17th position.

You can check to see that there are no other prices that work, if we continue to assume that the children only trade whole bars for each other. Notice that even though the price ratio 1:3 works, the opposite does not: Alice would rather keep her original combination than give up 3 Snickers for 1 measly Milky Way, and so Billy could never push through such an offer.

---

[2]Alice would also want to engage in a further trade on these terms, moving her to the 6th most preferred combination of having 2 Snickers and 4 Milky Ways. From analyzing Billy's point of view, we know that that won't occur. Some economists might say that therefore the price ratio of 1 Snickers for 2 Milky Ways doesn't lead to a true equilibrium, since Alice can only partially complete her desired transactions at this price. (Similar reasoning applies to Billy, for the hypothetical price ratio of 2 Snickers for 1 Milky Way.) This complication will make more sense to you after you study supply and demand curves in Lesson 11.

Summing up, what have we learned? We have seen that the underlying preference rankings and initial combinations of candy bars allow us to identify four different stable resting points, or equilibrium positions. Another way of describing our results is to say that we have identified four different outcomes in which *the gains from trade would be exhausted.* We also pointed out that for each of these four positions, there is a different price.

Economic logic alone can't tell us—with these specific numbers—how many candy bars Alice and Billy will have when they walk away from their trading session. We can't say for sure whether they will trade Snickers for Milky Ways at a ratio of 1:1, 2:1, 1:2, or 1:3. The actual outcome will depend on factors beyond the simple preference rankings and initial distribution of candy.

For example, if Alice really "drives a hard bargain" and Billy is relatively meek, then it's likely that she will push through the trade of 1 of her Snickers in exchange for 2 or 3 of Billy's Milky Ways. On the other hand, if Alice and Billy are equally skilled in the art of negotiation, then perhaps the even split will occur.

In the real world, it's possible that Alice and Billy make *no* exchanges, even if the table above correctly describes their preferences and candy holdings. Suppose Alice says, "Give me 2 Milky Ways and I'll give you 1 Snickers bar, or else I walk." Yet Billy thinks she is bluffing and says, "Nope, my best offer is to trade bars 1-for-1." In this case, it's certainly possible that Alice storms away, making good on her threat. In terms of our analysis, we would say that this isn't an "equilibrium" outcome, because there are still gains from trade that remain to be exploited—Alice and Billy can still both be happier if they swap their property around. So take care not to wrap too much significance around the economic concept of equilibrium—in the real world, **disequilibrium** occurs all the time!

Collapsing the Scope of Prices By Adding More Traders

Despite the complications, the above example laid out some basic principles in understanding how prices are formed in a barter market. In this final section we'll show that adding another trader can knock out some of the original possible prices. For this new twist, look at the table below, which reproduces the same rankings for Alice and Billy, but adds information about a third Trick or Treater, Christy:

Adding a Third Child Can Reduce the Number of Stable Outcomes

Preference Rank	Alice	Key	Billy	Christy
1	4S , 4M		4S , 4M	4S , 4M
2	4S , 3M		4S , 3M	4S , 3M
3	3S , 4M		3S , 4M	3S , 4M
4	**3S , 3M**		3S , 3M	4S , 2M
5	4S , 2M		4S , 2M	3S , 3M
6	**2S , 4M**		2S , 4M	4S , 1M
7	**3S , 2M**		3S , 2M	3S , 2M
8	2S , 3M		~~2S , 3M~~	2S , 4M
9	4S , 1M		4S , 1M	2S , 3M
10	1S , 4M	**Initial Combo**	1S , 4M	3S , 1M
11	~~2S , 2M~~	**Price: 1S for 1M**	~~2S , 2M~~	**2S , 2M**
12	3S , 1M	**Price: 2S for 1M**	3S , 1M	4S , 0M
13	1S , 3M	**Price: 1S for 2M**	1S , 3M	**1S , 4M**
14	~~2S , 1M~~	**Price: 1S for 3M**	2S , 1M	2S , 1M
15	1S , 2M		**1S , 2M**	1S , 3M
16	**4S , 0M**		4S , 0M	3S , 0M
17	1S , 1M		**1S , 1M**	1S , 2M
18	0S , 4M		**0S , 4M**	1S , 1M
19	3S , 0M		3S , 0M	2S , 0M
20	0S , 3M		0S , 3M	1S , 0M
21	2S , 0M		2S , 0M	0S , 4M
22	0S , 2M		0S , 2M	0S , 3M
23	1S , 0M		1S , 0M	0S , 2M
24	0S , 1M		0S , 1M	0S , 1M
25	0S , 0M		0S , 0M	0S , 0M

Notice that Christy's preferences for candy bars are not the same as Alice's and Billy's. Like them, Christy prefers more candy to less, and she also enjoys variety, other things equal. However, in everyday language people would say that Christy "likes Snickers bars a lot more than Alice and Billy." For example, Christy would rather have a *single* Snickers bar than have 4 Milky Ways! (Look at her 20th and 21st rankings.)

Of course, as someone trained in economic thinking, *you* know that there are situations where Christy would give up Snickers bars to obtain Milky Ways. For example, if she started with 4 Snickers, she would be willing to give up 2 of them to acquire 2 Milky Ways, as her 11th and 12th rankings demonstrate. But looking at her preference ranking compared to Alice's or Billy's, it is easy to see what the average person would mean by saying "Christy likes Snickers more than the others do," or perhaps, "Christy does *not* like Milky Ways nearly as much as the others do."

In the previous section we saw the various possible outcomes and barter prices with just Alice and Billy. What happens if Christy comes to the bargaining table before any deals are struck, and she's carrying 1 Snickers bar and 4 Milky Ways?

Before starting the analysis, let's lay the ground rules of how we're picturing the negotiating process. To keep things as simple as possible, we're going to look for outcomes where there is only one price for all the trades; in other words Alice can't charge Christy more Milky Ways than she charges Billy. We are also going to rule out any trade in which one of the children would object and make a better offer to one of the parties. So when Christy enters the scene, some of the possible "equilibrium positions" we discussed earlier break down.

For example, suppose Alice and Billy are about to trade Snickers for Milky Ways at a 1:1 price ratio. If Christy had never shown up, we already determined that Alice and Billy would each end up with 2 of each type of candy bar. At the price of 1:1, Christy would love to participate. After Billy and Alice had swapped 2 Snickers for 2 Milky Ways, Christy might say, "OK great, I would like to trade up to 3 of my Milky Ways for 3 Snickers bars from either of you guys." (These successive trades would move Christy from her original 13th ranked combination up to the 9th, 7th, and 6th ranked combinations.)

When Alice and Billy replied that they had done all the trading they wanted at the 1:1 ratio, Christy would be heartbroken. She could explain to Alice, "Why in the world did you trade away your Snickers at such a low price?! I would have gladly given you twice what Billy did."

For the purposes of our analysis in this lesson, we are going to say that this type of situation does *not* form a stable outcome or equilibrium. There is a sense in which Alice and Christy would both regret the outcome, if the price ratio of 1:1 occurred and Alice and Billy traded according to the original outcome when it was just the two of them. Loosely speaking we say that Christy comes on the scene and "knocks out" the 1:1 price.

Similar reasoning "knocks out" the other (original) stable outcome where Alice offered 2 Snickers to receive 1 Milky Way. It would be crazy for Alice to trade with Billy at such a disadvantage, when Christy would make her a much better offer.

The other two price ratios "survive" the arrival of Christy. At the 1:3 price, Christy remains a bystander. She sees Alice propose 1 of her Snickers for 3 of Billy's Milky Ways. He is tempted by the offer—it's better than nothing—but he turns to Christy and asks, "Can you do better than Alice?" Christy answers no, she wouldn't be willing to trade him her sole Snickers for only 2 Milky Ways. (We haven't included it because of space constraints, but the combination [0S, 6M] would be ranked far below [1S , 4M] for Christy.) Likewise, after the swap with Billy went through, Alice might ask Christy, "I'd be willing to give up another of my Snickers for 3 of *your* Milky Ways," but Christy would decline this offer too. So we see that 1:3 is still a stable or equilibrium price, but one on which Christy is content to "stay out of the market" and just eat the candy she personally collected from Trick or Treating.

The really interesting scenario is the price ratio of 1:2. Suppose Christy comes on the scene and observes that Alice is going to trade 1 Snickers for 2 of Billy's Milky Ways. Christy could say, "I'll take a piece of that action!" and Alice would be happy to oblige her. After the trades are complete, Alice ends up in her 6th ranked position, while Billy ends up in his 15th position and Christy in her 11th position. Once the candy bars have been rearranged in this fashion, there are no more gains from trade.

In this final scenario, the "equilibrium price" was 1 Snickers for 2 Milky Ways. At that price: (a) Alice sold 2 Snickers and bought 4 Milky Ways, (b)

Billy sold 2 Milky Ways and bought 1 Snickers, and (c) Christy sold 2 Milky Ways and bought 1 Snickers. Notice that the total number of Snickers sold equals the total number bought, and the same for Milky Ways. Also notice that at the equilibrium price, every child is able to complete the trades he or she wanted.[3]

As with the analysis when there were just two children, here we can't use economic logic alone to say what the resulting Snickers : Milky Way price will be. What we *can* say is that—with these specific numbers—Christy's presence collapsed the possible range of prices. Intuitively, Christy showed up with a large supply of Milky Ways and a strong demand for Snickers, and that ruled out some of the possible prices where Snickers were fairly cheap (namely 1:1 and especially 2:1).

Obviously the Halloween example was unrealistic in many ways, and there were many real-world considerations that we ignored. We focused on important principles that will show up in later lessons, after we introduce money and focus on Supply and Demand in markets. Generally speaking, in a large market with many buyers and sellers, there is a very narrow range of potential prices that are stable in the sense we've discussed above. For simplicity we will normally just talk of "the" equilibrium price, as determined by the preferences and initial property holdings of all the traders in the market. We went through the Halloween story in the present lesson to show you the basic foundation on which the more standard presentation—with supply and demand curves measuring prices in dollars—is based.

---

[3]On this point we again have to be careful because Alice can only partially complete her desired trades for the price of 1 Snickers for 3 Milky Ways. Although we didn't show it because of space constraints, Alice could very plausibly prefer a combination of (2S , 6M) to (3S , 3M), meaning that she would have preferred another round of trading in the gray equilibrium.

Lesson Recap . . .

- People trade with each other because they expect to gain from the exchange.
- So long as a trade is voluntary and honest, both parties expect to benefit. Trade leads to a win-win outcome.
- If an economist knows the preference rankings of a group of potential traders, he can describe how they would settle on the terms of their exchanges.

NEW TERMS

Money: A good that is accepted by everyone in the economy on one side of every trade.

Direct exchange / barter: Trading that occurs when people swap goods that they directly value.

Indirect exchange: Trading that occurs when at least one of the parties accepts an item that he or she does not intend to use personally, but instead will trade it away in the future to get something else.

Price: The terms of a trade, meaning how many units of one item are given up to acquire a unit of a different item.

Gains from trade: A situation in which two people can both gain (subjective) benefits from swapping their property with each other.

Equilibrium position: A stable situation in which there are no further gains from trade.

Disequilibrium: An unstable situation in which at least two people stand to benefit from an additional trade.

STUDY QUESTIONS

1. How is it possible for both parties to benefit from the same exchange?

2. *If a producer good only provides benefits indirectly, can a producer good be obtained via direct exchange?

3. Suppose the economy has only four goods: apples, oranges, bananas, and grapes. In barter, how many independent price ratios would exist? (E.g., the apple:orange ratio would not be independent of the orange:apple ratio.)

4. If Alice likes Snickers more than Milky Ways, does that mean she would always choose a Snickers over a Milky Way, if offered a choice between one or the other?

5. *In what sense did Christy's arrival "knock out" some of the possible equilibrium prices that could have formed between Alice and Billy?

LESSON 7

Indirect Exchange and the Appearance of Money

In this lesson you will learn:

- The limitations of direct exchange.
- The advantages of *indirect exchange* and *money*.
- The origin of money.

The Limitations of Direct Exchange

In Lesson 6 we learned the tremendous benefits of direct exchange. Because people often have different tastes (or preferences), and because they often start out with different amounts of various goods, there are gains from trade. People can voluntarily trade their property amongst each other, so that everyone ends up owning property that he or she values more than the original collection of property.

However, even though direct exchange benefits everyone who participates in it, there are limits to its effectiveness. In fact it's hard to imagine a world where people only engaged in *direct* exchange, versus *indirect* exchange (which we'll discuss in the next section). But in order to see the important difference, let's just imagine a world where people only make direct exchanges.

Remember, in a direct exchange each person must *directly* want to use the object being acquired. So we rule out any case where someone trades away something he originally owns, in order to acquire something that he then intends *to trade away to yet a third person*. It turns out that this limitation it actually quite restrictive.

For example, suppose a farmer goes into town to get his tattered shoes repaired, and to buy a new shirt. He brings with him several dozen eggs hoping to make a trade. Our poor farmer has to not only find a cobbler with the necessary skills to repair his shoes, but he needs to find a cobbler *who is that very same day looking to acquire eggs*. The same is true of our farmer's efforts to acquire a new shirt. He needs to find somebody who has a shirt that the farmer likes, *and* who is willing to trade away the shirt in exchange for the farmer's eggs (at an acceptable price).

But if you think things are tough on our farmer, they're even worse for the guy whose business is to produce stagecoaches. When he takes a finished stagecoach to market, he expects to get a large variety of goods and services in exchange for such a prized item. But if the world were limited to direct exchange, he would be unlikely to find a suitable trading partner. Not only would he have to find someone who owned an acceptable collection of meats, eggs, shirts, milk, ammunition, etc. that our manufacturer preferred to his stagecoach, but that special person would *also* have to be "in the market" for a stagecoach. What are the odds of that?

In reality, there would not *be* stagecoach producers, and probably not even shoe cobblers, in a world limited to direct exchange. People would not be able to specialize in certain professions, because it would be too risky. For example, a schoolteacher might instruct children in arithmetic and grammar, in exchange for milk, bread, and kerosene that the parents of the various children were willing to provide. But if one year there happened to not be any butchers who had school-age children, then the schoolteacher would have to go without meat the entire year!

So we see that in a world of direct exchange, people would probably live basically as Robinson Crusoe. As a default, they would have to provide for their own range of needs directly, acquiring their own food, making their own clothes, building their own shelter, and so on. Their standard of living would be much higher because of the benefits of trading with each other, but intensive specialization and large-scale production operations would be infeasible.

The Advantages of Indirect Exchange

We have seen the limitations of direct exchange. These limitations can be overcome when people begin to use *indirect* exchanges. In an indirect exchange, at least one of the traders gives up his own goods in return for something that he plans on swapping away for something *else* in the future. Once we allow this possibility, the limitations of direct exchange fall away.

For example, recall our farmer who went to town with a few dozen eggs, seeking shoe repair and a new shirt. Suppose the only cobbler in town told him, "Sorry I don't need any eggs right now." Under direct exchange, that would be that.

However, with the possibility of indirect exchange, the farmer can ask, "What *would* you be willing to trade away your shoe repair services for?" Suppose the cobbler answered, "I would fix your shoes if you could give me at least 6 pounds of butter, or 4 loaves of French bread, or a pound of bacon. Those are the things I'm really interested in right now."

This holds out hope for our farmer. He can now walk around town (in his tattered shoes) looking for someone who wants eggs, and is willing to trade butter *or* French bread *or* bacon for them. Instead of needing to find the perfect match—a cobbler who was looking for eggs that very day—the farmer can now add three more potential candidates who will work.

In fact, depending on how much time he wants to spend on the project, the farmer can take things a step further. Suppose he finds a butcher who has extra bacon that he's trying to sell, but that the butcher (like the cobbler) isn't interested in any more eggs that day. The butcher mentions that he *does* want some fish. A few minutes later, the farmer meets up with a fisherman just back from a long haul, and who is dying to have a big omelet. If you have ever dabbled with role-playing computer games, we don't need to spell out the opportunity this presents to our farmer.

Under direct exchange, the farmer needed to find a perfect match, namely a cobbler who wanted his eggs. Indirect exchange opens up a vast new range of beneficial trades, especially if traders are willing to operate at several "levels deep" of indirectness. The tremendous advantage of indirect exchange is that it facilitates rearrangements of property among multiple individuals, making them all better off, even though any single swap would have been vetoed by one of the required parties. The following diagram illustrates:

Rankings for *Direct* Use	Cobbler	Farmer	Butcher
1	Bacon	Repaired shoes	Eggs
2	Leisure	Eggs	Bacon
3	Eggs	Bacon	Repaired shoes

To keep things simple, in the diagram above we've left out the fisherman; we're assuming the farmer was able to find a butcher who wanted eggs in exchange for bacon. As the diagram indicates, all three of the men are happier when (1) the cobbler repairs the farmer's shoes, (2) the farmer gives his eggs to the butcher, and (3) the butcher gives his bacon to the cobbler. We know they're all better off, because they've moved from their 2nd ranked positions up to their 1st ranked positions. (Their original possessions are highlighted.)

However, notice that under direct exchange, this beneficial rearrangement of property (and performance of services) could not have occurred. We already know from the original story that there are no direct gains from trade between the cobbler and farmer; the diagram above reflects this fact, because the cobbler values his leisure time more than the eggs the farmer has to offer. The diagram also shows that the butcher values his bacon more than having the cobbler repair his shoes, and so there are no gains from direct exchange between those two. Finally, there are no *direct* gains from trade between the farmer and butcher, because the farmer's *direct* desire for bacon is ranked 3rd. If the farmer and butcher were the only people involved, then the farmer would not agree to the trade.

The beauty of indirect exchange is that it allows universally beneficial property (and service) transfers to get around the "bottlenecks" imposed by direct exchange. As the case of our hypothetical farmer illustrates, indirect exchange allows everyone to move much higher on his or her preference ranking, through suffering a temporary "hit" that is made up in the future by trading away the (directly) inferior object. When it comes to advantageous rearrangements of property, indirect exchange facilitates the principle of "one step back, two steps forward."

The Advantages of Money

We have seen the advantages of direct exchange, and the even greater advantages of indirect exchange. However, even if people begin accepting items in trade, planning to trade them away for what they ultimately desire, this process can still be quite cumbersome. To see why, just recall our illustration of the farmer with tattered shoes: Even though it all worked out in the end, he still had to go traipsing through town, looking for someone who was selling the items that the cobbler wanted to buy.

Besides the physical exertion involved, we should also point out the mental effort that traders would have to waste keeping track of dozens or possibly hundreds of important price ratios. For example, let's revisit our story of the farmer trying to find a buyer of his eggs so that he can give the cobbler enough bacon to fix his shoes. In the version of the story we told above, we simply assumed that once the farmer had run across the fisherman, that would be the end of the matter.

Yet in reality, our farmer may have held out for a better deal. If the fisherman were willing to trade 3 fish for 6 eggs, and the butcher were willing to trade a pound of bacon for 3 fish, then the farmer would realize, "Okay, I can ultimately get my shoes fixed by giving up 6 of my eggs."

If this were his only option, the farmer would think it well worth the price. But what if the town were quite large, with many different merchants and professionals? Suppose the farmer could find a baker who would be willing to give up 4 loaves of French bread for only 5 eggs. In this case, our farmer would realize, "Okay, I can ultimately get my shoes fixed by giving up 5 of my eggs." Notice that this is 1 egg cheaper than going through the route of trading eggs for fish.

Already you are probably getting lost in all the details. Yet in the real world, people would start keeping track of the exchange ratios of various goods against each other, in order to know whether they were getting a "good deal" on any particular trade. We see that the possibility of indirect exchange is thus a blessing and a curse: It's a blessing because it allows many people to make complicated (yet unanimously beneficial) rearrangements of their property. But it can also be a curse because people now can't merely consult their preferences of the *direct* use of goods when deciding whether and how much to trade. Before giving away something that they might personally find revolting, they first have to ask, "How much could I get for this if I held out for another buyer?"

What makes the above question particularly difficult is when traders need to reason two, three, or even more steps ahead to discover the ultimate "price" of the object they are trying to buy. In our story of the farmer, look at how complicated things got, even after introducing just a handful of different traders and their offers. In theory, for our farmer to be sure he obtained the cobbler's shoe repair services at the lowest possible price (measured in eggs), he would need to survey the entire town, writing down everyone's willingness to buy and sell various types of goods against each other. Then he would need a math whiz to help him solve a complex problem, showing him the (perhaps very long) chain of individual trades through which our farmer could give up the least possible number of eggs, in order to ultimately acquire 6 pounds of butter, 4 loaves of French bread, or 1 pound of bacon (which the cobbler insists on before repairing the shoes).

Of course, in the real world we don't have to go through such mental gymnastics every time we want to trade. Instead, we use **money**, which we can formally define as "a widely accepted medium of exchange." In plain language, *money* is a good that stands on one side of (virtually) every transaction. Rather than trading other goods directly against each other, people first sell all their wares to obtain money, and then they use the money to buy all their desired items.

When people in a community use money, they retain all the advantages of indirect exchange but considerably reduce its disadvantages. Rather than keeping track of dozens or even hundreds of price ratios of various goods offered and sought by various people, with money traders can simply keep track of the highest and lowest prices—quoted in money—of the items in which they're interested.

For example, if the town in our story above uses silver as its money, our farmer with the tattered shoes now has a relatively simple task. When he gets to town, he first searches for the person who will offer the most ounces of silver for his eggs. Then with the silver in hand, the farmer searches for the person who will repair his shoes for the fewest ounces of silver. So long as everyone in town buys and sells using silver, the above procedure ensures that the farmer obtains his shoe repair (and whatever else he wants to acquire) at the lowest possible sacrifice of his eggs. He no longer needs to write down the desires of every person he meets—he frankly doesn't *care* what others want to buy—and he no longer needs a math whiz to solve a complicated optimization problem.[1]

Who Invented Money?

The short answer is, "No one." As with a dirt trail through a forest, the English language, rock & roll, the rules of chess, and hairdos in the 1980s, no single person got up one day and invented money. Instead, money arose gradually over time as a cumulative result of the actions of many people. The institution of money is a classic example of what Austrian economist Friedrich Hayek called a **spontaneous order**, meaning that the use of money is a very complex and useful practice, even though it was not consciously planned by an expert or even a group of experts. Quoting the Scottish moral philosopher Adam Ferguson, Hayek described spontaneous orders (including money and spoken languages) as "the product of human action but not of human design."

Today almost everyone on the planet thinks of *money* as pieces of paper issued by governments. However this was not always so. Historically, money arose first in the marketplace, as an outgrowth of voluntary exchanges between regular traders. Kings and other political rulers saw the spoils to be reaped and gradually took over this market-created institution, as we will explain in greater detail in Lesson 21.

But without the intervention of a wise king, how could society have adopted the use of money? How would everyone decide what to use? After all, researchers tell us that throughout history different cultures have used all sorts of things as money: sea shells, rocks, cattle, salt, tobacco, gold, silver, and even cigarettes (in World War II P.O.W. camps). How would a group of people settle on a particular commodity to use as their money without resort to a political process?

---

[1]Strictly speaking, the astute trader would keep his or her eyes open for an **arbitrage opportunity**, even in a monetary economy. Yet even here, the calculations would be much easier than in an economy with no single medium of exchange lying on one side of each transaction. One of the exercises in the Teacher's Manual spells out this difference.

The answer is that it was probably a natural outgrowth of the efforts of people like our hypothetical farmer looking to get his shoes repaired. Recall that even though the farmer didn't *directly* have any use for fish or bacon—he didn't go to town to get either of those items—he ended up trading away his eggs for some fish, in order to trade the fish for bacon, in order to trade the bacon for a shoe repair. Notice that from the perspective of the fisherman and the butcher, they saw *an increase in the market for their products* because of indirect exchange. In other words, in addition to all the people who wanted to buy fish for their own direct use, the fisherman had a potential customer in the form of the farmer, who wanted to use the fish *indirectly* as a **medium of exchange**.

This process could snowball. In the beginning, when people were bartering goods against each other in a state of pure direct exchange, certain items (chickens, eggs, salt, etc.) would be widely desired in trade, while other items (telescopes, caviar, harpsichords, etc.) would be accepted by very few people. Then as the advantages of indirect exchange become obvious to more and more people, the initially more marketable goods would see a huge leap in their marketability. Even those people who didn't initially want the (highly marketable) goods for their direct use would nonetheless be willing to accept them in trade, because they would know it would be easy to trade them away for whatever they ultimately desired. If the snowballing process ever reached a point where a particular good were accepted in trade by almost everyone in the community, that would mark the birth of money—"a widely accepted medium of exchange."

To understand why some goods historically became money, and others did not, we can list some of the practical considerations, such as (1) ease of transport, (2) divisibility, (3) durability, and (4) convenient market value. When we consider these four criteria, we see why gold and silver have proven to be such excellent candidates of market-based money. For example, cattle are not very practical as money because they make smelly messes, they take up a lot of space, and you can't simply cut a steer in half to "make change" during a transaction. Popsicles also wouldn't stand the test of time as money, because they melt without proper care. Finally, a metal like bronze shares many of the excellent money-qualities of gold and silver, but because it is so plentiful, bronze has a much lower market value. That means a trader would need to carry a lot more bronze in his pockets (or in a cart) when making an expensive purchase, compared to how many gold and silver coins or bars he would need for the same trade.

There is nothing in economics that says gold and silver must be money, or that they are the only "natural" form of money. In a voluntary market, traders will end up adopting the money or monies that best suits their needs. We are merely explaining why, historically, gold and silver have so often been adopted by sophisticated merchants as money.

Lesson Recap . . .

- Although direct exchange is useful because it allows for win-win trades, it is limited because a trader needs to find someone who has the desired item *and* who wants to accept the good that the first trader wishes to give up. This limitation would make it very difficult for people to specialize in occupations: A dentist who wanted meat would need to find a butcher who had a toothache.

- Indirect exchange expands the opportunities of mutually beneficial trades. More complicated rearrangements of goods can occur, which make every participant better off. Indirect exchange eventually leads to the use of money, which makes it much easier for people to plan their trading activities.

- Nobody invented money. It arose spontaneously, almost "by accident," out of people's actions to improve their trading positions using indirect exchange.

NEW TERMS

Money: A good that is accepted by everyone in the economy on one side of every trade. In economics jargon, it is a widely (or universally) accepted medium of exchange.

Spontaneous order: A predictable pattern that is not planned by any one person. Examples would include the rules of grammar in the English language, the style of clothing that characterized the 1970s disco clubs, and the use of money.

Arbitrage opportunity: The ability to earn a "sure profit" when the same good sells at different prices at the same time.

Medium of exchange: An object that is accepted in a trade, not because the person receiving it wants to directly use it, but because he or she wants to trade it away in the future to acquire something else. Every indirect exchange requires a medium of exchange, which is the good through which the ultimate trade occurs. (Likewise, sound waves require a *medium* to travel through, in order to reach your ears. When it comes to sound waves, the medium will usually be the air, but it can also be water if you are in a pool with your head below the surface.)

STUDY QUESTIONS

1. What's the difference between direct and indirect exchange?

2. Why would specialization be impractical in a world limited to direct exchange?

3. How does indirect exchange facilitate the strategy of "one step back, two steps forward"?

4. What are the disadvantages of indirect exchange without money?

5. *Describe a society in which the people practice indirect exchange, but have not yet developed money.

LESSON 8

The Division of Labor and Specialization

In this lesson you will learn:

- The definitions of *division of labor (specialization)* and *productivity of labor*.
- The advantages of the division of labor.
- The principle of *comparative advantage.*

The Division of Labor and Specialization

In the last lesson we learned that the use of indirect exchange—especially when the practice is taken to its logical conclusion with the use of money—greatly enhances the scope for beneficial trades. However, a monetary economy doesn't merely facilitate the rearrangement of already-existing finished goods. One of its chief benefits is to foster the **division of labor,** which means that people **specialize** in different tasks in order to produce the goods in the first place.

To put it in other words, in the previous lesson we were taking it for granted that there was a person called a "butcher" who spent his time preparing and selling meats, and a person called a "cobbler" who spent all day selling shoes (and shoe repair services). Yet this was putting the cart before the horse, because without indirect exchange and especially the use of money, trading options would be so limited that people would have to be largely self-sufficient. In other words, if a community of people only engaged in direct exchange, then no individual could probably *afford* to become a shoe cobbler—he might get scurvy if no one with vegetables needed his shoes fixed for a few months.

As we have seen, the use of money overcomes these limitations. Very complex chains of production and trading can be arranged, since at each step the sellers can unload their wares for money and then look for the lowest prices in their role as buyers. A shoe cobbler can buy goods and services from dozens of other professionals, even though some of them may have no need for the cobbler's services. In effect, the use of money allows the cobbler to do a "favor" for a third party (say, a dentist) who then does a "favor" for the butcher (by fixing his teeth) who in turn does a "favor" for the cobbler (by giving him some of his bacon). Only through the use of money can very complex "favor swapping" occur, which makes it practical for people to "divide the labor" that needs to be done and allow individuals to specialize in particular tasks.

To grasp just how important the division of labor is, imagine a world without it. Rather than people specializing in various occupations and producing far more than they personally need, people instead try to be perfectly self-reliant. Each person (or each household at the very least) would grow his own food, make his own clothes, build his own furniture, perform his own dental and medical procedures, and so on. Clearly in such a world, most of the world's current population would die within a month or two, and the small band of survivors would live a primitive existence, especially as the tools they used wore out, machines broke down, and gasoline supplies ran out.

Why would modern civilization collapse without the division of labor? The quick answer is that the **productivity of labor** would plummet. Remember that Robinson Crusoe, alone on his desert island, was able to improve his lot—was able to achieve a life that he considered more pleasant—by using his *labor* to transform his environment. We saw that through saving and investment (in order to create a pole out of branches and vines), Crusoe could greatly increase the productivity of his labor, meaning that he could increase the number of coconuts he could acquire per hour of labor.

But saving and investment is only *one way* to increase the productivity of labor. Another way is through the division of labor, where "the work" is divided up into different types of tasks, and individual workers specialize in one or a few tasks. Rather than each person growing his own food, making his own clothes, performing his own dental work, etc., with specialization some people grow *all* the food, and some other people do *all* the dental work, etc. In our society, we have special names for these two groups of people: *farmers* and *dentists*.

The productivity of labor is magnified greatly when it is "divided" in this fashion. Simply put, people can produce more total stuff when they specialize in their tasks, rather than everyone trying to produce a small portion of each item in the total pile of stuff. By having special individuals devote themselves exclusively to farming, and others exclusively to dentistry, there is more total food produced, and more cavities pulled, per year than would be possible without the division of labor. Since there is more total stuff to go around, everyone can eat more, wear more clothes, and so forth under the division of labor.

Why Specialization Makes Labor More Productive

Most people agree that if they had to grow their own food, make their own clothes, etc., they would be plunged into abject poverty. Even though the conclusion is sensible, it's useful to spell out some of the specific reasons that specialization makes labor so much more productive:

- *Less time wasted switching between tasks.* Picture something as simple as three children cleaning up the table after dinner. Most likely, the kids can get the job done more quickly if they divide up the tasks and specialize, for the simple reason of cutting down on unnecessary walking. For example, one child can scrape the plates off into the garbage and carry the dishes to the sink. The second child can wash, and the third can dry. This system is much more efficient—they will all be done much sooner—than if each child grabbed a dish, scraped it into the garbage, then carried it over to the sink and washed it, then stepped to the right to dry the same dish and finally put it away. The same principle applies to other productive operations.

- *Promotes automation.* By taking a complicated task and breaking it down into its components, the division of labor promotes the use of automation (machinery). If everyone grew his own food in the backyard, it wouldn't make sense for anyone to develop tractors. Even if we just consider a particular factory, its output will be higher if the workers specialize in their jobs within the factory because it's then easier to incorporate machinery and tools to help them.

- *Economies of scale.* This is a generalization of the first two principles. For many operations, there are **economies of scale** at least up to a certain level of output. This principle means a doubling of inputs more than doubles the output. For example, if a chef switches from making enough pasta to feed one person to feeding fifty people, the time spent on preparation of the sauce, boiling the water, and so on certainly doesn't increase fifty times. This principle alone explains why it makes sense for roommates to alternate preparing meals, rather than each roommate cooking a whole meal for him or herself every night. Another everyday illustration of economies of scale involves making a cup of coffee: Whether you want to make one cup or four, the prep work is largely the same, which is why people often ask, "I'm making coffee, anyone else want some?"

- *Natural aptitude.* So far our principles have shown that even if the whole world were filled with identical people, there would still be advantages from specialization. In the real world, of course, people are *not* identical. Some people are simply born to be better farmers than others—and this natural advantage can include geographical factors. For example, a strong boy in Idaho would probably be able to grow more potatoes per year than a sickly, bed-ridden boy in Idaho, but at the same time a strong boy in Florida can grow more oranges per year than even a strong boy in Idaho. And the bed-ridden boy in Idaho might be born with a wonderful knack for language, and thus makes a much better copy editor or novelist than either of the healthy boys who are much better equipped to be farmers.

- *Acquired aptitude*. The true advantages of the division of labor occur when people *develop* their natural aptitudes through training and practice, practice, practice. Someone who's always had a "knack for numbers" in school would do a better job working at an accounting firm after graduating high school, compared to another high school graduate who always struggled with math. But if the student with good math skills then went to college and *majored* in accounting, his superiority would be even more pronounced. Finally, if we followed that same person and checked in at age 50, after he had spent twenty-eight years working as an accountant, then obviously he would be far more proficient at the job—meaning his labor would be much much more productive—than any other human who did not have such a background.

The above list is not meant to be exhaustive, but it lays out some of the main reasons that labor is so much more productive through specialization.

Enriching Everyone By Focusing on Comparative Advantage

It's important to emphasize that the benefits of specialization can only be reaped when people are able to *trade* with each other. If some people focus on growing food, while others focus on building houses, then this arrangement only works if the farmers are allowed to trade their surplus food in exchange for some of the builders' surplus houses. Otherwise the farmers will freeze and the builders will starve. Without the ability to move goods around the economy, the huge leap in "total output" (made possible by the division of labor) would be a hollow victory.

It's easy enough to see the mutual benefits of specialization and trade when two people have different areas of expertise. For example, if Joe is really good at planting and harvesting wheat, whereas Bill is an expert at sewing pants, then it's obvious that the two will both enjoy a higher standard of living if Joe concentrates on producing wheat while Bill concentrates on producing pants.

However, economists have discovered that the principle applies even in cases where one person is more productive *in every possible way*. In the jargon of economics, we can say that even if one person has an **absolute advantage** in every line of production, he or she still benefits by specializing in his or her **comparative advantage**, which is the field where the superiority is *relatively* greatest.

The principle of comparative advantage was traditionally used to illustrate the benefits of free trade in commodities between two nations, but for our purposes we can make the point quite easily with an example of two people in a monetary economy. Consider the table below:

Time It Takes to Perform Tasks in Clothing Store

	Tidy Up Store at Day's End	Convince Customer to Buy
John (hired help)	60 minutes	120 minutes
Marcia (owner)	30 minutes	15 minutes

In the table above, we see the hypothetical performance times at a clothing store in the mall for John (hired help) and Marcia (the store's owner). As the numbers indicate, Marcia is better at both making sales *and* at tidying up the store at the day's end, in preparation for opening the next morning.

Because Marcia has the *absolute advantage* in both making sales and tidying up, you might at first think that it is most efficient for her to spread her workday among the two tasks, rather than bringing John into the picture. But that's not correct. By hiring John and having him focus on taking out the trash, mopping the floors, etc. at the end of each day, Marcia can concentrate on her *comparative advantage*, which is making sales. In other words, Marcia can allow customers to stay in the store and browse for longer (thus making more sales), since she is delegating the necessary tidying up to John.

If Marcia is running her business in a monetary economy, it is quite simple for her to figure out whether it makes sense to hire outside help (John) or whether she should close the store early so that she can tidy up herself. For example, suppose that the typical customer purchase yields Marcia net earnings of $20.[1] That means for every 15 minutes that Marcia devotes to helping customers on the floor, on average she brings in an extra $20 that she can pay herself. If Marcia has to kick the customers out early, so that she can spend the last 30 minutes of each day tidying up, on average she thereby loses out on $40 in potential income from her business.

Does it make sense for Marcia to hire John, who runs a cleaning service catering to stores in the mall? It depends what John charges for his services. So long as he is willing to charge less than $40 to come in and clean up Marcia's store at the end of each day, it makes sense for Marcia to delegate these simple tasks to John. Since John is just a young guy with no significant skills, he is happy to charge just $15 for his hour of work. As these hypothetical numbers illustrate, there are large gains from trade between Marcia and John: It would be worth her while to pay someone up to $40 to tidy up her store, while John would be happy to do the job—which takes him an hour to complete—for anything more than $15. At any price in that range, both Marcia and John would consider the arrangement quite attractive.

Just to round out the discussion, notice that it would *not* make sense for Marcia to hire John to help her with making sales, or for John to quit the cleaning business and go into clothing retail. Because John is such a worse salesman than Marcia, he only makes a typical sale once every two hours (120 minutes). That means if John tried to replicate Marcia's business and devoted himself to selling clothes, his net earnings would work out to an average of $20 every two hours, or a mere $10 per hour. John can make much more than that cleaning.

Our example has illustrated the principle of comparative advantage: Even though Marcia is more productive at both tidying up her store and in

[1]For example, Marcia might sell $50 of clothes at the retail price, but she in turn had to spend $30 (all things considered) for those clothes in terms of the original wholesale price, as well as the overhead expenses of renting the store space, paying the electric bill, etc. In a more advanced textbook you can learn the precise ways that businesses treat different expenses and calculate the earnings from a particular sale.

making sales, she still benefits from associating with John. Marcia has the absolute advantage in both tasks, but only the comparative advantage in making sales. (John has the absolute advantage in neither task, but he *does* have the comparative advantage in cleaning.)

Specialization and trade showers benefits on all participants, even when one of them is more technically capable than the others. As we will see in Lesson 19, the principle of comparative advantage applies to international trade just as much as it does to Marcia and John.[2] A rich and productive country like the United States still benefits from trading with a "backward" country where the workers are less productive in every line of work and production.

---

[2]The Teacher's Manual contains an exercise explicitly illustrating the application of comparative advantage to international trade in Lesson 19.

Lesson Recap . . .

- One of the advantages of using money is that it allows people to specialize in different occupations.

- The division of labor (specialization) greatly enhances the productivity of labor. There is more total output when some people concentrate on growing food, others concentrate on building houses, others concentrate on treating illness, and so forth.

- Even someone who is more productive in every activity can still benefit from trading with people who are not as productive. Even in this case, both parties should focus on the areas in which they have the relative superiority—the comparative advantage—and trade some of the resulting output.

NEW TERMS

Division of labor / specialization: The situation where each person works on one or a few tasks, and then trades to obtain the things produced by others.

Productivity of labor: The amount of output a worker can produce in a certain period of time.

Economies of scale: A condition in which output will increase more than proportionally as inputs are increased. For example, there are economies of scale if doubling the amount of inputs leads to a tripling in output.

Absolute advantage: Occurs when a person can produce more units per hour in a particular task, compared to someone else.

Comparative advantage: Occurs when a person has the relative superiority in a particular task, when taking all other tasks into account. (Jim can have a comparative advantage in a certain task, even if Mary has the absolute advantage, because Mary might have an absolute advantage that's even *greater* in something else.)

STUDY QUESTIONS

1. What's the connection between specialization and the productivity of labor?

2. *If the world were filled with identical people, would specialization still be useful?

3. Why is trade important for the division of labor?

4. *Explain this statement: "The gains from trade in a case of absolute advantage are obvious, but they can be quite subtle in a case of comparative advantage."

5. Why is Marcia the storekeeper willing to pay up to $40 to have someone clean her store at the end of the day?

LESSON 9

Entrepreneurship and Competition

In this lesson you will learn:

- The role of entrepreneurs in a market economy.
- How competition guides entrepreneurs.
- Why workers tend to get paid the full value of what they contribute.

Entrepreneurship

The entrepreneur is the driving force of a market economy. It is the **entrepreneur** who judges that something is missing in the market, and decides to start a new business or develop a new product. The entrepreneur uses savings (either personal or borrowed from capitalists[1]) to hire workers, rent land and equipment, and purchase raw materials, electricity, semi-finished goods, and other inputs. The entrepreneur then gives

[1]In the real world, the distinction between entrepreneurs and capitalists is blurry. If a business loan were truly risk-free, then the capitalist would earn a guaranteed return on his or her loan and would be selling "services" for an agreed-upon price just as the utility company sells electricity to the entrepreneur. Yet in reality, the capitalist who lends to a new business always partakes in the entrepreneurial risk of the venture, regardless of the terms of the contract. It's always possible that the business fails and the capitalist loses everything.

instructions to the hired help to use the tools, machinery, and inputs to produce goods and services which in turn are sold to customers.

The customers of a particular business may be other entrepreneurs or the final consumer. For example, one entrepreneur might open a bakery, where he uses a large oven, flour, water, and a bunch of teenagers to produce crusty French bread for local families. But there is another entrepreneur whose business is the production of industrial-scale ovens, and his customers are other entrepreneurs such as the baker and the owner of a restaurant.

Revenues are the money that customers pay to the entrepreneur for his products and services. **Expenses** are the money that the entrepreneur must pay out to workers, suppliers, landlords, and others in order to continue producing his goods and services. When revenues are higher than expenses, the entrepreneur earns a monetary **profit**. If expenses are higher than revenues, the entrepreneur suffers a monetary **loss**. Although entrepreneurs may be motivated by factors other than monetary profits and losses, when people refer to a "successful business" they mean one that is profitable.[2] On the other hand, if someone appeared to be running an operation year in and year out, constantly suffering monetary losses with no apparent end in sight, then the operation would probably be a hobby or a charity, rather than an actual business, and the would-be entrepreneur would actually be a consumer.[3]

---

[2]We are referring to *monetary* profit and loss to avoid confusion with the broader concepts of *subjective* (or *psychic*) profit and loss, which are ultimately what the entrepreneur cares about. For example, if an entrepreneur spends 60 hours a week putting his heart and soul into a new business, and ends up with monetary profits of $100 per month, then he will probably abandon the business. Even though he is taking in more dollars than he pays out, his *opportunity cost* of using his labor in such a manner is quite high. The entrepreneur could earn much more than $100 per month by closing his own business and working for someone else—namely, a more successful entrepreneur!

[3]Once again, the distinction between these roles can be blurry in the real world. For example, a retired man might operate a Little League baseball field and charge the young children a modest fee to defray the expenses of hiring umpires and buying t-shirts, but the whole effort could be recreational for the man, who simply loves baseball. Especially if the man spent his own money to transform his (huge)

The Contribution of the Entrepreneur

"What distinguishes the successful entrepreneur and promoter from other people is precisely the fact that he does not let himself be guided by what was and is, but arranges his affairs on the ground of his opinion about the future. He sees the past and the present as other people do; but he judges the future in a different way."

—Ludwig von Mises, *Human Action*, p. 582.

Competition Protects Customers

If entrepreneurs are the driving force in a market economy, competition is what regulates and motivates them. **Competition** ensures that entrepreneurs constantly strive to provide customers with goods and services at the quality they want for the lowest possible price.

In a pure market economy, every transaction is voluntary. No matter how rich a particular entrepreneur becomes, he can't literally *force* a customer to buy his products. Customers always have the option of taking their business elsewhere, meaning that even the most successful entrepreneurs must continually earn their patronage day in, day out.

The competitive process unfolds through a process of imitation and innovation. An insightful entrepreneur surveys the status quo and has a good idea to improve on the way that other entrepreneurs are currently serving their customers. The idea might be grand, such as the invention of a completely new product. But often the innovation is quite modest, such as switching to a plastic (and unbreakable) ketchup bottle, or changing the system of passenger seating for airline flights. Many innovations also occur on the production side, when an entrepreneur discovers a cheaper source of raw materials, or discovers a use for by-products that were previously

backyard into a baseball field, it would be clear that the operation wasn't really a for-profit business and that the man wasn't looking for a certain monetary return on his investment.

thrown out. When magnified in large-scale operations, even tiny reductions in expenses can translate into huge differences in profits.

The story does not stop there. When a particular entrepreneur comes up with a successful innovation, he earns relatively high profits. Other entrepreneurs see his success, and they begin to imitate it—while looking for further ways to make slight modifications and introduce yet more innovations. The business world never sleeps. Even those firms that are "on top" in their respective industries are constantly researching new ways to stay ahead of the competition. Over time, there is a tendency for businesses to produce goods and services of rising quality and falling prices.

The ultimate beneficiaries of the competitive process are not the entrepreneurs, but their customers. When a particular entrepreneur makes a successful innovation and earns extraordinary profits, the success is temporary. Over time, his competitors discover how to lower their expenses, or improve the quality of the product, as he has done. Many critics of the market economy are horrified at the huge "markups" that sometimes occur, meaning that there is a large gap between the price an entrepreneur charges for a product, versus the money he himself had to pay to produce the item. But so long as there is competition, monetary profit (and hence "markups") will be whittled away, as competitors try to gain market share by offering a similar product at a slightly lower price. Only by constantly introducing further innovations can a particular entrepreneur enjoy a steady stream of monetary profits.

In practice, most entrepreneurs are motivated by the desire to earn monetary profits. Yet in a market economy, the only way to earn profits is to serve customers (while keeping expenses down). One of the most beautiful aspects of a market economy is that it harnesses some of the most selfish, ambitious, and talented people in society, and makes it in their direct financial interest to worry at night about pleasing others. Entrepreneurs drive the market economy, but competition *among* entrepreneurs keeps them honest.

Competition Protects Workers

In the previous section we saw that competition protects consumers from arbitrarily high prices. If a particular entrepreneur is charging his customers a large markup relative to his expenses, in a free market he can't prevent a competitor from offering the same product at a slightly lower price to win over his customers. In the long run, competition ensures that customers do not "overpay" for the goods and services they desire. Customers are charged a "fair" price for products and services, in the sense that at the moment of sale, some of the brightest minds in society had not yet come up with a way to deliver those items at lower prices—even though they would have reaped financial rewards from doing so.[4]

On the other side of the business, competition protects workers from arbitrarily low wages. It is true that a particular worker—especially with a family to feed—may not have much "bargaining power" and will have to accept a very low wage if that's the only offer available. Yet in a pure market economy, a tight-fisted employer can't prevent a competitor from coming along and offering a slightly higher wage to win over the underpaid employees and drive the tight-fisted entrepreneur out of business. In the long run, competition ensures that employers do not "underpay" for the labor services—and other resources—that they must hire or purchase in their operations.

In order to judge whether an employee is getting paid a "fair" wage, we need to understand the employee's actual contribution.[5] After all, some employees are more productive (and hence valuable) than others, so it makes sense that different employees will be paid different wages. How then does an employer decide what he's willing to pay a potential new hire?

Economists say that the employer should try to calculate the **marginal productivity** of the potential new worker. This means that the employer should look at his total business output, with and without the new worker. Then the employer uses this information to calculate how much extra revenue his operation will bring in, because of the additional output. These

[4]We have put "fair" in quotation marks because in a pure market economy, *every* transaction is voluntary and *fair* in a very important sense. Even if an entrepreneur sells a product for a price much higher than the amount of money he spent in procuring the item, the customer still values the product more than the money he spends on it—both the customer and the entrepreneur subjectively benefit from the trade.

[5]Again, we have put "fair" in quotation marks because *every* labor contract is fair in the free market, in the sense that it is voluntary and the worker subjectively values the wages more than the leisure he or she gives up by accepting the job.

calculations provide a ceiling, an upper limit of how much the employer would be willing to pay for the new worker.

Of course, in practice the employer will try to pay less than the marginal productivity of a potential new worker—just as in practice he will try to charge his customers a large markup. But competition ensures that he can't get away with "underpaying" employees for very long, just as it prevents him from "overcharging" his customers for very long.

For example, suppose Rita owns a restaurant that is very busy. Rita notices that a major bottleneck in her operation is the cleaning of a table after the customers leave. At any given time, there are several tables in the restaurant that are dirty, meaning the hostess has to ask incoming customers to wait a few minutes before being seated. Rita realizes that it makes sense for her to hire an additional busboy to help the current busboy clean tables and get them ready for new customers.

Rita finds a candidate, Bob, who has had previous experience as a busboy at a busy restaurant, and who seems to be very courteous and responsible. Rita estimates that if she offers Bob the busboy position, after a week of getting used to the new job his presence will allow her restaurant, on average, to serve an extra 2 tables per hour. (Perhaps instead of there being 4 dirty tables at any time, now there are only 3, and each group of diners takes an average of 30 minutes to order their food, eat the meal, and leave.) If the typical table of patrons pays $26 to Rita for a meal that costs her $20 to prepare—not counting the paycheck she gives to Bob—then Rita would be willing to pay Bob up to $12 per hour.

Of course, Rita would hope to hire Bob for less than $12 per hour. But if she offered him only $4, then Bob would surely be able to sell his services to a competitor restaurant for, say, $5 per hour. Ultimately, the only logical stopping point would occur when Bob was being paid according to how much extra money his services brought in to the employer.[6] Competition

[6]Things are not as simple as we made them sound in the text above. In some cases there are several factors that are indispensable for the final output, so it is difficult to isolate the "marginal productivity" of any one factor. (How do The Beatles split up the proceeds from their concert performances and record contracts? It wouldn't really work to ask, "How much would sales fall if Paul McCartney didn't play?" because then McCartney and Lennon would each seem to deserve

among entrepreneurs provides a tendency for workers to be paid for their contributions.

more than half of the proceeds.) Another complication is that the addition of more workers can change the marginal productivity of the original workers, meaning that competition will have to change their wages too if they had previously been paid a "fair" amount. Finally there is the complication that workers won't have the same marginal productivity in different businesses. For example, if Bob the busboy would add $12 to Rita's operation, but only $10 to the next restaurant that needs a busboy, then competition really only ensures that Bob gets paid at least $10. You will need to consult a more advanced book on economics to learn the solution to these complications.

Lesson Recap . . .

- Entrepreneurs are the driving force in a market economy. They hire workers and buy resources, in order to produce goods and services for sale to the consumers.

- Competition pushes entrepreneurs to produce goods and services that their customers value, and to charge the lowest possible price for the level of quality that the customers desire.

- Competition also pushes entrepreneurs to pay workers the full value of their contribution to the business. If they underpay, then another employer—who only wants to make more money himself—can offer higher pay and entice the worker away.

NEW TERMS

Entrepreneur: The person in a market economy who hires workers and buys resources in order to produce goods and services.

Revenues: The amount of money customers spend on an entrepreneur's output during a period of time.

Expenses: The amount of money an entrepreneur spends on labor, raw materials, and other inputs during a period of time.

Monetary profit: The amount by which revenues are greater than expenses.

Monetary loss: The amount by which expenses are greater than revenues.

Competition: The rivalry that exists between entrepreneurs who have the option of hiring the same workers and buying the same resources, in order to produce goods and services to be sold to the same customers.

Marginal productivity: The increased revenues that result from hiring an extra worker.

STUDY QUESTIONS

1. Why is the entrepreneur the "driving force" of a market economy?

2. *In the real world, why are all capitalists also entrepreneurs?

3. What motivates and regulates entrepreneurs in a market economy?

4. How does the competitive process unfold through "imitation and innovation"?

5. How does competition protect workers?

LESSON 10

Income, Saving, and Investment

In this lesson you will learn:

- The definitions of *income, saving,* and *investment* in a monetary economy.
- How saving and investment increase an individual's future income.
- How saving and investment increase an economy's future output.

Income, Saving, and Investment

In Lesson 4, we saw that even Robinson Crusoe, stranded on his island and with no one to trade with (except Nature), could classify his actions with the concepts of income, savings, and investment.

In a modern economy with many individuals who use money, the concepts are similar but easier to define. For an individual, **income** typically refers to how much money he or she can spend on consumption during a certain period of time, due to the sale of labor services and the earnings of assets that the individual owns. For a business firm, **income** (or **earnings**) is defined as revenues minus expenses. We recall from the previous lesson that revenues are the total amount of money customers spend on the business' products and services. Expenses are the total amount of money the business spends in producing those goods and services.[1]

When an individual spends less on consumption than his or her income during a certain period, the difference becomes **savings**. (If saving is negative—meaning the individual consumes more than his or her income—then it is called **borrowing** or **dissaving**.) When the individual spends some of his or her savings in order to generate more *future* income, it is called **investment**.[2,3]

Investment Increases Future Income

The downside of saving (and investment) is that it reduces how much consumption you can enjoy today. On the other hand, the benefit of saving (and investment) is that it *increases* how much you can consume in the future. The tables on the following page illustrate the pros and cons of investment by looking at two hypothetical people, Prodigal Paul and Frugal Freddy.

---

[1]Note that because we are still in the section of the book describing a pure market economy, we are not discussing taxes. In the real world, various definitions of *income* account for pre- and after-tax calculations.

[2]Business firms too can invest in order to boost future earnings. We do not discuss this in the text, however, because it would quickly lead to many accounting technicalities that are beyond the scope of this discussion.

[3]In any period of time, investment can't be higher than savings. Some economists would say that investment can be *lower* than savings, however. For example, if someone earns $100,000 in income, spends $80,000 on consumption, and invests $15,000 in stocks, then some economists would say the remaining $5,000 sitting in the bank account is part of savings but not part of investment. However, other economists would argue that investment is necessarily always equal to saving. In our example, they would say that the person had $20,000 of total savings, and invested $15,000 in stocks and the other $5,000 in "cash." This hair-splitting debate is relevant when economists argue over whether an economy can get stuck in a situation where savings is higher than investment.

PRODIGAL PAUL'S FINANCES

Year	1	2	3	4	...	25	26	27	...	47	48	49
Total Market Value of Assets	$ -	$ 2,500	$ 5,006	$ 7,519		$ 61,757	$ 64,411	$ 67,072		$ 121,712	$ 124,517	$ 127,328
Labor Income (paycheck)	$ 50,000	$ 50,000	$ 50,000	$ 50,000		$ 50,000	$ 50,000	$ 50,000		$ 50,000	$ 50,000	$ 50,000
Earnings From Assets (5% interest)	$ -	$ 125	$ 250	$ 376		$ 3,088	$ 3,221	$ 3,354		$ 6,086	$ 6,226	$ 6,366
Total Income	$ 50,000	$ 50,125	$ 50,250	$ 50,376		$ 53,088	$ 53,221	$ 53,354		$ 56,086	$ 56,226	$ 56,366
Consumption (95% of income)	$ 47,500	$ 47,619	$ 47,738	$ 47,857		$ 50,433	$ 50,560	$ 50,686		$ 53,281	$ 53,415	$ 53,548
Saving (5% of income)	$ 2,500	$ 2,506	$ 2,513	$ 2,519		$ 2,654	$ 2,661	$ 2,668		$ 2,804	$ 2,811	$ 2,818
Investment in Assets (=Saving)	$ 2,500	$ 2,506	$ 2,513	$ 2,519		$ 2,654	$ 2,661	$ 2,668		$ 2,804	$ 2,811	$ 2,818

FRUGAL FREDDY'S FINANCES

Year	**1**	**2**	**3**	**4**	**...**	**25**	**26**	**27**	**...**	**47**	**48**	**49**
Total Market Value of Assets	$ -	$ 15,000	$ 30,225	$ 45,678		$429,503	$450,945	$ 472,710		$ 983,526	$ 1,013,279	$ 1,043,478
Labor Income (paycheck)	$ 50,000	$ 50,000	$ 50,000	$ 50,000		$ 50,000	$ 50,000	$ 50,000		$ 50,000	$ 50,000	$ 50,000
Earnings From Assets (5% interest)	$ -	$ 750	$ 1,511	$ 2,284		$ 21,475	$ 22,547	$ 23,635		$ 49,176	$ 50,664	$ 52,174
Total Income	$ 50,000	$ 50,750	$ 51,511	$ 52,284		$ 71,475	$ 72,547	$ 73,635		$ 99,176	$ 100,664	$ 102,174
Consumption (70% of income)	$ 35,000	$ 35,525	$ 36,058	$ 36,599		$ 50,033	$ 50,783	$ 51,545		$ 69,423	$ 70,465	$ 71,522
Saving (30% of income)	$ 15,000	$ 15,225	$ 15,453	$ 15,685		$ 21,443	$ 21,764	$ 22,091		$ 29,753	$ 30,199	$ 30,652
Investment in Assets (=Saving)	$ 15,000	$ 15,225	$ 15,453	$ 15,685		$ 21,443	$ 21,764	$ 22,091		$ 29,753	$ 30,199	$ 30,652

The tables track the financial activity of Paul and Freddy throughout their lives. They hold comparable jobs and earn a steady paycheck of $50,000 each year from selling their labor services. However, both men save some of their income and invest it in assets that pay 5% **interest** per year. We will discuss debt and interest payments in more detail in Lesson 12, but for now you just need to know that in any given year, in addition to their paychecks Paul and Freddy earn interest income equal to 5% of the total market value of their investments.

Paul and Freddy are identical, except for the proportion of their incomes that they save. Prodigal Paul only saves 5% of his income each year, and spends the rest on consumption—going out to dinner, flashy jewelry, vacations to Tahiti, and so forth. Frugal Freddy, on the other hand, sets aside 30% of his total income each year, and plows it into his financial assets.

The tables illustrate the different lifestyles caused by these savings decisions. In the earlier years, Paul enjoys more consumption than Freddy. He is able to attend more parties, wear nicer clothes, and generally have more fun. However, as the years pass, the gap between the two men constantly shrinks. Even though Frugal Freddy always consumes a much lower proportion of his income, his *income itself* is growing much faster than Prodigal Paul's. In fact, by the 26th year, Freddy's consumption of $50,783 is greater than Paul's consumption of $50,560. From that point forward, Freddy can spend more on immediate enjoyments than Paul can afford. Remember, the two men have identical incomes from their labor services every year—they both earn the same paychecks from their jobs. But Freddy's middle-aged years are much more prosperous, because he has been so frugal in his early working years.

One last interesting observation is that in the 48th year of his career, Freddy's financial assets break the $1 million mark. Many people think that only "rich people" can ever get their hands on a million dollars. But as the table illustrates, even someone making $50,000 per year, and who invests in moderately safe assets, can eventually accumulate $1 million simply by habitually saving a large fraction of his income—at least in a world without taxes!

Retirement

On the following set of tables we look at what happens after Paul and Freddy stop working, and their paychecks drop to $0. (We assume this

PRODIGAL PAUL'S RETIREMENT

Year	50	51	52	53	...	63	64	65	...	74	75
Total Market Value of Assets	$ 130,146	$ 132,972	$ 135,804	$ 127,594		$ 19,169	$ 5,128	$ -		$ -	$ -
Labor Income (paycheck)	$ 50,000	$ 50,000	$ -	$ -		$ -	$ -	$ -		$ -	$ -
Earnings From Assets (5% interest)	$ 6,507	$ 6,649	$ 6,790	$ 6,380		$ 958	$ 256	$ -		$ -	$ -
Total Income	$ 56,507	$ 56,649	$ 6,790	$ 6,380		$ 958	$ 256	$ -		$ -	$ -
Consumption (95% of income)	$ 53,682	$ 53,816	$ 15,000	$ 15,000		$ 15,000	$ 5,384	???		???	???
Saving (5% of income)	$ 2,825	$ 2,832	$ (8,210)	$ (8,620)		$ (14,042)	$ (5,128)	$ -		$ -	$ -
Investment in Assets (=Saving)	$ 2,825	$ 2,832	$ (8,210)	$ (8,620)		$ (14,042)	$ (5,128)	$ -		$ -	$ -

FRUGAL FREDDY'S RETIREMENT

Year	50	51	52	53	...	63	64	65	...	74	75
Total Market Value of Assets	$ 1,074,130	$ 1,105,242	$ 1,136,821	$ 1,123,662		$ 949,875	$ 927,368	$ 903,737		$ 630,133	$ 591,640
Labor Income (paycheck)	$ 50,000	$ 50,000	$ -	$ -		$ -	$ -	$ -		$ -	$ -
Earnings From Assets (5% interest)	$ 53,707	$ 55,262	$ 56,841	$ 56,183		$ 47,494	$ 46,368	$ 45,187		$ 31,507	$ 29,582
Total Income	$ 103,707	$ 105,262	$ 56,841	$ 56,183		$ 47,494	$ 46,368	$ 45,187		$ 31,507	$ 29,582
Consumption (70% of income)	$ 72,595	$ 73,683	$ 70,000	$ 70,000		$ 70,000	$ 70,000	$ 70,000		$ 70,000	$ 70,000
Saving (30% of income)	$ 31,112	$ 31,579	$ (13,159)	$ (13,817)		$ (22,506)	$ (23,632)	$ (24,813)		$(38,493)	$(40,418)
Investment in Assets (=Saving)	$ 31,112	$ 31,579	$ (13,159)	$ (13,817)		$ (22,506)	$ (23,632)	$ (24,813)		$(38,493)	$(40,418)

happens in the 52nd year after they have entered the work force.) Both men now begin *dissaving*, meaning that they consume more than their incomes each year.[4] This is possible because they have accumulated a stockpile of financial assets. Not only can the men spend money that is generated by the interest earnings on these assets, but they can also sell off a portion of the assets and consume the proceeds of the sale. (This is called *reducing the principal* of one's assets or savings.)

At this point we really see the benefits of Freddy's relative frugality. During his retirement years, he can easily afford to maintain a constant level of consumption of $70,000 per year. This is a tad lower than what he was used to just before he retired, but it is still a quite comfortable lifestyle—and it's 40% more than his whole *paycheck* was during his working years!

In contrast, Prodigal Paul has to sharply cut back on his consumption spending once he stops going to work. He drops down to $15,000 in annual consumption. The reason Paul is in such dire straits is that at the time of retirement, he had only accumulated about $136,000 in assets, whereas Frugal Freddy had over $1.1 million. Thus Freddy not only has a much larger annual income from investment earnings during retirement, but he also has a much larger stockpile of assets to "draw down" and fund his retirement lifestyle.

As the tables show, the real crunch for Paul comes in Year 64. At this point, he can't even eke out his $15,000 consumption for the year, because he has exhausted all of his financial assets. After living on an austerity budget of $5,384 this year, Paul is flat broke. If he doesn't want to go back to work, he will need to get money for consumption from relatives, churches, or some other philanthropic organization. (We are still describing a pure market economy, so there are no government relief programs.)

Again in sharp contrast, Frugal Freddy can continue his very comfortable retirement lifestyle up until the 75th year after he began working, when we assume he passes away. Not only has Freddy's frugality allowed him to fund his own retirement without relying on the generosity of others, but he even has almost $592,000 left in his estate to bequeath to his heirs.

---

[4]In the tables, note that parentheses are an accounting convention to denote negative numbers.

How Saving and Investment Increase An Economy's Future Output

Everyone who has held a job and a bank account understands the potential benefit of postponing consumption today in order to enjoy greater consumption in the future. However, many people—if pressed—would explain this increase to the saver's income by an offsetting reduction in the income of a borrower somewhere in the economy.

This is certainly a possibility. For example, if Bill (the borrower) forgets his lunch money on Monday, he might ask his coworker Sally (the saver), "Can you lend me $10 and I'll pay you back $11 tomorrow?" If Sally agrees, then it's clear that her $1 in interest on the personal loan was paid out of Bill's reduced income for that month. In other words, if Bill's take-home pay that month were $5,000, then he would actually only have $4,999 to work with, because of his $1 expenditure in "buying a loan" from Sally. At the same time, if Sally's normal paycheck were also $5,000, then this particular month she would actually have $5,001 to work with, after earning $1 in providing "lending services" to Bill.

In the scenario above, what basically happened is that Bill financed his consumption with an "advance" made by Sally. On the Monday in question, when Bill left his wallet at home, Sally had to have in her pocket enough spare cash to lend $10 to Bill. Perhaps this made her rearrange her planned spending that day, or perhaps it simply meant that Sally carried less cash in her own purse than she originally had desired. In any event, Sally provided a definite service to Bill. Given his mistake, both parties benefited from the voluntary loan transaction. Even though it might seem from a quick look as if Bill lost and Sally gained, in reality both parties benefited. In a sense Bill's total monthly consumption was lower, but he *preferred* having $1 less in order to obtain his usual $10 lunch on the particular Monday. There is nothing irrational or "uneconomical" about Bill's decision to pay $1 for Sally's loan.

Making loans so that borrowers can finance their present consumption (at the expense of future consumption) is certainly part of what happens in a market economy on a grand scheme; it constitutes a large portion of the credit card industry. However, you should *not* conclude that all savings and investments are of this nature. When we consider the lifetime savings plan outlined in the previous section, *there doesn't need to be* one or more borrowers who grow ever deeper in debt as the decades roll on. In fact, it is possible that *every single person in a market economy provides for a comfortable retirement* through saving and investment during his or her working career.

How is this possible? For every Sally who saves and earns ever-growing streams of interest income, doesn't there have to be a Bill somewhere who borrows and *pays* ever-growing streams of income? Yes and no. The key is that the loans or investments can be made in *productive enterprises*, rather than simply being lent to an individual who increases his consumption in the present. If the savings are channeled into expanding production (rather than merely financing consumption), then "total output" grows over time, in principle allowing every member of society to enjoy larger incomes.

In Lesson 12 we will go over the mechanics of credit and debt more carefully, but for now we just need to understand the big picture of what would happen if everyone in society suddenly decided to save a large fraction of his or her income. In order to save more, each person would cut back on consumption. That means people would spend less on fancy restaurants, sports cars, electronic gadgets, and designer clothes. At the same time, people would increase the amount of money they lent and invested in businesses, either directly (through buying corporate stock or bonds) or indirectly (by depositing the money with banks which then advanced loans to businesses).

These large swings in how people spent their incomes—diverting it away from consumption and toward investments—would ultimately steer workers and other resources out of industries catering to immediate consumption, and toward industries catering to long-range production. For example, high-end retail and jewelry stores would see their sales plummet, and they would lay off workers and cut back on their inventory. Fancy restaurants too would lay off workers and close down some of their locations.

The laid-off workers would look for jobs in other industries, and this extra competition would push down wage rates in those sectors. At the lower wage rates, businesses in these other industries would be willing to hire the displaced workers. Other resources besides laid-off workers would be redirected to new uses, as well. For example, the owners of now-vacant buildings (which used to house clothing stores and other retailers) would lower their asking price for rents, making it easier for other businesses to expand their operations by filling the buildings.

If we ignore the real-world disruptions that would occur during the transition, even a large and sudden increase in the savings rate wouldn't affect "total spending." It's true that *consumption* spending would (initially) be much lower, but *investment* spending by businesses would be correspondingly higher. The total number of jobs (eventually) would also be the same, because the laid-off waiters and mall employees would now be working in factories producing drill presses and backhoe loaders.

The essential insight is that a sudden increase in savings allows the economy's output to shift away from consumption goods and into capital goods. Just as Robinson Crusoe was able to enhance the power of his bare hands through the wise use of saving and investment—even though he had nobody to "lend to" on the island—so too can the whole population enhance each other's labor productivity by channeling more resources into the production of machinery and tools. There is no "cheating" going on here; everyone's income can grow larger over the years when everyone is more physically productive because of the growing stockpile of capital goods.

In Lesson 12 we will give a longer explanation of how interest rates are determined. This is a very complex area. For example, the accumulation of capital goods directly raises workers' incomes through higher *wages* (because each hour of work—with the better tools—now produces more output). In the present lesson, we are only making the important point that it's possible for everyone to grow richer through saving. It is not true that a lender grows rich only when a borrower grows poor.

Lesson Recap . . .

- Because of interest, an individual can save and invest today, in order to increase his or her income in the future. A small decrease in consumption today, can lead to a much greater amount of consumption in the future.

- When individuals save and invest, the economy is physically transformed. Instead of channeling labor and other resources into making television sets and DVDs, production is redirected toward making tools and equipment. This reduces the amount of consumer goods produced in the present, but the new tools make workers more productive in the future.

- One person's saving and investment doesn't force someone else to sink ever deeper into debt. It is possible for every single person in the economy to save large sums and enjoy a much higher future income.

NEW TERMS

Income (individual): The amount of money that can be spent on consumption goods in a certain period, from the sale of labor and the earnings of other assets (such as stocks).

Income / earnings (business): Revenues minus expenses.

Savings: The amount by which income is greater than spending on consumption.

Borrowing / dissaving: The amount by which consumption spending is greater than income.

Investment: Savings that are spent in the hopes of increasing future income.

Interest: The income earned during a period of time from lending savings to others. Interest is usually quoted as a percentage of the principal (the amount of money originally lent) earned per year. For example, if someone lends $1,000 today and is paid back $1,050 twelve months later, then the principal is $1,000, the interest earned is $50, and the interest rate is 5%.

STUDY QUESTIONS

1. Can investment occur without saving?

2. What are the pros and cons of saving a high fraction of your income?

3. What's the connection between saving and retirement?

4. If someone borrows in order to buy today rather than waiting to pay cash, is this an example of uneconomical behavior?

5. *Is it possible for every individual in the community to accumulate assets for retirement—or does one person's rising wealth translate into someone else's rising debt?

LESSON 11

Supply and Demand

In this lesson you will learn:

- The definitions of *supply* and *demand*.
- The *law of supply* and the *law of demand*.
- How economists use supply and demand to explain market prices.

Supply and Demand: The Purpose

An old joke says that if you taught a parrot to say, "Supply and demand," it could answer any economics question. This is almost right—to be truly a good economist, the parrot would also need to be trained to disagree with half of the other parrots.

The lessons contained in this book are designed to give you a solid foundation in economic thinking. Its pages are not covered with the graphs you will find in a typical economics textbook. The one exception to this rule is the famous supply and demand graph. In addition to the concepts underlying the graph, we provide diagrams because it makes some of the points easier to grasp. However, you should never ascribe too much importance to the particular supply and demand curves we will draw in this (and subsequent) lessons. They are simply convenient ways to give a concrete example of a particular point, just as the specific numbers used in some of our stories in previous lessons were not crucial to the general economic principles that we were illustrating.

Keep in mind that economists don't rely on a *theory* of supply and demand; they rather use them as *tools*. The concepts of supply and demand are ways of viewing the world. They allow economists to group different forces or causes into two different categories, in order to think clearly and systematically about changes in the world and how they will impact market prices.

Because supply and demand are conceptual tools, not an empirical theory, there will never be evidence that demonstrates that "supply and demand" is somehow *false*. What might happen is that future economists decide that "supply and demand" is no longer the most useful approach to thinking about prices. For now, virtually all practicing economists use supply and demand to explain market prices, because superior tools have yet to be discovered.

Demand: Its Definition and Its Law

Demand is the relationship between various hypothetical market prices for a good or service, and the total number of units that consumers want to purchase at each hypothetical price. To remind us that *demand* is not a specific number, but rather a *relationship among many numbers*, economists often use the term **demand schedule**. A demand schedule can be constructed for one person or for many people. The following table illustrates Jennifer's demand schedule for gasoline.

The demand schedule that follows lists the amount of gasoline that Jennifer would buy at various hypothetical prices. We have stressed that this is a *snapshot in time*, namely, on a particular Tuesday afternoon. It is important to remember that someone's demand for a good or service can change from moment to moment, depending on the person's subjective preferences as well as other factors.

The situation we had in mind for the numbers that follow is that Jennifer's car is almost out of gas, and she plans on stopping at a station on her way home from work. At a price of $4 or higher per gallon, Jennifer would not buy *any* gasoline, because that would strike her as an unusually high price and she would hope to fill up at a different station the following day. To motivate the other numbers, we have further assumed that Jennifer only has $16 in her purse, and that her car has a 15-gallon tank (which is

Jennifer's Demand for Gasoline on Tuesday Afternoon

Price (dollars / gallon)	Quantity (gallons)
$5.00	0.0
$4.00	0.0
$3.50	1.5
$3.00	2.5
$2.50	4.0
$2.00	8.0
$1.50	10.7
$1.00	14.7
$0.50	14.7

almost empty). At the prices of $3.50 and $3.00 per gallon, Jennifer would only buy a small amount of gas, enough to get her back and forth to work the next day (though she gives herself a bigger cushion at the lower price). At $2.50 she would buy more gasoline because of the better deal, while at $2.00 and $1.50 she would spend all of her cash. Finally, at $1.00 and $0.50, she would fill up her car completely.

The only "rule" that the schedule above obeys is the **Law of Demand**, which states that holding other influences constant, a lower price will lead a consumer to buy either the same or a greater amount of the good or service.[1]

[1]Some economists view the "law" of demand as an empirical tendency, similar to a physicist who observes, "Gravity tends to make things fall." In this view, there are occasional exceptions to the law of demand, because we can imagine someone buying fewer silver bars if their price were very low, or buying fewer units of a designer handbag if its price were too low and hence it ceased to be a status symbol. Other economists interpret the *Law* of Demand as just that—a law. For them, it is not an empirical tendency, referring to physical objects and sales figures. Rather, they prove the Law of Demand is true by thinking through the logic of economizing action. As a consumer buys more units of a good, each successive unit is less important, and so it is only natural that a consumer who spends his or her money in order to satisfy the most important goals, will necessarily buy at least the same number of units as a good's price falls. The apparent counterexamples

In the table below, we retain Jennifer's demand but add in the demand schedules for several other people:

Individual and Market Demands for Gasoline on Tuesday Afternoon

Price	Jennifer	Beth	Jim	Dave	Hank	Jill	MARKET
$7.00	0.0	0.0	0.5	1.0	13.0	0.0	14.5
$6.50	0.0	0.0	0.5	1.5	13.0	0.0	15.0
$6.00	0.0	0.0	1.0	2.5	13.0	0.0	16.5
$5.50	0.0	0.0	1.0	3.0	13.0	0.0	17.0
$5.00	0.0	0.0	1.0	3.0	13.0	0.0	17.0
$4.50	0.0	0.0	2.0	5.0	13.0	0.0	20.0
$4.00	0.0	0.0	2.0	5.0	13.0	0.0	20.0
$3.50	1.5	0.0	2.0	5.0	13.0	0.0	21.5
$3.00	2.5	0.0	4.0	15.0	13.0	0.0	34.5
$2.50	4.0	0.0	4.0	15.0	13.0	0.0	36.0
$2.00	8.0	0.0	8.0	15.0	13.0	0.0	44.0
$1.50	10.7	6.3	8.0	15.0	13.0	0.0	53.0
$1.00	14.7	6.3	8.0	15.0	13.0	0.0	57.0
$0.50	14.7	6.3	8.0	15.0	13.0	0.0	57.0
$0.00	14.7	6.3	8.0	15.0	13.0	0.0	57.0

are explained away as "different goods," because it's not the physical properties of a designer handbag that matter, but the subjective happiness it gives to the buyer. In this book we won't take a stand on this controversy, and will avoid any confusion by having *all* supply and demand schedules and curves obey their respective "laws."

Again, the only specific rule that the above table obeys is the Law of Demand. Since it is true in each individual's case, it is also true for the *market* demand for gasoline, because "the market" is simply the combination of the individuals. The only explanatory comments for the numbers in the table are that Hank is on a road trip for his company, and his travel expenses will be reimbursed, so he fills up his tank regardless of the price. Jill doesn't own a car, so she buys no gasoline regardless of the price.

Once we have the market demand schedule, it's a simple matter of plotting points to graph the market's **demand curve**:

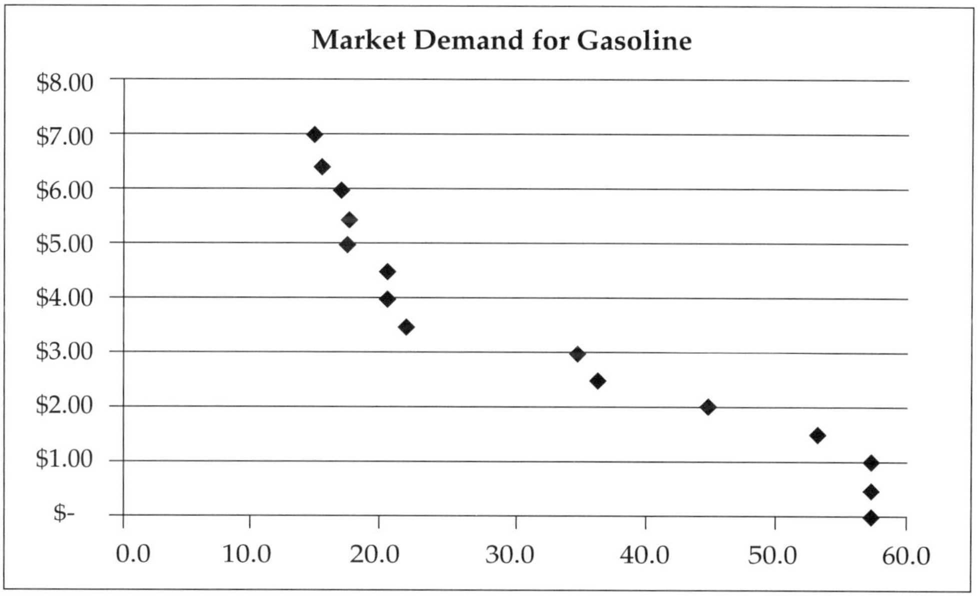

The above graph doesn't look very pretty. That's why economists cheat when they are using generic demand curves, and draw something like this:

Generic Demand Curve

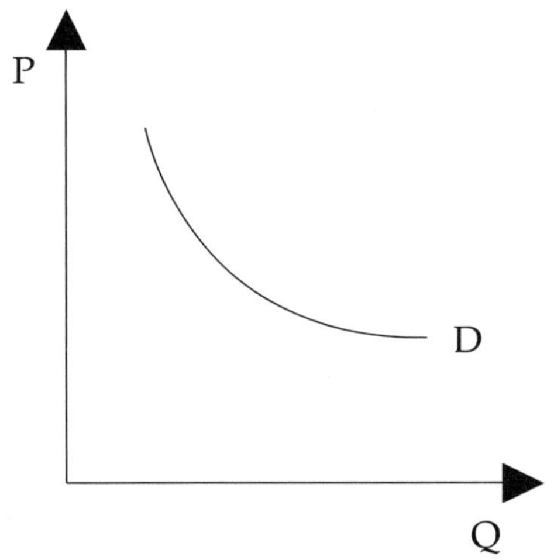

or

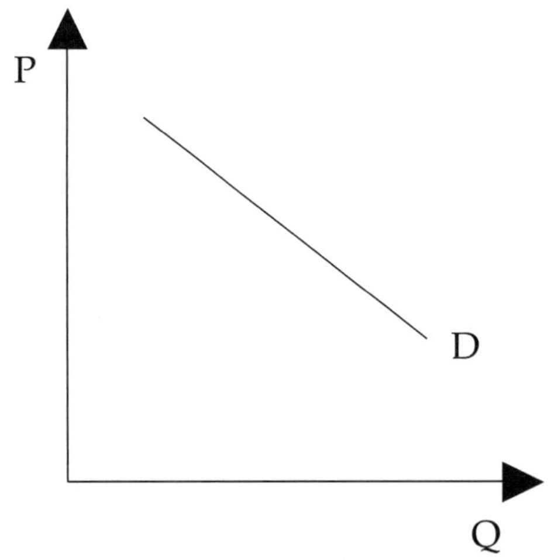

Supply: Its Definition and Its Law

Once you understand demand, supply is easy to explain: **Supply** is the relationship between various hypothetical market prices for a good or service, and the total number of units that producers want to sell at each hypothetical price. As with demand, we can construct a **supply schedule** and a **supply curve** to illustrate this relationship for an individual or group, at a particular snapshot in time. The following table shows the supply schedule for our hypothetical community (on the same Tuesday afternoon), followed by the corresponding supply curve.

Individual and Market Supplies of Gasoline (Tuesday afternoon)

Price	Quik Mart	Fill 'Er Up	Farmer Jim	MARKET
$7.00	50.0	200.0	20.0	270.0
$6.50	50.0	200.0	20.0	270.0
$6.00	50.0	200.0	20.0	270.0
$5.50	50.0	180.0	0.0	230.0
$5.00	50.0	160.0	0.0	210.0
$4.50	50.0	130.0	0.0	180.0
$4.00	40.0	115.0	0.0	155.0
$3.50	35.0	95.0	0.0	130.0
$3.00	25.0	85.0	0.0	110.0
$2.50	10.0	26.0	0.0	36.0
$2.00	0.0	10.0	0.0	10.0
$1.50	0.0	5.0	0.0	5.0
$1.00	0.0	0.0	0.0	0.0
$0.50	0.0	0.0	0.0	0.0
$0.00	0.0	0.0	0.0	0.0

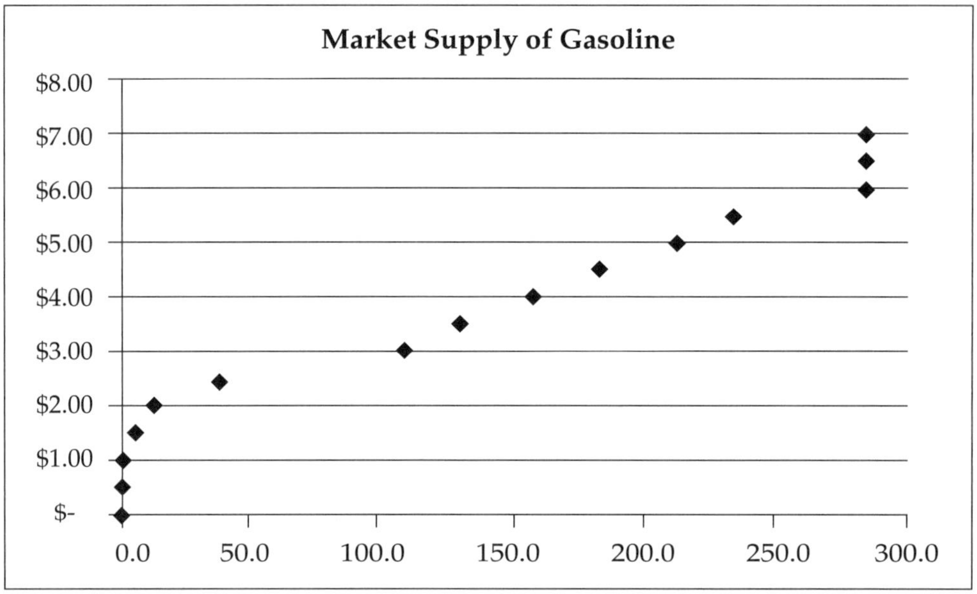

The story behind the above figures is that there are two single-pump gasoline stations in town, the Quik Mart and Fill 'Er Up. The owners arrange for the periodic replenishing of their underground fuel tanks—one of which has a capacity of 50 gallons, the other of 200 gallons—assuming a market price between $2.50 and $3.00 per gallon. If the price should fall too low, they simply shut their stores and hope they can fetch a better deal in the near future. As the price rises, they use various techniques to sell larger quantities—such as working through their lunch breaks, keeping the store open longer, and rushing outside whenever a customer pulls up in order to pump the gas at no additional charge (and thus clear out the pump for the next potential customer). At a price of $6.00 per gallon or higher, Farmer Jim finds it worthwhile to enter the market. He has backup gasoline on hand to run his equipment, and at a high enough price he leaves his farm work to set up a roadside stand and sell some of the gasoline back to other motorists.

Our hypothetical numbers obey the **Law of Supply**, which states that as the market price of a good or service rises, producers offer the same or greater number of units. Here is what a generic supply curve looks like:

Generic Supply Curve

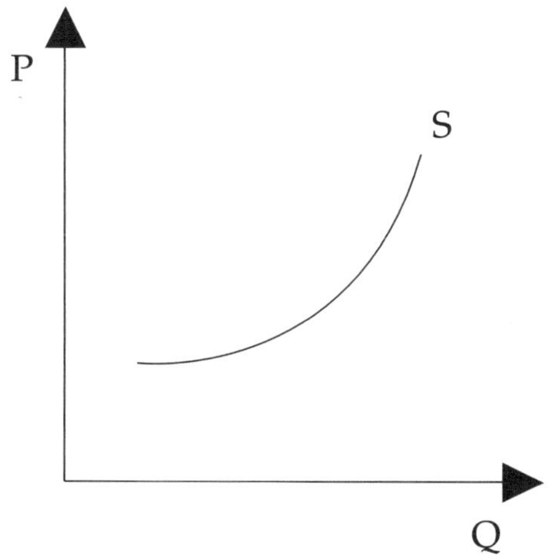

or

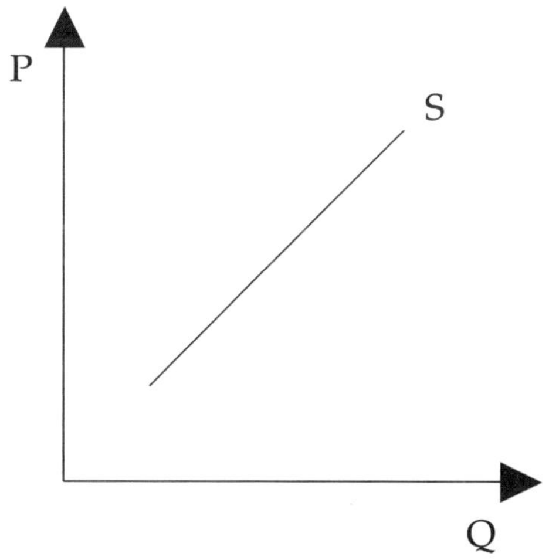

Using Supply and Demand to Explain the Market Price

The whole purpose of using the concepts of supply and demand is to organize our thinking around different changes and how they will affect market prices. When something changes—such as consumer tastes, or the availability of a certain resource—we methodically walk through the impacts on supply and demand for a particular good or service, and then we can gauge the ultimate impact on the market price. But before we give some examples (in the next section), you first need to see the standard demonstration of how *stable* supply and demand curves provide a target or an anchor for the market price.

Let's finish up with our gasoline market example from above. In the table below, we've combined the information from the demand and supply schedules for the whole market, and we've also added two new calculations for each hypothetical price:

Market for Gasoline (Tuesday Afternoon)

Price	Supply	Demand	Surplus	Shortage
$ 7.00	270.0	14.5	255.5	0.0
$ 6.50	270.0	15.0	255.0	0.0
$ 6.00	270.0	16.5	253.5	0.0
$ 5.50	230.0	17.0	213.0	0.0
$ 5.00	210.0	17.0	193.0	0.0
$ 4.50	180.0	20.0	160.0	0.0
$ 4.00	155.0	20.0	135.0	0.0
$ 3.50	130.0	21.5	108.5	0.0
$ 3.00	110.0	34.5	75.5	0.0
$ 2.50	36.0	36.0	0.0	0.0
$ 2.00	10.0	44.0	0.0	34.0
$ 1.50	5.0	53.0	0.0	48.0
$ 1.00	0.0	57.0	0.0	57.0
$ 0.50	0.0	57.0	0.0	57.0
$ -	0.0	57.0	0.0	57.0

A **surplus** (or a "**glut**") occurs when producers are trying to sell more units of a good or service than consumers want to purchase (at a particular price). A **shortage** occurs when consumers want to buy more units than producers want to sell (at a particular price). In this context, the **equilibrium price** (or the **market-clearing price**) is the one at which the amount supplied exactly equals the amount demanded. If the market is in equilibrium, there is no surplus and no shortage.

In our example, the equilibrium market price is $2.50 per gallon of gasoline. This price is *in equilibrium* because it balances the pressures of the consumers and the producers. (In physics, a ball at rest on a table is in *equilibrium* because the downward force of gravity is exactly counterbalanced by the upward force of the table pushing against the ball.) The idea is that if the price for some reason happened to be *more* than $2.50 per gallon, market forces would push it down.

For example, if producers thought the market price on this Tuesday afternoon would be $3.50, they would plan on selling a total of 130 gallons of gasoline. But at this posted price, consumers would only start buying at a pace to purchase a total of 21.5 gallons during the course of the day. If the owners of the Quik Mart and Fill 'Er Up stubbornly clung to the price of $3.50, they would end up with a surplus of 108.5 gallons that they had planned on selling but couldn't. The definition of supply (at various prices) is how many units producers would sell *if they actually received that hypothetical price for every supplied unit*. Because the owners of our gas stations would soon realize that they had misjudged the market—meaning that they would *not* be able to sell a combined 130 gallons for $3.50 each—they would reduce the posted gasoline price and revise their ambitious sales projections.[2]

On the other hand, if the market price should happen to be below $2.50 on this Tuesday afternoon, market forces would tend to push it up. Specifically, the owners would realize that customers were buying gasoline in larger quantities than the owners had planned on selling at the low price. Consequently the owners would raise the posted price, so that they could

[2]Of course in the real world, different markets have different degrees of price "stickiness." A gasoline station can actually change prices very quickly, even from minute to minute if need be. Other markets, such as housing, usually see much slower price changes. The same principles apply, but to be realistic the story would involve a home buyer lowering his or her asking price after (say) several *months* of finding no buyers.

earn more profits and avoid the awkward situation of having to shut down the store early and send customers away with no gas.

Our intuitive arguments show that the only "stable" or equilibrium price for gasoline is $2.50 per gallon. Especially if we assume that the supply and demand schedules remained fairly stable in our hypothetical community, we would expect that in practice the actual market price would be $2.50 (or very close to it). At this price, producers want to sell exactly as many gallons as consumers want to buy—36 gallons with our specific numbers. This is the **equilibrium quantity**.

In a generic supply and demand graph, the equilibrium price and quantity line up with the intersection of the curves, as we show below. In many textbooks, these items are denoted P^* and Q^*.

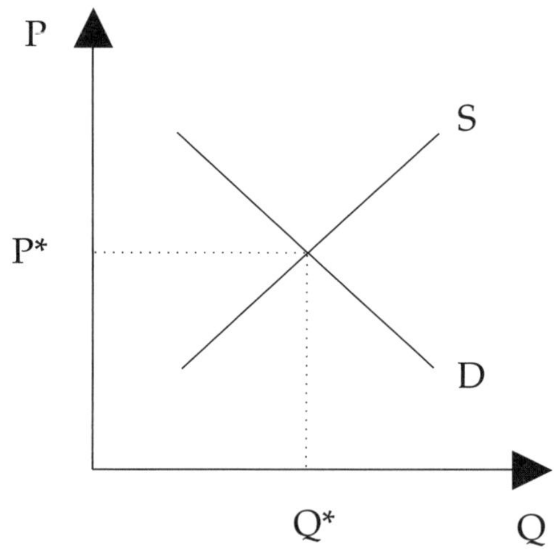

We can also use the generic graph to denote a surplus (from a price P^H that is too high) and a shortage (from a price P^L that is too low). The sizes of the surplus and shortage are also indicated by the respective brackets.

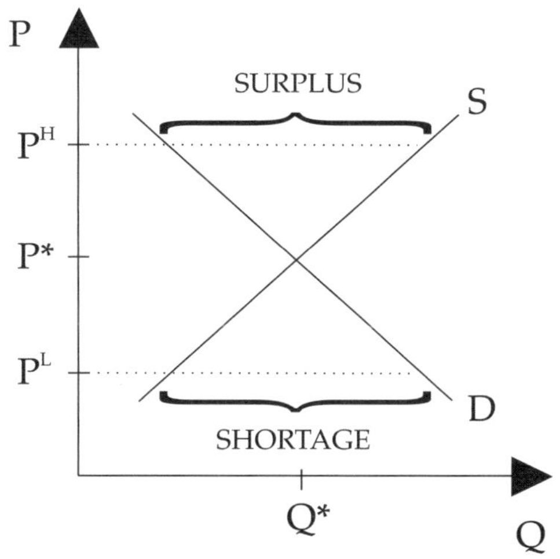

Using Supply and Demand to Understand Price Changes

People who are untrained in economic thinking often tie themselves in knots when they try to analyze some world event and its impact on prices. For example, if OPEC countries announce that they are reducing their output of oil, many people—sometimes even newspaper reporters!—will say nonsense like this:

> "The OPEC announcement means a reduction in the supply of oil, which will raise prices. However, at the higher prices there will be less demand for oil, which will lower prices."

Thus we apparently conclude that the OPEC announcement will both raise *and* lower oil prices! Now that you are armed with the tools of supply and demand analysis, you can avoid such silliness. We'll first deal with two examples of changes on the supply side, and then we'll deal with two examples of changes on the demand side. Our fifth example will involve simultaneous changes to supply and demand.

Example 1: Supply Reduction

For this first example, let's deal with the oil example we just discussed. Suppose that the OPEC countries announce that they are cutting their production of oil by several hundred thousand barrels per day. What effect will this have on the oil market?

If all we want to figure out is the *direction* of the (equilibrium) price and quantity change, we can use generic supply and demand curves. (This will be our strategy for all of the examples in the remainder of this lesson.) We'll first draw two arbitrary curves and come up with P^* and Q^* for the situation just *before* the OPEC announcement:

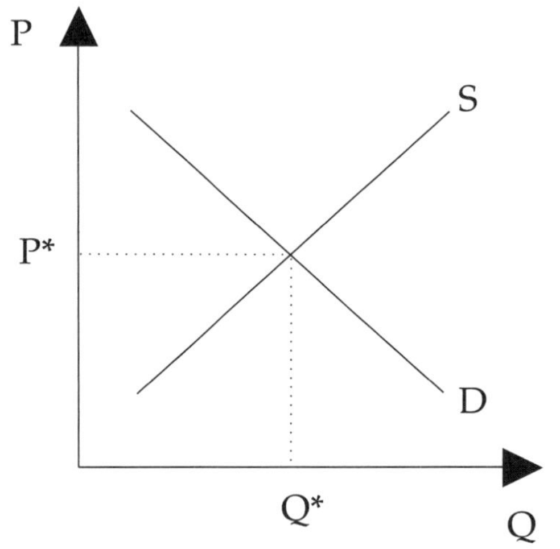

Oil Market

Now we want to examine the impact of the OPEC announcement. Does their decision affect the supply curve, the demand curve, or both?

The OPEC ministers are clearly reducing the supply of oil. We can translate their statement like this: "Before we had various quantities of barrels of oil that we would sell, depending on the price of oil. Now we have changed our minds, and for each hypothetical price, we will sell *fewer* barrels than we would have yesterday." Economists refer to this as a **reduction in supply** or a **leftward shift in the supply curve.** The reason for the latter phrase is simple enough: Graphically, a reduction in supply appears as a leftward movement in the supply curve. Really what's happening is that we're drawing a *new* curve altogether, but visually the new curve looks like the old curve "shifted to the left."

Before drawing our new graph, we should ask: Will the OPEC announcement affect the *demand* for oil? Here we need to be careful. When you think of "demand," remember that it is *the entire relationship* between hypothetical prices and quantities—demand is *not* simply one number. (Think of the *demand schedule*—i.e., the whole table—to keep this straight.) As we'll see, the OPEC announcement will definitely affect the *equilibrium quantity of oil purchased*, but that by itself doesn't mean that *demand* has shifted. No, the vast majority of buyers of oil don't *directly* care about how many barrels OPEC is producing. This information is only relevant to them because they know (from basic economics) that the OPEC decision will affect the price of oil. But as far as their willingness to buy more or fewer barrels at various hypothetical prices—i.e., their demand schedule—the OPEC announcement probably won't have much of an effect.[3] So in our graph below, we'll keep the demand curve the same.

As the following chart indicates, the leftward shift in supply leads to a higher (equilibrium) price of oil and a lower (equilibrium) quantity of oil produced and purchased. To be precise, economists would say that the *demand* for oil remained constant, but the *quantity demanded* declined. Another way of making this crucial distinction is to say that we moved the supply curve itself, while we merely *moved along* the same demand curve. Our hypothetical journalist above—who ended up concluding that the OPEC announcement would lead to both higher and lower oil prices—got confused on this essential point; he mixed up a shift in demand, with a movement along the demand curve.

---

[3]In reality, we could come up with complicated stories of why some oil purchasers—particularly speculators who might stockpile oil based on their estimates of future prices—might have their individual demand schedules change because of the OPEC announcement itself. However, this is a subtle mechanism and lies outside the scope of our basic discussion in the text. Clearly the OPEC announcement is much more about a supply shift than a demand shift.

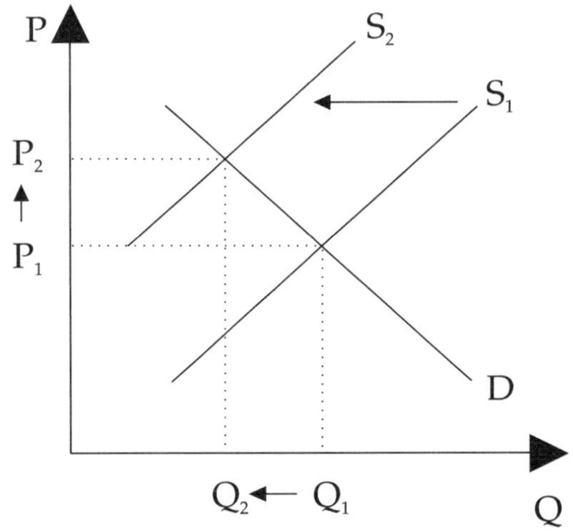

Oil Market

We already see the tremendous benefit of carefully defining supply and demand. What economists have basically done is first take everything that could possibly affect producers' decisions to sell various quantities of a good. This list of causes could be huge, including the weather, the producers' forecasts of future customer behavior, and even the possibility of civil war. Then, after they have come up with a list of all the different factors that could influence producers' decisions on how much to sell, the economists hold every single one of those influences constant, *except* they allow the price of the good to change. The supply schedule (and curve) is then the tracing out of the thought experiment where *only the price of the good* is allowed to change, while all the other influences are held constant. So to repeat, economists are *not* saying that the price of a good is the only thing that affects the quantity that producers want to sell. But when economists construct a supply schedule or draw a supply curve, they are holding all the other influences constant in order to isolate the effects of the change in price.

Similarly, the demand schedule (and curve) traces out the thought experiment where economists hold constant all factors that could possibly affect consumers' desires to purchase quantities of a good, *except* the price of the good. By varying that one element, and holding everything else constant, economists can map out the demand for the good.

When we're trying to analyze the impact of some change, then, what we're doing is trying to figure out which list the factor belongs in. Is it something that will influence producers and how much they would be willing to sell the good in question? Is it a factor that will influence how much consumers would be willing to purchase of the good in question? Or both? Let's move on to another example.

Example 2: Supply Increase

Suppose the weather is very accommodating and the orange crop is unusually large. What effect will this have on the price of oranges?

The unusually good weather means that farmers will have more oranges than they normally have after their harvest. Consequently, they will probably be willing to sell more oranges at various hypothetical prices than they would have in the case of normal weather. In other words, supply has increased, meaning the supply curve shifts to the right.

At the same time, the weather per se probably doesn't have a very big effect on consumers' willingness to buy oranges at various prices. For all practical purposes, we can say that the unusual weather won't influence the demand for oranges.

As the graph shows, a rightward shift in supply, coupled with a stable demand, leads to a lower (equilibrium) price and a higher (equilibrium) quantity:

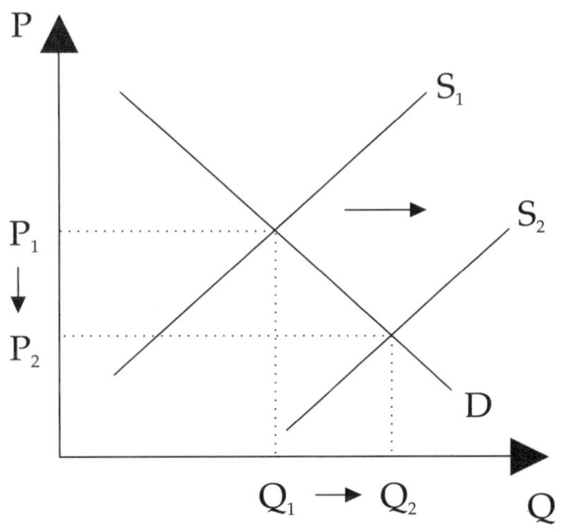

Orange Market

Example 3: Demand Decrease

Let's continue with the example above, and assume that great weather in Florida has yielded a bumper crop of oranges. What effect, if any, will this have on the market price of *apples*, if we assume that the apple orchards experience a normal year?

The perfect combination of sunshine and rainfall in Florida, by assumption, doesn't translate into a bigger apple crop among the major orchards. It's hard to see how the bumper orange crop would directly affect the supply schedule of apples, so we'll assume it stays the same.

However, it *does* make sense to think that the Florida weather will affect consumers and their demand *for apples.* For many consumers, apples and oranges are **substitutes**, meaning that one or the other can satisfy the consumers' ultimate objectives (in this case, the desire for fruit).[4] When the price of a good goes down, the demand *for its substitutes* goes down as well. In our case, the flow of cause-and-effect runs like this: The unusual weather leads to a bumper crop of oranges in Florida, which increases the supply of oranges and doesn't affect the demand for oranges. This means the price of oranges falls. The lower price of oranges doesn't affect the supply of apples, but it *does* affect the demand for apples, by shifting it to the left.

This is a subtle point that sometimes confuses people who are new to the economic way of thinking. Remember that supply and demand curves vary the price *of the good in question* while keeping everything else the same. So one of the elements of "everything else" is the price of *other goods.* To put it in other words: When the price of apples changes, this doesn't affect the demand for apples; all that happens is we move *along* the demand curve for apples. However, when the price of *oranges* changes, this can indeed shift the entire demand curve for apples (to the left).

In the following chart we show the effect of a generic reduction in demand while supply is held constant:

---

[4]On the other hand, a **complement** is a good that goes hand-in-hand with another. For example, peanut butter is a complement to jelly. If other influences stay the same, a fall in the price of jelly will *increase* the demand for peanut butter. So the connection between price and demand for complements is the opposite of the connection in the case of substitutes.

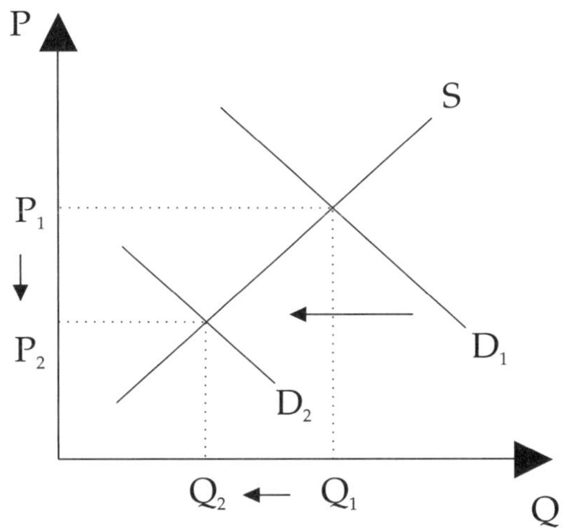

Market for Apples

Example 4: Demand Increase

Suppose the actor Robert Pattinson moves into an apartment complex. What will be the likely effect on the rental price of the apartments in the building?

In this example the analysis is straightforward. The supply of apartments in the building is unchanged; the owner of the building can't sell more units than physically exist, and Pattinson's decision to rent one of the units presumably won't make the landlord decide to rent out *fewer* units. On the other hand, there are plenty of consumers (mostly female) who would love to live in the same building as the *Twilight* star. The fact that he now lives in the building would increase the market demand for apartments in that complex:

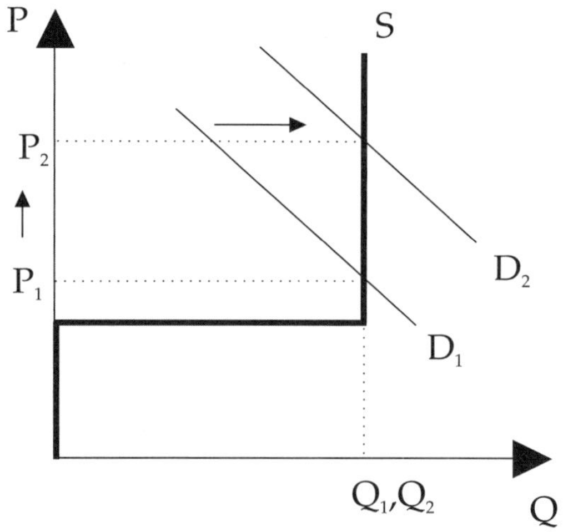

Market for Apartment Units

The only complication in our diagram above is the odd-shaped supply curve. We are taking the opportunity in this example not merely to show the effects of a demand increase, but also to show the possibility of a fixed (unchanging) supply. With a more typical supply curve, an increase in demand moves price *and* quantity up, but in our example, only the price has increased, since the quantity of apartments cannot increase, at least not anytime soon.[5]

The graph above also shows that if the price falls low enough, the owner of the building doesn't bother renting any units out to tenants. Instead, he prefers to keep the building empty and avoid the headaches of dealing with customers who complain of no hot water, loud parties, and so on. But since the whole point of owning the building is to make money, even at a relatively low price the landlord is willing to rent out all the units.

[5]A standard economics textbook will usually distinguish between short-run and long-run supply curves. We will not go down this route because it would involve more graphical analysis.

Example 5: A Simultaneous Change in Supply and Demand

In the previous examples we have analyzed situations where a change clearly had a large effect on *either* supply *or* demand, but a minor impact on the other. What happens when a change has significant impacts on both supply and demand at the same time?

For example, suppose that a new medical report shows that leather shoes pose serious health risks to those who come in frequent contact with them. What will happen to the equilibrium price and quantity of leather shoes?

The new report will (eventually) cause the supply curve of leather shoes to shift to the left.[6] If the entrepreneurs are directly involved with handling the shoes, they won't be as eager to handle as many pairs per day. But even if they merely hire others to sell the shoes, they will still have to pay higher wages as workers prefer to take other, safer jobs. The higher wages of workers will raise the expenses of selling shoes, making the supply curve shift left.

But for obvious reasons, the medical report will also significantly affect the demand for shoes, shifting it to the left as well. In this case, we can confidently say that the equilibrium *quantity* will decline, but we don't know what will happen to the equilibrium price of leather shoes. The leftward supply shift would tend to raise the price, but the leftward demand shift would tend to lower it. Only if we had exact numbers could we say which effect would be larger. Generically speaking, a reduction in supply *and* demand at the same time can make the equilibrium price go up or down:

---

[6]We say *eventually* the supply curve will shift left because it's possible that the most paranoid of leather shoe owners try to unload their inventory the day of the announcement, at whatever price they can get. This technically would constitute a rightward shift in the supply curve. But in the text we are focusing on the more permanent situation, looking at producers who stay in business and continue to sell shoes months after the initial announcement.

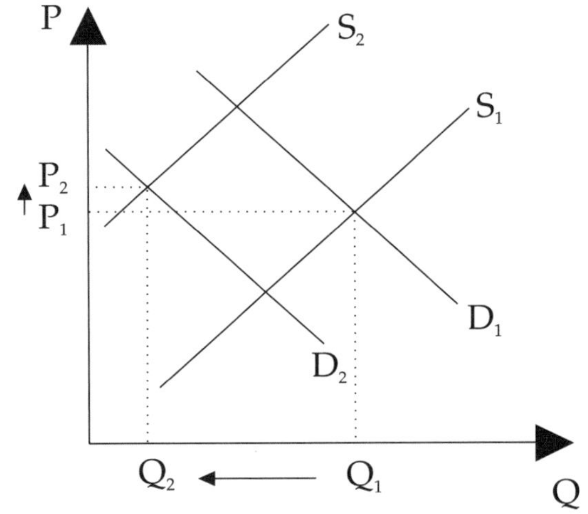

Market for Shoes

or

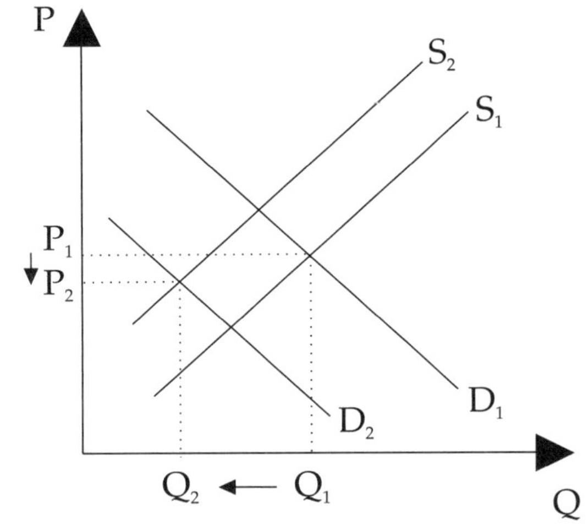

Market for Shoes

In the exercises accompanying this lesson you will work through other combinations of changes in supply and demand that occur at the same time. In each case, either price *or* quantity will move in a certain direction without a doubt, but then the other item's movement will be uncertain.[7]

[7]In other words, in a given exercise you will be able to decide (a) that the quantity definitely goes up, but you won't know for sure which way the price moves,

Lesson Recap . . .

- Economists use supply and demand to explain market prices and the amounts of goods and services produced. Supply and demand aren't "theories" but instead provide a mental framework for understanding how changes in the economy will affect prices and amounts.

- Supply and demand schedules (and graphs or "curves") illustrate the hypothetical effects of keeping every other influence the same, and allowing only the price of the good to change. To repeat, this isn't a "theory" about what things influence people in the economy, it is simply a framework for economists to organize their thinking.

- The Law of Supply says that if other influences stay the same, then an increase in the price will lead producers to sell more units, while a decrease in price will lead producers to sell fewer units. The Law of Demand says that if other influences stay the same, then an increase in price will lead consumers to buy fewer units, while a decrease in price will lead them to buy more units.

(b) that the quantity definitely goes down, but you won't know about the price, (c) that the price definitely moves up, but you won't know which way quantity moves, or (d) that the price definitely goes down, but you won't be sure which way the quantity moves.

NEW TERMS

Demand: The relationship between the price of a good (or service), and the number of units that consumers want to purchase at each hypothetical price.

Demand schedule: A table that illustrates the demand relationship either for an individual or a group.

Law of Demand: If other influences stay the same, then a lower price will lead consumers to buy more units of a good (or service), while a higher price will lead them to buy fewer units.

Demand curve: A graphical illustration of the demand relationship, with price placed on the vertical axis and quantity on the horizontal axis. Sometimes a generic demand curve is drawn as a smooth, curved line or even as a simple straight line. Demand curves are "downward sloping," meaning that they start in the upper left and move down and to the right.

Supply: The relationship between the price of a good (or service), and the number of units that producers want to sell at each hypothetical price.

Supply schedule: A table illustrating the supply relationship, either for an individual or group of producers.

Supply curve: A graphical illustration of the supply relationship, with price placed on the vertical axis and quantity on the horizontal axis. Sometimes a generic supply curve is drawn as a smooth, curved line or even as a simple straight line. Supply curves are "upward sloping," meaning that they start in the bottom left and move up and to the right.

Law of Supply: If other influences stay the same, then a higher price will lead producers to sell more units of a good (or service), while a lower price will lead producers to sell fewer units.

Surplus / glut: A situation where producers want to sell more units of a good (or service) than consumers want to purchase. This occurs when the actual price is higher than the market-clearing price.

Shortage: A situation where consumers want to buy more units than producers want to sell. This occurs when the actual price is below the market-clearing price.

Equilibrium price / market-clearing price: The price at which producers want to sell exactly the number of units that consumers want to purchase. On a graph, the equilibrium price occurs at the intersection of the supply and demand curves.

Equilibrium quantity: The number of units that producers want to sell, and consumers want to buy, at the equilibrium price. On a graph, the equilibrium quantity occurs at the intersection of the supply and demand curves.

Reduction in supply / leftward shift in the supply curve: A situation in which a change *besides* the price of a good (or service) causes producers to reduce the number of units they want to sell, at various possible prices. On a graph, this change causes the supply curve itself to move to the left. (In a similar way, an *increase* in supply or a *rightward* shift in the supply curve, occurs when a change causes producers to *increase* the number of units they want to sell, at various possible prices.)

Reduction in demand / leftward shift in the demand curve: A situation in which a change *besides* the price of a good (or service) causes consumers to reduce the number of units they want to purchase, at various possible prices. On a graph, this change causes the demand curve itself to move to the left.

Substitutes: Goods (or services) that consumers use for similar purposes. For example, Coke and Pepsi might be substitutes if someone goes to the store looking to buy soda. A change in the price of one good tends to cause a change in the same direction in the demand for a substitute. (A reduction in the price of Coke will probably cause a reduction in the demand for Pepsi.)

Complements: Goods (or services) that consumers use together. For example, hot dogs and mustard might be complements if someone goes to the store in preparation for a cookout. A change in the price of one good tends to cause a change in the opposite direction in the demand for a complement. (A reduction in the price of hot dogs will probably cause an increase in the demand for mustard.)

STUDY QUESTIONS

1. Why does the text say that supply and demand can never be proven false?

2. Why does the text say that demand is a snapshot in time?

3. How do you go from individual demand or supply schedules, to market demand and supply schedules?

4. Explain how the market process tends to push prices toward their equilibrium levels.

5. If supply increases while demand decreases, what can we say about the change in (equilibrium) price? What about the change in (equilibrium) quantity?

ADVANCED LESSON 12

Interest, Credit, and Debt

In this lesson you will learn:

- The function of *interest* in a market economy.
- Common types of *credit transactions.*
- The pros and cons of going into *debt.*

Interest: It's About Time

As we have already learned in Lesson 10, interest is the amount of money paid to a lender above and beyond the return of the *principal*. For example, if someone lends out $1,000 and receives $1,080 back one year later, the principal is $1,000 and the lender has earned $80 in interest. Usually people discuss the *interest rate*, which is the interest expressed as a percentage of the principal, and is also usually quoted on a yearly basis. In our example, the loan carried an 8% annual interest rate.

The subject of interest, and the explanation of how markets determine particular interest rates, can be one of the most complicated areas in economic theory. In the present lesson we will obviously just cover the basics. Essentially, interest has to do with *time*. Lenders must be compensated (with interest) to give up money available to them *now*, in exchange for a promise to be paid back with money not available until the *future*. On the other hand, the reason borrowers are willing to *pay* interest is that they value having money (and the things it can buy) right now, rather than having to put off their purchases until the future. A positive interest rate goes hand in hand with **time preference**, which is the desire (other things equal) to enjoy goods sooner rather than later.

The interest rate tells us how much the market price of a current dollar is, compared to a future dollar. Right now, the "market price" of a $100 bill is, well, $100. But how much *right now* is an ironclad guarantee that a crisp $100 bill will be delivered in exactly one year? It's certainly not worth a full $100; except under very unusual circumstances, nobody would give up a $100 bill today, in exchange for receiving the same $100 bill back in 12 months. We know that in practice, people pay *less than* $100 today, in order to receive a promise—even a very reliable promise from a trustworthy borrower—of a future payment of $100. The *market interest rate* shows us exactly what the **discount** on future dollars is, or (equivalently) what the premium on current dollars is. For example, at an interest rate of 5%, people would pay about $95.24 today, in order to receive an ironclad claim on a $100 payment in exactly one year.[1]

In a sense, the interest rate is an **exchange rate** between currencies, except that the two currencies are "current U.S. dollars" and "future U.S. dollars." A normal exchange rate shows how many current U.S. dollar bills trade for one euro or Mexican peso, whereas an interest rate shows how many "2010" US dollar bills trade for one "2011" U.S. dollar bill, if the current year is 2010.

A business firm needs to use exchange rates if it operates in several countries, in order to keep its accounts in a common denominator. For example, if a firm buys certain Chinese components priced in yuan, pays pesos to workers in Mexico to assemble the parts into finished goods, and finally sells the products in the United States for dollars, then the firm's accountants will need to translate the three currencies into a common denominator (presumably U.S. dollars) to tell if the business is making a profit.

By the same token, interest rates for varying time durations or **maturities** allow businesses to keep track of their books for operations that unfold over several years (not countries). If the firm buys raw materials from U.S. suppliers in 2010, then pays American workers to process the materials during

[1]You can check that $95.24 x 1.05 = $100.00.

2011, and finally sells the finished goods gradually during the course of 2012, the firm's accountants cannot ignore the time element for the various expenditures and revenues. The dollars paid for materials in 2010, as well as the dollars paid for labor in 2011, have a higher market value than the dollars received from customers in 2012, and so the accountants need to *discount* the later money. Market interest rates help them determine the appropriate discount to apply, in order to look at the entire three-year operation and decide, "Did we turn a profit?"

It is important to point out that the higher the interest rate, the more *present-oriented* business operations will be. If there is a very long operation, requiring inputs of labor and raw materials for many years before the finished product emerges, then the higher the interest rate, the less profitable such an operation will be. This is because the entrepreneur running the operation will spend money today and for many years, in the hopes of receiving revenue at some far future date. The higher the interest rate, the bigger the "penalty" on the duration of an operation, and the greater the encouragement that the market gives to entrepreneurs to quickly convert their resources into final goods for their customers.

On the other hand, a low interest rate gives a "green light" to entrepreneurs to start longer production processes. Even if we keep all of the prices for materials and the final product the same, a given project can appear unprofitable at a high interest rate, but profitable at a lower interest rate. Like all other market prices, interest rates guide entrepreneurs to invest their limited resources efficiently.

Savings, Investment, and Economic Growth

Remember that in Lesson 10 we saw how an increase in savings allows more investment and faster economic growth. We are now in a position to show how the market interest rate helps this process.

First, imagine an initial scenario where the interest rate is 8%. We can use supply and demand curves (as discussed in Lesson 11) to illustrate this initial equilibrium interest rate for the **loanable funds market**:

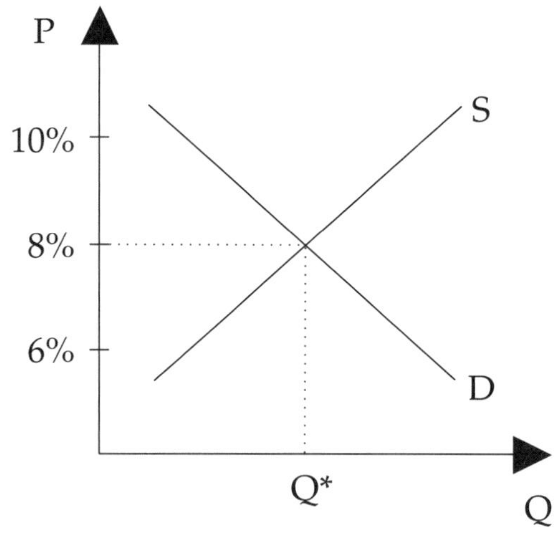

Market for Loanable Funds

Notice that the x-axis on the above refers to the total amount of money being borrowed (demanded) and lent (supplied). The y-axis refers to the price of the loan, which is the same thing as the interest rate. Some people say that interest is the "price of money," but that is inaccurate; it is the price of *borrowing* money. In our example, to borrow $100 for a year carries a price of $8; after a person borrows and repays the loan principal, he still has to fork out an additional $8 fee.

The equilibrium interest rate equates the quantity demanded of borrowed money with the quantity supplied of money to be lent. If the interest rate were too high, then lenders would want to lend out more money than borrowers wanted to borrow. (Convince yourself that at higher interest rates—other things equal—lenders would want to supply more funds while borrowers would demand fewer funds.) On the other hand, if the interest rate were below 8% in our chart above, then there would be a shortage of loanable funds, as borrowers would seek to borrow more (measured in total dollars) than lenders collectively would be willing to supply. With our supply and demand curves as shown above, only at an interest rate of 8% do we have an equilibrium, where the lenders want to provide exactly as much money in loans as people wish to borrow.

Now what happens if most people in the community decide to save more? In a supply and demand framework, we illustrate this change by shifting the supply curve of loanable funds to the right, because at every hypothetical interest rate (price), the suppliers are willing to bring more of their saved funds to the market to lend out to borrowers. Suppose that the community's increased willingness to save leads to a fall in the rate of interest (the price of a loan) down to 6%, and an increase in the total amount of dollars lent and borrowed.

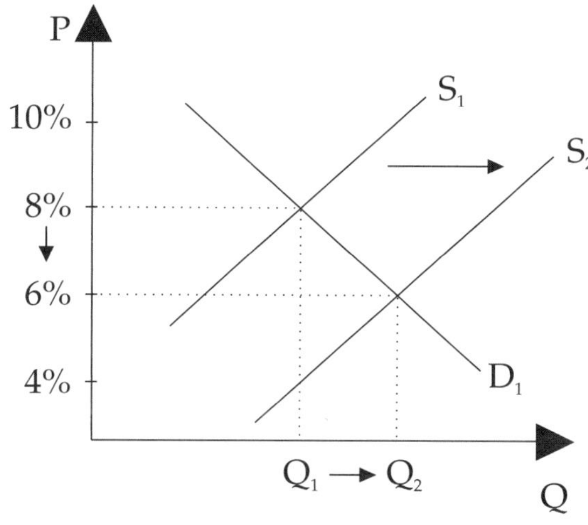

Market for Loanable Funds

We now have a more complete understanding of the process described in Lesson 10. When a community saves more in general, this pushes down interest rates and leads to more total funds available for borrowers. The lower interest rates send a signal to entrepreneurs to engage in longer-term projects that are now profitable. In Lesson 10 we already saw that when people in the community on average reduced their present consumption (spending on restaurant meals, vacations, electronics goods, etc.), this frugality freed up physical resources and allowed for increased investment in machinery, tools, and other capital goods that would eventually boost future output. But now we see how the market interest rate plays a role in helping the entrepreneurs adjust to the new preferences of their customers, and guides them into shifting the entire structure of production to become more future-oriented.

Common Credit Transactions

In a simple **credit transaction**, one party trades money that he has saved in exchange for a claim (or a promise) from another party that she will give a specified payment of money at a future date, or a stream of money payments at various specified dates.[2]

In the examples we discuss in this section, *credit transactions do not create money*, they simply shift money from one holder to another.[3] When someone buys a pack of gum, money isn't created; the buyer hands over money in exchange for the pack of gum. In the same way, a simple credit transaction doesn't create money either—the lender hands over money in exchange for an I.O.U. from the borrower. Because of this fact, credit transactions *per se* do not tend to "push prices up" as many people believe. The borrower is able to spend more in the present than he otherwise would be able to, it's true, but the lender can spend that much less. At the time of the repayment, the borrower must restrict his spending in order to pay back the principal (plus interest), but the influx of money gives that much more spending ability to the lender.

Bonds

When a company wishes to borrow money, it sells a **bond** which is a legal claim entitling the bondholder to a stream of cash payments from the bond issuer (i.e., the company). There is nothing mysterious behind

[2]Note that if a merchant allows a customer to buy merchandise "on credit," you can break the overall transaction into two separate events: First the merchant lends money to the customer on certain terms, and then the customer uses the borrowed money to buy merchandise from the merchant.

[3]In modern times, most governments have institutionalized the practice of **fractional reserve banking**, in which banks really do create new money when they advance a loan. This is a complex topic that we will not discuss in this introductory book.

"issuing" a bond; it is simply a standardized contract in which a company borrows money from someone else in the community. The person "buying the bond" is really doing nothing more than lending money (the bond price) in exchange for the company's official promise to make interest payments at regular intervals and eventually return the principal.

Banks

When an individual wants to borrow money, he can make individual arrangements with various people. However, in many cases borrowers use the services of a **credit intermediary**, such as a **bank.** The bank is an intermediary between the ultimate lenders and borrowers in the market. First, the bank acts as a borrower, when **depositors** lend their funds to the bank (and earn a certain interest rate on their deposits). Second, the bank uses these funds to act as a lender to people in the market who wish to borrow from the bank (and pay a certain, higher interest rate on their loans).

A successful bank is able to earn enough money on the **spread** (the difference between the interest rate it charges borrowers and the interest rate it pays to depositors) in order to pay its staff and other expenses, as well as provide an income to the entrepreneur(s) running the bank. One of the main reasons the bank is able to maintain this spread is that different borrowers have different degrees of **credit risk.**

Consider a young couple who want a **mortgage** to buy a new house for $200,000. Ultimately, they are going to borrow the money from various savers scattered throughout the community. But if the prospective borrowers went knocking door to door, trying to find 200 people who would each put up $1,000 in exchange for the couple's signatures on a loan contract, they probably wouldn't find many takers, or if they did, the interest rate they charged would be quite high. The problem is that the individual saver doesn't really know the couple very well, and even if the couple is hardworking and sincere, a job layoff or medical condition could make them **default** on the loan.

Now we understand the function of a credit intermediary such as a bank. People in the community are willing to deposit their money with the bank, because it is much less likely to lose their savings than any individual borrower. Thus they are willing to lend at a much lower contractual interest rate than they would have insisted from the couple trying to buy a house. On the other hand, the bank can afford to lend to the couple, because it has experts whose job is to evaluate the likelihood that the couple will make their mortgage payments on time. By making mortgage loans not just to one couple, but to hundreds or thousands of home buyers, the bank reduces the damage of any particular loan default. So long as the bank has properly estimated the credit risks of its various borrowers, the bank will absorb the expected number of **delinquencies** and defaults as part of the cost of doing business. The interest rates it charges in its various mortgage and other loan contracts will have already reflected the riskiness of each borrower.

When the savers in a community lend to the borrowers *through* credit intermediaries such as banks, it allows the risks to be pooled and distributed more uniformly. If, say, 1% of the couples borrowing money for a home purchase end up defaulting on the mortgage payments, that loss doesn't fall entirely on an unlucky 1% of the lenders who lose their life savings. On the contrary—assuming the banks have done their jobs properly—the loss in contractual mortgage payments is spread evenly among all the lenders, reflected in the fact that they earn a lower interest rate on their bank deposits than the ultimate borrowers are paying on their mortgages.

Credit Cards

A popular form of credit transactions nowadays involves the use of a **credit card**. When a customer buys, say, a pair of shoes at the mall and swipes her credit card at the register, what actually happens is that the credit card issuer pays money to the store, and then records the loan on the customer's account. As with the other transactions discussed above, here too *no new money is created.* In principle, the transaction is equivalent to one where a representative of the credit card company walks into the store, hands the customer the money in exchange for a signature promising to pay it back with interest, and then the customer hands the newly-borrowed money to the store clerk. The familiar use of plastic cards is just a matter of convenience, allowing the cumbersome two-step process to be executed in a matter of seconds.

As with other lenders, credit card issuers must be careful when lending money to borrowers. When someone applies for a credit card, the issuing company will review the applicant's **credit history** to judge the likelihood that the applicant will pay back any borrowed money. There are several companies that provide the service of keeping up with borrowers' debts and repayment history. These companies sell lenders "scores" on each applicant, to make it easier for the lender to determine if the borrower is likely to repay on time. Applicants with "good credit" (meaning a high **credit score**) have shown that they are responsible and can be trusted to pay off their credit card balances. On the other hand, an applicant who has a high amount of debt with other companies, and has a history of missing payments, will have "poor credit" (meaning a low credit score) and may not be approved for a new card, or will be granted a card but with a very modest **credit limit**. Ironically, someone who has never had a credit card or otherwise borrowed money may find it difficult to secure a card with a high credit limit, because there is no history that the issuer can review to see how this applicant handles debt.

The Pros and Cons of Debt

Some people understandably warn that "you should never get into debt," and that "if you can't pay cash for something, then you can't afford it." Indeed there is much truth to this warning, and many people would testify that excessive credit card debt ruined their lives. In a free market, if a consumer chooses to buy on credit this is a voluntary action, and the consumer thought at the time of purchase that the benefits of the immediate availability outweighed the costs of having to pay back the loan (with interest) in the future. So when some criticize the wisdom of credit purchases, they are relying on the fact that people can often *regret* their previous, voluntary choices.

When it comes to consumer purchases on credit, there is an important distinction between a **secured** versus an **unsecured loan**. A secured loan has **collateral** backing it up, often the object being purchased with the loan. Typical examples include a mortgage, in which the house (and land on which it sits) serves as collateral, or a car loan in which the vehicle is the collateral. Although these are credit transactions too, it certainly changes our evaluation of the wisdom of a large increase in debt if we find out that there is a valuable new asset being acquired. For example, if someone borrowed $10,000 to take a cruise, there would be nothing (except memories) to show for it down the road, whereas someone borrowing $10,000 to buy a new car could sell the car and pay off most of the remaining debt if his circumstances changed.[4]

The most obvious example of what is called **productive debt** occurs when an entrepreneur borrows money in order to expand his or her business operations. For example, a large corporation may decide to issue $10 million in new bonds in order to finance the construction of a new factory. So long as things go according to plan, what happens is that the corporation borrows $10 million from savers in the community, and uses the lent funds to purchase raw materials, equipment, and labor services from workers. After the factory is up and running, the corporation's revenues are higher than they otherwise would have been, and out of this surplus the corporation can make its periodic interest payments to the new bondholders, and eventually eliminate the debt completely by paying back the principal. In many respects, debt is simply one way that businesses can raise funds for new investment spending, with another method being the issuance of stock, a topic we address in Lesson 14.

Individuals too can borrow productive debt, if they receive loans to put themselves through college or medical school. The essential feature of productive debt is that the borrowed money is invested in order to increase the borrower's future income, so that paying back the loan will not be a burden.

---

[4]Strictly speaking, the distinction between a secured and an unsecured loan doesn't match up perfectly with the different types of borrowing behavior. For example, someone could get a secured loan with his car (which he previously purchased with cash) serving as the collateral, and then use the money to finance a vacation cruise. On the other hand, a dentist could use her personal credit card in order to purchase a new computer for her office receptionist. It's still the case, however, that a person's credit report will penalize him or her more heavily if a given amount of debt is unsecured, because there are no assets "backing up" the loans.

Lesson Recap . . .

- In a market economy, interest rates help to coordinate consumers' preferences to enjoy goods sooner versus later, with producers' investments in projects that take shorter or longer to complete. If people are impatient, then the interest rate will be high and producers will invest in relatively quick projects. If people are willing to postpone immediate gratification by saving, then the interest rate will be low and producers can invest in longer projects.

- Common credit transactions include cases where corporations borrow money by issuing bonds, homebuyers take out mortgages from banks, and individuals pay for purchases using credit cards.

- There are pros and cons of going into debt. On the positive side, debt allows the borrower to make purchases sooner. On the negative side, a higher debt load forces the borrower to devote more of his income to paying interest (or "finance charges") to the lender, leaving less income available for enjoyments in the future. In some situations taking on debt can be "productive" if the borrowed money is invested rather than spent on immediate enjoyments.

NEW TERMS

Time preference: The degree to which people prefer to consume sooner rather than later; a gauge of people's impatience to receive enjoyments.

Discount: The percentage by which the value of a unit of money is reduced, because it will not be received until the future.

Exchange rate: The "price" of one currency in terms of another, or how many units of one currency will trade for one unit of another currency.

Maturity: The time duration of a specific loan, and the interest rate that applies to it. (Loans and their corresponding bonds can have shorter or longer maturities.)

Loanable funds market: The market in which lenders give money to borrowers at an agreed-upon interest rate.

Credit transaction: An exchange where one person gives up something (such as money) today, while the other person promises to give up something (such as money) in the future.

Bond: A corporation's IOU, which is a legally binding promise to repay borrowed money plus interest. The buyer of a bond gives money to the corporation today, in the hopes of receiving back the principal plus interest in the future.

Fractional reserve banking: The typical practice where banks do not keep all of their customers' deposits in the vault. In other words, all of the bank's customers have more money on deposit, than the bank has cash in the vault.

Credit intermediary: A person or organization that is the "middleman" between lenders and borrowers.

Bank: A common credit intermediary, which takes deposits from many different lenders and makes loans to many different borrowers.

Depositors: People who give their money to a bank.

Spread: The difference between the interest rate that a credit intermediary (such as a bank) earns from its borrowers, compared to the interest rate it pays to its lenders or depositors. A positive spread allows the credit intermediary to earn income from its activities, so long as it has correctly estimated the likelihood of default by its borrowers.

Credit risk: The likelihood that a borrower will be unable to pay back a loan.

Mortgage: A special type of loan in which the borrower buys a house (or other real estate) with the funds. Usually the property serves as collateral for the mortgage.

Default: A situation when a borrower stops making repayments on a loan.

Delinquencies: Cases where borrowers are not in good standing with the lender (such as a bank), because they have not been keeping up with their required payments.

Credit card: A device that allows the borrower to achieve virtually instant loans from the credit card company when making purchases.

Credit history: A person's record of borrowing and repayment behavior.

Credit score: A number that an agency will assign to a person based on his or her credit history, which helps potential lenders decide on the riskiness of lending money to the person.

Credit limit: The maximum amount of money that a person can borrow from a pre-approved source (such as a credit card).

Secured loan: A loan that has an asset (such as a house, car, etc.) pledged as collateral, in case the borrower defaults. The advantage to the borrower is that the interest rate is lower than it would be for a comparable unsecured loan.

Unsecured loan: A loan that has no collateral serving as a backup. If the borrower defaults, the lender has no other options. The advantage to the borrower is that none of his or her other assets can be seized (or "repossessed") in the case of default.

Collateral: An asset that a borrower "puts up" when applying for a loan. If the borrower defaults, the lender may take possession of the collateral as compensation. (For example, if a borrower wants money to buy a house or a car, these items themselves can serve as the collateral, meaning that if the borrower fails to make his or her payments on schedule, the lender can take control of the house or car.)

Productive debt: Debt used to finance investments. Ideally, the extra income from the investment spending will allow the borrower to make the interest payments resulting from the increase in debt, so that the extra borrowing "pays for itself."

STUDY QUESTIONS

1. Why is the first section titled, "Interest: It's About Time"?

2. *What is the connection between interest rates and currency exchange rates?

3. Why does a low interest rate give a "green light" to long production processes?

4. What is exchanged in a credit transaction?

5. What is "productive debt"?

ADVANCED LESSON 13

Profit and Loss Accounting

In this lesson you will learn:

- The distinction between interest and profit.
- The social function of profit and loss accounting.
- The limits of profit and loss accounting.

Profit and Loss Guide Entrepreneurs

In previous lessons we have shown how market prices guide the actions of everyone in a market economy. For example, if an unexpected cold snap decimates the orange crop, then the sudden drop in supply will cause the prices of oranges and orange juice to rise,[1] which in turn will lead consumers to buy fewer oranges and cartons of orange juice. For a different example, if people become more concerned about having straight teeth, the demand for braces will rise, which will ultimately lead to more students

[1]We are speaking loosely. Technically, a cold snap *per se* doesn't cause prices to rise, and even a reduction in physical supply doesn't cause prices to rise. More accurately, we should say that the cold snap changes the situation of the orange producers, and then their new subjective valuations interact with the original subjective valuations of buyers in the market, such that the equilibrium price of oranges is higher than it was before. But it is obviously much simpler to say, "Supply fell so the price rose."

choosing a career in orthodontics.[2] Market prices act as signals about underlying changes in both the physical world and subjective preferences, allowing people to adjust their behavior in light of new realities.

Entrepreneurs do not respond to particular prices but rather to the *difference* between certain prices. Specifically, entrepreneurs estimate the amount they must spend on their ingredients or inputs (hired workers, raw materials, electricity bill, etc.), and then *forecast* the total revenues they will receive from customers when selling their finished products or services. In short entrepreneurs estimate whether their proposed course of action will yield a *profit* or a *loss*, where this calculation involves current and future market prices.

Generally speaking, activities that generate high (monetary) profits will attract more entrepreneurs, while those that cause losses will repel entrepreneurs. In a market economy with open competition, there is a tendency for monetary profits and losses to be whittled away over time, as entrepreneurs adjust to the situation. When more entrepreneurs flock into a highly profitable activity, their efforts to buy the necessary inputs cause their prices to rise, while the increased output of the finished good or service causes the price to the consumer to fall. The gap between the two sets of prices—which was driving the originally high profit margin—tends to shrink, so that the monetary profits disappear as well.

The reverse occurs when an activity is plagued by recurring losses. New entrepreneurs will shy away from the industry, and entrepreneurs who are originally in the industry will either scale back their operations or abandon them and move to a different line of work. The entrepreneurs' total demand for the necessary inputs drops, leading to lower prices for the workers, raw materials, and other items used in this particular activity. On the other hand, the diminished supply of the finished good or service

---

[2]As always, these examples should be interpreted as *tendencies* that will only lead to actual changes so long as other things remain equal. If the drop in orange supply were accompanied by a new report showing that orange juice causes cancer, then the price of orange juice might end up falling. On the other hand, even if the earnings of orthodontists rise because of a higher demand for braces, it's still possible that fewer students go into the field if a popular movie depicts orthodontists as having dirty and unfulfilling jobs.

tends to raise the price that the consumer must pay. This process continues until the finished price has risen enough, and the input prices have fallen enough, so that the remaining entrepreneurs no longer suffer losses from producing the good or service in question.

Interest versus Profit

We have explained that when an entrepreneur calculates whether or not his business is turning a profit, he must consider the prices of the various inputs he uses in his operations. For example, if he runs a factory that produces television sets, he must take account of (a) the wages he pays to his assembly line workers, (b) the prices for the metals and plastics that he buys in bulk, and even (c) the payments that he makes to the utility company for the electricity his operation requires. Only if the revenues he earns from selling television sets is great enough to cover these expenses will the operation be profitable.

However, up until now we have ignored a very important "input" into any long-term business operation: the financial capital invested in it, and the associated "price" of this investment as expressed by interest payments. To see how interest payments factor into profitability, it's easiest to use a concrete illustration.

Suppose someone can spend $10,000 in January buying a plot of land that contains a young crop of Christmas trees. The new owner doesn't need to spend any more money. All she has to do is *wait* until December when she can sell the 100 mature trees for an average of $30 apiece. After the trees have all been sold, she can also sell the bare land for $7,300. From the revenue from the trees and the land sale, the entrepreneur would have turned her original $10,000 investment into $3,000 + $7,300 = $10,300, which is certainly more money than she started out with. Can we conclude that the Christmas tree venture was profitable?

Before answering the question, our tree entrepreneur needs to consider interest payments. For example, if she originally *borrowed* the $10,000 from someone at a 5% annual interest rate, then she actually *lost* money on the whole arrangement. With her $10,300 in hand, she tries to pay off the creditor who lent her the money, and finds that she still owes a balance of \$200.[3]

Even if the tree entrepreneur uses her own saved funds, most economists would say she still "lost" money on the deal, if alternative investments yielded a rate of return higher (and less risky) than the implicit 3% return in the Christmas tree business. For example, back in January if the woman could have taken \$10,000 out of her savings and purchased a 12-month corporate bond yielding 5%—*and* if the woman viewed this investment at least as "safe" as plowing her money into a crop of Christmas trees—then in a sense she would be \$200 poorer if she invested the money in the land with the young crop of trees. In this case the monetary "loss" would not show up in the official records compiled by her accountant, because the \$500 in forfeited interest on the corporate bond would be an *opportunity cost*, rather than an explicit out-of-pocket expenditure.

In Lesson 12 we learned that people usually attach a higher value to current dollars (and other forms of money) over future dollars, meaning that interest rates are positive. We need to keep this fact in mind when discussing competition and its impacts on profit margins. Even in the long run, it is not true that competition will *completely* whittle away the gap between the revenues an entrepreneur receives from selling his product or service, versus the out-of-pocket expenditures on inputs such as labor and raw materials. This is because a portion of what is called the **gross profit** (or **accounting profit**) must go to pay interest on the financial capital invested in the business. When we say that a high profit attracts more entrepreneurs into an industry, to be correct we mean high **net profit** (or **economic profit**), i.e., the profit when an implicit interest payment on invested capital has been included as one of the "inputs" into the operation.[4]

---

[3]We're ignoring the slight complication that she can pay back most of the loan before 12 months have actually passed, in which case the interest expense would not be a full \$500.

[4]Most economists would also include the implicit salary that the entrepreneur "pays herself" as an item to be subtracted from gross or accounting profit, to compute net or economic profit. But in the Christmas tree example, we assumed that the owner didn't have to do any work except wait 12 months for the trees to mature.

The Social Function of Profit and Loss Accounting

Many naïve observers of the market economy dismiss concern with the "bottom line" as a purely arbitrary social convention. To these critics, it seems senseless that a factory producing, say, medicine or shoes for toddlers stops at the point when the owner decides that profit has been maximized. It would certainly be *physically possible* to produce more bottles of aspirin or more shoes in size 3T, yet the boss doesn't allow it, because to do so would "lose money." On the other hand, many apparently superfluous gadgets and unnecessary luxury items are produced every day in a market economy, because they are profitable. Observers who are outraged by this system may adopt the slogan: "Production for people, not profit!"

Such critics do not appreciate the indispensable service that the profit-and-loss test provides to members of a market economy. *Whatever* the social system in place, the regrettable fact is that the material world is one of *scarcity*—there are not enough resources to produce all the goods and services that people desire. Because of scarcity, every economic decision involves *tradeoffs*. When scarce resources are devoted to producing more bottles of aspirin, for example, there are necessarily fewer resources available to produce everything else. It's not enough to ask, "Would the world be a better place if there were more medicine?" The relevant question is, "Would the world be a better place if there were more medicine *and less of the other goods and services* that would have to be sacrificed to produce more medicine?"

In standard introductory textbooks, they often define the **economic problem** as society's decision on how to allocate scarce resources into the production of particular goods and services. In reality, "society" doesn't decide anything; individual members of society make decisions that interact to determine the ultimate fate of all the resources at humanity's disposal. In the pure market economy that we are studying in this section of the book, everyone in society obeys the rules of private property which assign ownership claims to particular units of resources. In this context, market prices are formed when individuals engage in voluntary exchanges with each other. The resulting prices in turn give entrepreneurs the ability to calculate (expected) profits and losses from various possible activities. It is the interaction of property owners in voluntary trades that "determines" what goods and services get produced, but the signals provided by market prices—and the resulting calculations of profit and loss—help the property owners make *informed* decisions.

It might be useful to step back and look at the big picture. The entrepreneurs offer money to the owners of labor services, capital goods, and natural resources. The entrepreneurs then use these inputs to produce goods and services which they sell to consumers for money (see figure on the next page).

The Customer Is Always Right

The real bosses [under capitalism] are the consumers. They, by their buying and by their abstention from buying, decide who should own the capital and run the plants. They determine what should be produced and in what quantity and quality. Their attitudes result either in profit or in loss for the enterpriser. They make poor men rich and rich men poor. They are no easy bosses. They are full of whims and fancies, changeable and unpredictable. They do not care a whit for past merit. As soon as something is offered to them that they like better or is cheaper, they desert their old purveyors.

— Ludwig von Mises, *Bureaucracy*, p. 227

When a particular entrepreneurial venture goes "out of business," what that ultimately means is that consumers were not willing to spend enough money on its finished output, to cover the offers the entrepreneur needed to make in order to bid the scarce inputs away from *other* entrepreneurs who wanted the inputs for *their* enterprises.

To see this principle more concretely, let's work with a silly example. Suppose a successful builder dies and passes on his business to his foolish son. The son gets the bright idea to build new apartment buildings covered with pure gold. He correctly estimates that there would be high demand for apartments where the elevator, hallways, and kitchen shelves were coated

The Big Picture: Entrepreneurs Buy Inputs to Make Goods and Services for Consumers

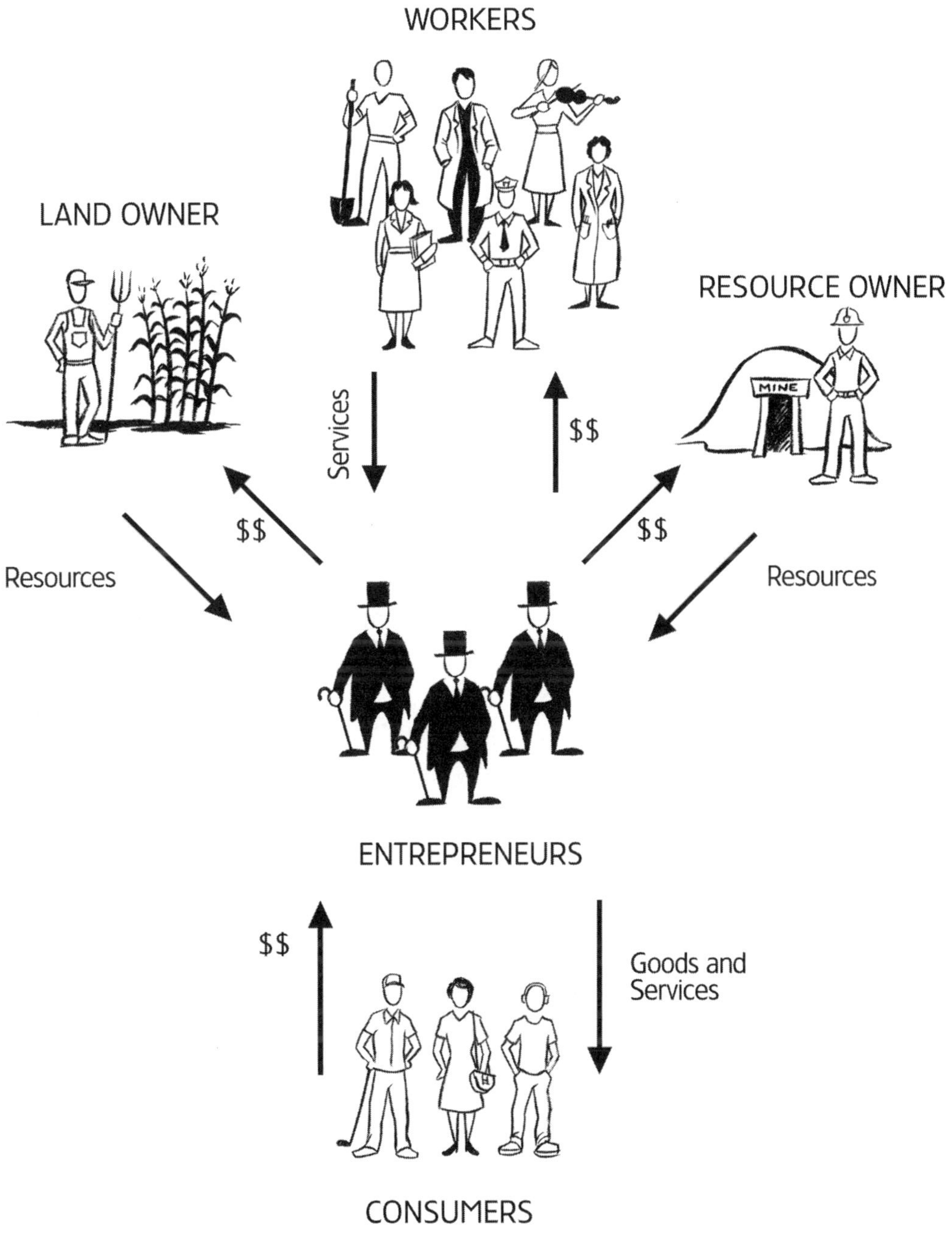

with gold. In fact the son can rent his units for much higher monthly fees than the owners of normal apartments in similar locations.

Of course, this isn't the whole story. Even though his revenues are very high, the foolish son's production costs are astronomical. In addition to the labor, wood, concrete, and other items, he must spend hundreds of millions of dollars buying large quantities of gold. His accountants inform him that despite the higher revenues, he is losing incredible amounts of money because of his decision to coat the apartments with gold. The son will have to either wisen up quickly, or he will squander all of his wealth. Either way, he won't be building apartments coated with gold for very long.

Now if we were to interview the son and ask him what happened, he might say, "It's too expensive to use gold in my business." But notice that this can't be true for *all* entrepreneurs. After all, the *reason* gold is so expensive is that *other buyers are paying such high prices for it*. For example, jewelers still find it profitable to buy gold in order to make necklaces and earrings, and dentists still find it profitable to use gold for fillings. No *jeweler* would say, "It's too expensive to use gold in my business."

Loosely speaking, the profit and loss system communicates the desires of consumers to the resource owners and entrepreneurs when they are deciding how many resources to send into each potential line of production. It's ultimately not the owners of gold mines nor the captains of industry who determine how gold will be used in a market economy. Instead, these decisions are largely guided by the spending decisions of the *consumers*. It is the consumers' demands for normal versus gold-coated apartments, in conjunction with their demands for silver versus gold-coated necklaces, that leads to the outcome that gold-coated apartments are ridiculously unprofitable while gold-coated necklaces are perfectly sensible.

The profit and loss test provides structure to the free enterprise system. People are free to start new businesses, and to sell their resources (including the labor services of their bodies) to whomever they wish. In a market based on the institution of private property, profits occur when an entrepreneur takes resources of a certain market value and transforms them into finished goods (or services) of a *higher* market value. This is the important sense in which profitable entrepreneurs are providing a definite service to others in the economy. Without the feedback of profit and loss calculations, entrepreneurs would have no idea if they were making *economical* use of the resources used up by their business operations.

The Social Function of Profits

"In a free economy, in which wages, costs, and prices are left to the free play of the competitive market, the prospect of profits decides what articles will be made, and in what quantities—and what articles will not be made at all. If there is no profit in making an article, it is a sign that the labor and capital devoted to its production are misdirected: the value of the resources that must be used up in making the article is greater than the value of the article itself.

"One function of profits, in brief, is to guide and channel the factors of production so as to apportion the relative output of thousands of different commodities in accordance with demand. No bureaucrat, no matter how brilliant, can solve this problem arbitrarily."

—Henry Hazlitt, *Economics In One Lesson*
(New York: Crown Trade Paperbacks, 1979), pp. 161–62

The Limits of Profit and Loss Accounting

Profit and loss calculations do not *determine* the actions of people in a market economy, but merely *guide* them. The rules of accounting are a mental *tool* similar to the more fundamental tool of arithmetic. Young students are forced to memorize the times tables, but most people recognize that there is nothing arbitrary about these "rules"—they are simply shortcuts to expressing objective truths about *reality*. Adults are free to ignore multiplication if they want, but they will probably not get very far in life. If too many people decided they no longer "believed in" arithmetic, civilization would come crashing down.

In an analogous fashion, entrepreneurs (or their accountants or the programmers who design their business software) must learn the proper way to construct a balance sheet and an income statement to understand if their enterprises are profitable. These techniques are not arbitrary, and they express truths about the physical world as well as other people's (subjective) preferences. Any particular entrepreneur can choose to ignore the bottom line if he wishes, but he won't be in business for long. And if too many entrepreneurs went this route, there would soon be mass starvation.

Notwithstanding the tremendous importance of mental tools such as arithmetic and financial accounting, there are limits to their usefulness. After all, young students learn much more than math—depending on their background, they might also memorize the Ten Commandments, read Aristotle, and study the French Revolution, in order to become responsible members of society. Arithmetic (or mathematics more generally) helps guide people's decisions, but obviously such knowledge only goes so far in what it can say.

A similar limitation applies to financial accounting and the profit and loss test. Entrepreneurs in a market economy aren't slaves to profit maximization; a business owner can close the shop from Christmas Eve through New Year's, and spend the holidays with his family. An entrepreneur is also perfectly free to give discounts to the elderly, or to perform services for free for the indigent, as acts of charity. There is nothing "uneconomical" or "inefficient" about such decisions.

However, the crucial point is that financial accounting allows the entrepreneurs to realize *just how expensive* these decisions are. Someone who owns a movie theater probably *won't* close it down during the holiday season, simply because the potential revenues are so lucrative.[5] Yet this

[5]Of course, the owner might hire workers to run the theater while he stays home with his family. In this case, we have to understand why the workers find it "profitable" to agree to such a shift instead of spending all of Christmas Day with their own families.

seemingly deplorable fact—that the profit motive "forces" some merchants to work even on Christmas!—is really just a reflection of how much consumers enjoy going to movies during the holidays.

In terms of a social institution, private property (and its offshoots of market prices and profit and loss accounting) is extremely beneficial to mankind because it provides coherence to economic activities. To recognize this fact is *not* to say that, "Profit makes right." For example, many consumers may be willing to spend large sums of money on things that are immoral, and the resulting profitability of producing these items or services doesn't wash away their flaws. Economics does *not* say, "A movie studio must produce violent films if they make the most money." In practice, it probably *will* be the case that entrepreneurs will enter an industry and produce those things which command the highest profits, but strictly speaking economic science does not instruct entrepreneurs to devote their lives to the accumulation of as much money as possible.

Even in cases where many people consider certain profitable activities to be immoral, it is not the profit motive per se that is at fault, but rather consumer demands for iniquitous ends. For example, it is true that large amounts of arable land are devoted to tobacco rather than tomatoes. But ultimately it is not the capitalist system that "forces" farmers to plant so much tobacco, it is instead the willingness of so many consumers to spend their money on cigarettes rather than salads. Critics of this unhealthful outcome really have a problem not with private property per se, but with the voluntary choices of smokers.

There is more to the good life than earning profits, and not everything can be reduced to dollars and cents. However, the money prices formed in a market economy allow individuals to put their affairs into perspective, in order to realize just *how much* they are ignoring the desires of others when they use their property in particular ways.

Lesson Recap . . .

- *Interest* refers to the normal return from lending or investing savings in a project, which could just as well have been earned in other projects. *Economic profit* refers to the extra return an entrepreneur earns from a particular project, over and above the normal interest return on the invested capital that could have been earned on similar projects.

- Profits and losses help guide entrepreneurs to use scarce resources in ways that best satisfy the preferences of their customers. If an activity is profitable, it is a signal that the entrepreneur is transforming resources into goods and services of higher value. If an entrepreneur is losing money, it is a signal that consumers would prefer that resources stop flowing into the losing operation, and go elsewhere to create more valuable goods and services.

- Profit and loss accounting can only reflect the monetary aspects of an operation. An entrepreneur may continue operating a business that "loses money" because he gets personal enjoyment from it, and there is nothing "uneconomical" about this decision. Even so, accurate profit and loss accounting allows entrepreneurs to make informed decisions about the use of scarce resources; it lets them take into account other people's preferences about how those resources shall be used.

NEW TERMS

Gross profit / accounting profit: The excess of revenues over out-of-pocket expenses. This is what newspapers mean when they report on a corporation's "profits" for a given time period.

Net profit / economic profit: The portion of gross profits over and above the normal interest return on the invested capital.

Economic problem: How to allocate society's scarce resources (including labor) in order to produce the combination of goods and services that best satisfies people's preferences.

STUDY QUESTIONS

1. Explain: "Entrepreneurs do not respond to particular prices but rather to the *difference* between certain prices."

2. Explain: "In a market economy with open competition, there is a tendency for monetary profits and losses to be whittled away over time, as entrepreneurs adjust to the situation."

3. *How does interest relate to profit, specifically the difference between accounting and economic profit?

4. In what sense do consumers—rather than the "captains of industry"—guide the production decisions in a market economy?

5. Does a market economy force entrepreneurs to do whatever makes the most profit?

ADVANCED LESSON 14

The Stock Market

In this lesson you will learn:

- The definition of the *stock market.*
- The difference between corporate debt and *equity*.
- The social function of stock *speculation.*

The Stock Market

In everyday conversation, people often refer to "the market" and ask whether it is "up or down." What they mean is not the overall market economy, but rather the stock market. The **stock market** is a particular market in which buyers and sellers trade **shares of corporate stock**, which are legally transferable *fractions of ownership* of corporations. For example, if someone owns 50 shares of stock in the Acme Corporation, and there is a total of 1,000 shares outstanding, then this person owns 5% of the Acme Corporation itself. He and the other shareholders have proportional claims on the assets and income earned by the Acme Corporation.

Purchases and sales of stock shares occur on **stock exchanges,** such as the New York Stock Exchange (located at 11 Wall Street, New York, N.Y.) or the London Stock Exchange. You have probably seen frantic traders yelling out bids as stock prices scroll across a large display screen. With the development of the internet, it has become much easier for average people to buy and sell stocks (through **stock brokerages**) without physically visiting a stock exchange.

When people refer to a particular stock's price, they usually mean the price at which the last trade was conducted. In many settings unrelated to the stock market, a seller will fix a price and wait a long time to see how many he sells, before adjusting the price. For example, a couple trying to sell a home will list their price and probably wait at least one month before considering a reduction. A grocery store might update the price it charges for milk or eggs much more frequently, but even here a shopper doesn't usually see prices for these items change from hour to hour. Things are different on the stock market, where billions of individual stock shares may change hands every day, and where prices may be extremely volatile, changing from moment to moment as new information hits "the market."

Why Issue Stock? (Debt versus Equity)

In Lesson 12 we learned that entrepreneurs sometimes borrow money from others in order to accelerate the growth of their businesses. If a business is a **sole proprietorship**, the individual owner who wants outside funds might ask friends and family for loans, relying on informal contracts and their trust in his character.

However, an alternate method is to **raise capital** by selling *ownership claims* to the business. In this case the existing owner or owners can **go public** by **incorporating** the business and selling shares to others in an **initial public offering** (IPO). Or, an existing corporation can raise more capital by selling additional shares of stock (thus diluting the ownership claims of the original shareholders).

There are various regulatory, legal, and tax reasons that favor incorporation over other business forms for certain companies. In this lesson, our goal is merely to understand the basic distinction between a corporation raising new funds by **issuing debt versus stock**. The latter move is also called issuing **equity**, because it confers ownership in the corporation.

For concreteness, let's imagine the Acme Corporation is doing quite well and wants to raise $100 million to expand its operations. One way to do that is to sell new bonds to lenders, which (say) promise to pay them 5% interest annually, and a return of the principal in ten years. Under this route, Acme gets its desired $100 million right away, and then must make ten annual payments of $5 million before paying out the $100 million and retiring the bonds. (If Acme doesn't want to come up with $100 million at that future point, it may of course try to **roll over the debt** by issuing new bonds—this is like **refinancing** for a homeowner.)

There are pros and cons for Acme raising the funds by issuing new debt. If things go as planned, the $100 million injection of new funds (to be spent on a new plant, advertising, recruitment of skilled managers, etc.) will allow Acme to boost its revenues by more than $5 million each year, meaning the debt issuance will "pay for itself." That is to say, the increase in Acme's revenues will allow it to more than cover the interest payments, so that in the long run the owners of Acme (i.e., the shareholders) will be richer, because of their decision to issue debt. Whether the decision turns out to be just a good one or a fantastic one, Acme still has to pay the same fixed 5% interest payments on the borrowed money.

The downside of taking on additional debt is that Acme has to pay its creditors (i.e., the bondholders) whether or not the expansion is profitable. If the $100 million in new funds doesn't allow Acme to generate at least an additional $5 million per year (on average), then Acme's owners will be poorer because of their bad decision. Had they properly forecast the fate of their company, they would not have agreed to borrow money at a 5% interest rate, yet once the bonds are sold they can't avoid their contractual obligations. They are locked into making the annual $5 million interest payments, regardless of Acme's health.[1]

Rather than issue new debt, the Acme Corporation instead can sell new shares of stock. For example, suppose that originally Acme has 2 million outstanding shares, owned by various people in the community. If Acme then issues 2 million new shares at $50 each, it will raise the desired $100 million in new funds for its expansion. But now that the total number of Acme shares has risen to 4 million, the proportional ownership of the

[1]We are ignoring such complications as the possibility that Acme's bonds are **callable**, meaning that Acme has the contractual ability to pay off the $100 million earlier than the original ten-year schedule specifies, and hence avoid being locked into the 5% rate for the entire time.

original shareholders has been diluted. For example, if Bill Johnson owns a block of 200,000 shares, he originally owned 10% of Acme. But after the new issuance of stock, Bill's original 200,000 shares only represent (200,000 / 4 million) = 5% of Acme.[2]

By expanding the pool of ownership in Acme itself, the issuance of new shares does *not* commit the corporation to a fixed stream of payments (the way the bonds would have). As part owners, the new shareholders share in the "upside" if the expansion goes well and the corporation enjoys substantial earnings, but on the other hand they suffer proportional losses if Acme does poorly in the upcoming years. Because shareholders are **residual claimants**, their stocks entitle them to a fractional share of ownership in Acme's assets only *after* the other creditors have been satisfied. For example, out of their revenues in a given year, Acme officials will first have to pay contractual interest payments to their bondholders, before sending a **dividend** to the shareholders.

Economists and other financial analysts have different theories and rules of thumb to explain the ideal balance between debt and equity for a given corporation. For our purposes here, it is enough that you understand a new issuance of debt (versus equity) increases the possible returns to the existing shareholders, but it carries greater risk. In contrast, if the existing shareholders issue more stock and spread their ownership over a bigger pool of people, then their scope for high returns is diminished but at the same time they can share the pain of losses with more people as well.

---

[2]Note that the market value of Bill's stock may very well increase because of the deal, even though his proportional share in Acme itself has fallen. It's true that (loosely speaking) Acme's assets now must be divided into 4 million pieces instead of 2 million, and in that respect the market price of each share would be expected to fall. On the other hand, the new stock issuance brought in an additional $100 million which Acme officials intend to use to make the corporation more productive. This would tend to drive *up* the stock price, and hence the market value of Bill's 200,000 shares. Only time will tell if Acme's decision is wise, but the point for our purposes is that existing shareholders do not necessarily find their financial interests hurt whenever a corporation issues new stock. Unfortunately financial press accounts often give this impression when a corporation in the real world issues new stock.

A firm's **leverage** refers to the relative size of its debt compared to the equity held by the owners. The higher a firm's leverage, the greater the potential returns for its owners, but the greater potential it has to go **bankrupt**. In the financial world, firms differ in the amount of leverage they take on. Certain investors buy stock in (or lend money to) conservative companies with little leverage, whereas other, more aggressive investors are interested in companies carrying high debt loads but with a sound business plan.

The Social Function of Stock Speculation

From the individual investor's viewpoint, corporate stocks are a particular avenue for his saved funds. Rather than keep money under his mattress or lend it to a bank, the investor can choose to purchase shares of stock in one or more corporations. His hope is that the market value of his investment will grow over time, either because of periodic dividend payments—in which the corporation distributes some of its excess earnings to shareholders—and/or because the market price of his stock rises. Many people invest at least a portion of their savings in corporate stock, because it typically offers a higher rate of return than bonds.[3]

Although there is in fact no clear dividing line, people often distinguish between stock investors versus stock speculators. A **speculator** buys a particular stock *not* because of the long-run potential growth of the corporation, but rather because he expects the share price to rise in the near future. The speculator does not seek out sound companies to invest in, but rather looks for *underpriced stocks* to turn a quick profit.[4] In the eyes of many, stock

[3]Of course, corporate stock is *riskier* than bonds. The market price of a stock can be very volatile, whereas the return on a bond is contractually fixed, meaning the investor (lender) only must face the risk of the bond issuer defaulting. (Bond investors also face **interest rate risk**, which is the risk that interest rates will change and affect the current market price of the bonds they hold. But so long as the investor holds a given bond to maturity, his flow of cash payments is fixed, absent a default by the issuer.)

[4]Even here, the distinction is blurry. Someone might think a particular stock is underpriced *because* the company has such strong "fundamentals" and is likely to

investing is a perfectly respectable and indeed crucial feature of a market economy, whereas stock *speculation* is deemed unethical and harmful.

This popular condemnation of stock speculation fails to appreciate the genuine contribution of this activity. In Advanced Lesson 13, we learned that the successful entrepreneur buys resources at a low price and transforms them into finished goods and services that fetch a higher price. The greater the profits an entrepreneur reaps, the bigger this gap or mismatch between resource and consumer goods prices must have been. The entrepreneur thus serves a vital social role in channeling scarce resources into those activities where (loosely speaking) the most market value can be added.

The stock speculator is just a particular type of entrepreneur. After all, the motto of the speculator is to "buy low, sell high." The astute speculator identifies stocks that are *mispriced* before others notice the problem, and benefits accordingly, if and when other investors begin to see things as the speculator. For example, suppose Acme's stock is selling for $40 per share but Sam the speculator believes this is far too low, and that the price will rise to $45 by the end of the week when a new report comes out. (The report will have favorable news that will cause many investors to revise their expectations about the future earnings of Acme. These changed expectations will lead investors to bid more *right now* for Acme stock, because these shares represent partial ownership claims on Acme's future earnings.) In anticipation of this appreciation, Sam buys 10,000 shares of Acme. If his hunch is correct and the report causes the stock price to rise to $45, Sam can then sell his shares and pocket the $50,000 gain from his speculation. Of course, if Sam had been *wrong* and Acme shares fell to $35, he would be *down* $50,000 if he sold his holdings at the end of the week.

Many observers liken stock speculation to pure gambling, but there is an essential difference: When someone bets $1,000 on red at the roulette wheel, this action doesn't influence the movement of the wheel—at least not in an honest casino! However, when Sam the speculator buys 10,000 shares of Acme because he believes its price of $40 is too low, his very action tends to

---

enjoy strong earnings in the future. Such a person could be classified as a speculator if he bought the stock, not because he wanted to partake in a long stream of dividend payments, but because he expected other investors to soon see things from his perspective, and bid up the price of the stock.

push up the price of Acme stock. After all, the demand for Acme shares has suddenly increased while the supply of shares is the same, and so (other things equal) the price of Acme stock will rise. So we see that when speculators believe that a stock will rise in the future, their attempt to profit from their prediction causes the underpriced stock to rise in value.

On the other hand, if speculators believe a certain stock is *overpriced*, then their actions will tend to push down the price. For example, suppose an Acme shareholder believes his stock is overpriced at $40. He can sell off 10,000 shares, and then buy them back if and when the price falls to $38. He ends up with the same number of Acme shares in his possession, but he also has an additional $20,000 because of his speculative move.[5] In this case too, the speculator's efforts to gain personal profit end up moving the stock price in the correct direction, because (other things equal) his selling at $40 would tend to push down the price of Acme shares.

To summarize, successful stock speculators identify and correct mispriced stocks. Although their motivation is presumably personal financial gain, nonetheless their activities are socially useful for several reasons. First and most obvious, speculators—if they are successful—actually *reduce* the volatility of stock prices. After all, their actions pull up prices when they are too low, and they push down prices when they are too high. Speculators keep stock prices from straying too far from where they "ought" to be, and in that sense reduce the day-to-day movements in stock prices. The presence of speculators makes the stock market as a whole more orderly and safer for average investors, who don't need to worry as much about a particular stock dropping 30% after a "surprise" announcement—the speculators will usually have sniffed out the story weeks in advance and already moved prices accordingly.

More fundamentally, it's important for stocks to be accurately priced because they represent something real—they are partial ownership claims on corporations, which in turn possess scarce physical assets and produce goods and services for their customers. Recall that the relatively high

[5]Even speculators who originally own no shares of Acme can profit from a perceived overvaluation. They can engage in a **short sale** in which they borrow shares of stock from existing owners, sell them to collect the current market price of $40, and then buy the shares back at a lower price and return them to the original owners.

market price of gold acts as a signal telling entrepreneurs, "Only use me in very important projects where the customer is willing to pay much more for the use of gold." In a similar fashion, a very valuable corporation needs to have a very high market price (i.e., share price times the number of total shares) to ensure that it ends up in the hands of serious owners who will make good decisions affecting the fate of the corporation.

To take a silly example: If for some reason Microsoft shares suddenly plummeted so that with a measly $1 an investor could purchase an entire block of 1 million shares, then that would mean someone could purchase *Microsoft itself* if he were willing to plunk down about $9,000. Thus the fate of hundreds of millions of PC users would be at the mercy of anyone with $9,000 and an idea of "a better way to run Microsoft." In reality, of course, the market value of Microsoft is (as of this writing) hundreds of billions of dollars. Its major shareholders may make critical mistakes when they assemble a Board of Directors and decide other issues, but the high share price ensures that the people making such decisions will take their responsibilities very seriously.[6]

Finally, recall what we learned in the previous section: One of the ways a corporation can raise new funds is to issue more stock. By improving the accuracy of stock prices, speculators help allocate the flow of new savings into corporations, so that those corporations with the best prospects will have higher stock prices and thus tend to receive more funds for expansion.

---

[6]Even very rich investors will likely hold a relatively small portion of Microsoft, if they are not knowledgeable in the computer industry. Rather than holding a large share of the company (and having to vote on important decisions affecting software development and so forth) such investors would probably diversify their savings among the stock of many other corporations, deferring to true experts in any particular one.

Lesson Recap . . .

- The stock market (located at physical exchanges but also on computer networks) brings together buyers and sellers of ownership shares of corporations. The stock market determines what group of people are the actual owners of corporations, and who therefore are ultimately responsible for how these organizations conduct business.

- When a corporation issues debt, it sells bonds in order to borrow funds from lenders. It owes a contractual amount of interest payments and the return of principal, regardless of the success of the corporation. On the other hand, when a corporation issues equity, it sells shares in order to raise funds from investors. These investors are entitled to their share of the corporation's earnings, which are tied to the success (or failure) of the corporation.

- Stock speculators try to "buy low, sell high" (or "sell high, buy low"). Successful speculators fix "mispriced" stocks, because their actions push up stocks that are underpriced and push down stocks that are overpriced.

NEW TERMS

Stock market: A special type of market in which buyers and sellers exchange shares of corporate stock.

Corporate stock: Partial ownership claims to a corporation. If there are 100,000 total shares of stock in a corporation, someone who buys 5,000 shares owns 5% of the corporation itself.

Stock exchanges: Particular locations or venues where stocks are traded. The most famous example is the New York Stock Exchange, located on Wall Street.

Stock brokerages: Companies that help individuals buy and sell stocks. The broker will act on behalf of the client and execute his or her orders to buy and sell shares.

Sole proprietorship: A business owned by a single person.

Raise capital: The process of obtaining funds for a growing business by selling partial ownership of the business to outside investors.

Going public: Allowing the general public to buy shares of stock in a corporation, as opposed to restricting ownership to those specifically invited by the owners.

Incorporation: Transforming a business into a corporation, so that its ownership is allotted by shares of stock.

Initial public offering (IPO): The auction of shares to the general public when a corporation first decides to go public.

Issuing debt: Raising funds by selling bonds to lenders.

Issuing stock / issuing equity: Raising funds by selling stock shares to investors.

Rolling over debt: Paying off an old set of bondholders by issuing new bonds.

Refinancing (a mortgage): The situation that occurs when a homeowner gets a new mortgage from the bank (perhaps at a lower interest rate or with lower monthly payments) and uses it to pay off the current mortgage.

Callable bonds: Bonds that the issuer (borrower) has the right to pay off ahead of schedule.

Residual claimants: Refers to stockholders, who are entitled to the earnings of a corporation only after the other creditors have first been paid.

Dividend: A disbursement of a portion of a corporation's net earnings to the stockholders.

Leverage: Enhancing the potential returns from an investment by using borrowed money.

Bankrupt: The situation that occurs when a business has liabilities greater than its assets.

Speculator: A person who buys an asset (such as a corporate stock) thinking its price will rise, or who sells an asset thinking its price will fall.

Interest rate risk: The risk bondholders face because rising interest rates will reduce the market value of their bonds.

Short sale: A transaction in which a person borrows an asset (such as a share of stock) from an existing owner, in order to sell it at the current price. The person eventually must buy back the asset to return it to the original owner.

STUDY QUESTIONS

1. If Jim owns 200 shares of a corporation, can we figure out how much of the corporation Jim owns?

2. What are the two basic options a corporation can take to raise new funds?

3. Who gets first dibs on the earnings of a corporation—the bondholders or the stockholders?

4. If a corporation is highly leveraged, will its stock be more likely to appeal to a conservative or an aggressive investor?

5. *How do successful speculators *reduce* the volatility of stock prices?

Part III

SOCIALISM: THE COMMAND ECONOMY

LESSON 15

The Failures of Socialism—Theory

In this lesson you will learn:

- The definitions of *socialism* and a *command economy*.
- The *incentive problem* of socialism.
- The *calculation problem* of socialism.

The Vision of Pure Socialism

In Part II of this book, we explained the basic structure and functioning of a pure market economy. In this lesson, we will explain the idea of a pure **command economy**, or what is also called a **command-and-control economy**. Remember that in a pure market economy, the ownership of resources is dispersed among private citizens, and economic outcomes are determined through the combination of actions taken by all of the resource owners. In contrast, in a pure command economy the government owns all the resources and makes all the decisions of what to produce with them. Depending on the writer, socialist theorists have proposed different methods by which government officials would reach such decisions, perhaps taking into account the desires of workers and the preferences of consumers. Yet ultimately, in a pure command economy it is the government that must assign jobs to workers, and give orders to factories and farmers.

Although granting such awesome powers to government officials[1] may sound frightening to many readers, the historical appeal of a command economy is the possibility of avoiding the seemingly unjust outcomes that occur in a system based on private property. Indeed the very terminology is emotionally laden: A market economy is called *capitalism*, whereas a command economy is called **socialism**. Such labels imply that a market economy exists to serve the interests of the small class of capitalists (i.e., large property holders), whereas a command economy supposedly organizes the structure of production in order to serve the interests of all of society. Just as political revolutions swept away the monarchical and aristocratic power structures that had favored an elite minority, so too did socialist reforms champion **economic democracy** in which important economic decisions would be decided by the people (as represented by government officials) rather than by a rich minority who owned most of the (private) property.

Despite the good intentions of many socialist reformers, there are serious flaws with their proposals. In the present lesson, we will explain the major *theoretical* problems with a society that abandons the institution of private property and tries to replace it with socialism. In other words, using our knowledge of economics we will try to simply *think through* the idea of socialism and highlight some major problems that will occur any time it is implemented.

In the next lesson, we will briefly examine the historical record to see what happened *in practice* when some countries actually tried to implement socialist reforms. As we will see, the results ranged from bad to horrible, and will help to confirm the theoretical arguments we make below.

---

[1]There are some socialist thinkers who are also **anarchists**, meaning they propose the abolition of the State along with the abolition of private property. Obviously this type of socialist does not advocate that the government seize control of all resources. To keep things simple we will continue to assume in the text that we are dealing with government control, but much of the economic analysis would apply to the "anarcho-socialist" proposals as well. You should be aware, however, that many self-described socialists would deny that their system entails State power over workers.

Socialism's Incentive Problem

The most obvious problem with socialism is that it alters the incentives that both producers and consumers face, which could cripple the performance of any socialized economy. If a government really tried to implement the Marxist slogan, "From each according to his abilities, to each according to his needs," it's likely that most people would eventually not work nearly as hard as they did under a capitalist framework.

One of the key principles of a pure socialist system is the separation of production from consumption, meaning that workers use resources to first produce a pile of output, and then the government distributes the goods (such as residential housing) to various recipients according to criteria that are considered just or fair (such as how large a particular family is). Yet many observers would say that human nature itself implies that people won't work nearly as hard in order to help society at large, as they will when they get to keep the fruits of their efforts. If these critics are right, then a socialist system might distribute its goods more "fairly" than a capitalist system according to a reformer's criteria, but there will be far fewer goods to be distributed.

Who Picks Up the Garbage?

The problem of coaxing workers to put in long hours is related to the problem of distasteful jobs. Simply put, under a socialist system, who will pick up the trash and who will clean the public restrooms? In a market economy, wages can adjust to attract more workers to a particular occupation. It's true, most 8-year-olds don't announce, "I want to be a janitor when I grow up," but the reason some people become janitors is that the job pays more than many other jobs requiring similar education and experience.

Under pure socialism—at least as phrased in Marx's famous slogan—what people get to *consume* should have no relation to what they *produce* as workers. This takes away the most obvious method by which the socialist government can get "volunteers" for the distasteful jobs that must be performed. Naturally, socialist theorists have proposed other types of compensatory schemes, such as rewarding the comrades who work in the coal mines with more vacation days per year or with longer lunch breaks.

This might help somewhat, but it still could lead to absurdities in the use of scarce labor power. For example, a market economy might induce 100 men in a certain city to voluntarily agree to set their alarms every morning to collect trash for 8 straight hours, because they are paid enough money to afford a nice lifestyle. In essence, other members of the market economy strike a bargain, saying, "If you will deal with my trash every week, I'll produce medical services / cook you a steak dinner / teach your kids algebra / etc."

To repeat, this type of voluntary bargain is not available if the socialist leaders truly wish to depart from the methods of capitalism and private property. If the amount of personal consumption is to be based on considerations *other* than a worker's contribution to total output—in other words, if workers are to be rewarded in a way different from what would happen under capitalism—then the leaders must tinker with the other characteristics of jobs in order to get enough volunteers for each occupation. For example, rather than having 100 men pick up trash and earn enough money to buy a fancy car, the socialist system might need *200* men devoted to trash collection, who only work 4 hours a day, and drive a boring car just like every other worker. Though the problem of trash collection could be solved in this way—by cutting hours—the socialist leaders now have 100 fewer workers for every *other* occupation compared to the capitalist system. This is just a particular manifestation of the broader problem—that under socialism, it is likely that many or most workers would not put forth the same effort that they would under a capitalist system in which their lifestyles were directly tied to job performance.

Of course, an obvious "solution" to the problems of **shirking** and the performance of undesirable jobs is that the government could simply *force* people to fulfill particular tasks. Just as the socialist leaders have the authority to decide what crops should be planted on each acre of farmland, in principle they could also tell each "unit" of labor what role he or she would play in the grand economy-wide production plan. Historically, some of the more naïve reformers thought that a socialist government could retain the worker's right to choose his or her occupation, but other thinkers were far more candid about the duties of workers in a socialist society.

Yet even if we allow for the use of punishment, a socialist government would still face the problem of a drop in overall output because of the lack of cooperation from many of its workers. In a market economy, the allure of large financial rewards causes the best and brightest to rise up from the crowd, as it were, and demonstrate their talents and ambition. Even if they were willing to use draconian penalties, socialist rulers wouldn't have been able to identify the potential output of a Bill Gates when looking at him and his peers at 20 years old. They could have threatened to whip or imprison the young Gates if he didn't process enough statistical reports per hour, but it wouldn't have occurred to them to demand, "You'd better come up with some computer ideas that will revolutionize the world, or else we'll kill your family." This is because no one had any idea of the genius lying inside the young Bill Gates (and Thomas Edison, Henry Ford, etc.) until he stepped forward and demonstrated it in the market economy.

Allocating "Capital" to New "Firms"

Everyone can immediately recognize the potential incentive problem under socialism when it comes to workers and shirking. An equally important, though far less obvious, incentive problem involves the allocation of "capital" to new "firms" in a socialist system. We are putting the terms in quotation marks, because strictly speaking there *is no* financial capital in a purely socialist system, and there aren't independent firms, either. Under socialism, there's just a massive collection of natural resources, capital goods, and workers with various skills, which the government planners must take as a starting point when they draw up a complex blueprint for the entire economy.

Even so, the socialist planners would face challenges *similar to those solved by the financial markets* under capitalism. For example, in a market economy the scientists employed by an oil company might convince their managers that it would be well worth it to spend $2 billion developing an offshore platform in a certain location in the Gulf of Mexico (and with extra safety measures in light of the BP spill). The managers would in turn make the case to *their* superiors and so forth, until finally the shareholders either explicitly or implicitly gave their approval. If the company didn't have enough spare cash, it would have to issue either more bonds or stock in order to finance the project. Yet whether the project were funded internally or with outside assistance, ultimately private capitalists would need to put their own saved funds at risk in the hope that the project would bring enough new oil to market to justify the huge expenses.

Notice that the potential risks and rewards of the offshore project still exist under socialism; they are not mere artifacts of a market economy. The socialist planners would not be omniscient; they too would have to rely on the guidance of scientists and other experts to estimate how many barrels of oil a proposed new platform would make available for future economic planning. Yet we now see the crux of the problem: How do the socialist planners responsibly pick the "winning" projects out of the thousands of *competing* proposals? After all, there are all sorts of ways one *might* deliver more barrels of oil—or energy in other forms—into the hands of future planners, but the current planners obviously cannot "fund" all of them, because there aren't enough resources to go around. When it comes to this problem of choosing which risky ventures to approve and which to veto, the different incentives between capitalism and socialism manifest themselves once more.

To see why, suppose the government planners decided to naïvely fund those projects that promised the greatest return—whether measured in barrels of oil, minivans, gallons of milk, etc.—for a standardized contribution of current resources. This would simply give project managers the incentive to exaggerate the merits of their pet proposals. Note that they wouldn't even necessarily be *lying*—though some obviously would—but rather they would understandably cite the most favorable studies and would not ask their staffs to spend much time dwelling on possible pitfalls in their proposal. The result would lead to a squandering of society's scarce resources, as they were mobilized according to a central plan relying on the forecasts of the most unscrupulous and/or reckless promoters.

On the other hand, the government planners would also face the danger of establishing an incentive scheme that stifled creativity and risk taking. For example, the planners might follow a procedure whereby they took the advice of formally trained scientists and other objective experts on various things, but that if anyone ever turned out to be horribly wrong in one of his or her predictions, then the planners would never again allow this particular expert to influence the grand economic plan. Such a rule would certainly get rid of the snake oil salesmen, but it would also render the legitimate advisors far too conservative. People with bold ideas would be afraid to challenge the consensus of their peers, especially if their scheme would likely fail but had a small chance of being extremely successful.

Of course, the socialist planners could try to avoid both extremes by establishing incentives that both encouraged sensible risk-taking but weeded out the demonstrably incompetent. For example, the planners could take the total amount of resources they intended to devote to "new project development" and assign responsibility for a certain fraction of the resources to an individual expert, based on that expert's overall track record. Any particular mistake would not disqualify an expert, so long as his or her successes had more than compensated for the failures. To motivate the experts to take risks when they believed there was a chance for great payoff, the planners could also stipulate that the standard of living of the experts would itself be proportional to their overall track record in handling society's scarce resources.

We hope that you have noticed what's happening. In the effort to correct the flaws with various ways of implementing socialism, our hypothetical central planners are led step by step to reinvent...*capitalism*.[2]

One Giant Monopoly

Thus far we have focused on the incentive problem the socialist government would face in motivating its citizens to participate in the desired fashion in the economic plan. But there are enormous incentive problems going the other way, too. Specifically, the government officials would have little incentive to take the preferences of the citizens (both as workers and consumers) into account when drawing up the grand economic plan. It is extremely ironic that many socialist reformers warn of the dangers of capitalist "monopolies" in particular industries, when their recommendation would establish one giant monopolist—the government—in control of *all* industries.

---

[2]The great Austrian economist Ludwig von Mises made this argument in his classic work *Socialism*, originally written in German in 1922 (Indianapolis: Liberty Fund, 1981, pp. 192–94).

Even in nominally capitalist countries, we can nowadays see this principle in operation. For example, it is a common joke that the Department of Motor Vehicles (DMV) is not staffed by the friendliest of employees. In many cities the subway facilities are in various stages of disrepair. The condition of government-run hospitals for military veterans—let alone for committed psychiatric patients—can be downright scandalous. As a final example, notice that during the hot summer months, beer companies and air conditioner technicians welcome the huge volume of business with open arms, whereas government-regulated utilities scold their customers for using too much electricity or water.

There is a simple explanation for this undeniable pattern: When government agencies (or favored organizations in the private sector) provide goods and services to the public, they can't be fired. People have to go to the DMV to get their licenses renewed and so forth; they can't take their license business elsewhere to a company with friendlier staff. The manager of a grocery store has an incentive to keep surly employees away from customers, but the manager of a branch of the DMV doesn't face nearly the same motivation. If *his* superiors were really interested in customer satisfaction, they could establish a compensation scheme whereby each DMV branch manager in a particular city were paid a bonus proportional to how many residents decided to take their "business" to that manager's particular branch. But this simply pushes the problem back one stage: Why would the branch manager's superiors care about keeping motorists happy, with all of the other things they have to worry about? It's not as if the city government will take in more revenues from people who decide to become drivers due to the friendly DMV employees.[3]

To be sure, the people in a socialist society could vote in new government officials if they lived in a democracy, and they could ultimately undertake a violent revolution no matter *what* the form of government. All government officials—whether in a limited state presiding over a largely market economy, or even in a totalitarian socialist state run by a dictator—want to keep the public happy, generally speaking. Even so, the difference in incentives facing the people "in charge" between a pure market economy and a

[3]Even if this were to happen, the people in charge of compensating DMV branch managers wouldn't *themselves* be able to pocket the extra revenues from issuing more licenses.

pure command economy is colossal. The very worst a capitalist "tyrant" can do is fire you (if you're an employee) or refuse to sell to you (if you're a customer). In contrast, if the government makes *all* hiring decisions in the entire economy, and controls *all* the grocery stores, it can intimidate critics quite effectively by shipping them off to work in Siberia or starving them. And don't expect the newspapers or other media to document the abuses—the government owns them, too.

Socialism's Calculation Problem

In the historical debates over socialism, its opponents would raise the incentive problems described above (or in other forms) and the proponents would usually respond by arguing that people growing up in a socialist paradise would learn to work for the benefit of their neighbors. They claimed that a new "Socialist Man" would emerge, who was not selfish as people under capitalism were. The central idea was that in their natural state humans were benevolent and altruistic, but that the institution of private property *conditioned them* to become greedy and callous. Perhaps if the workers didn't need to worry about providing for their families—so the socialists argued—they would have no qualms about going to the factories every day in service to the common good.

In this context, the opponents of socialism developed a much more fundamental critique.[4] Even if there were no problems of incentives—so that the workers happily performed whatever tasks they were assigned, and the socialist planners truly had nothing but the best of intentions for their citizens—socialism *still* would do a very poor job of using society's resources efficiently.

Because the socialist government would *own all of the resources*, there wouldn't be any markets for them. In other words, people wouldn't be trading money for tractors, plots of farmland, barrels of oil, and so forth. This means that under pure socialism, there would be no prices for natural resources, labor, and capital goods. Without prices for their inputs, the socialist planners would have no way of estimating the total monetary cost

[4]Ludwig von Mises systematically laid out the calculation objection, which we are about to summarize in the text, in a 1920 article.

of their projects. Therefore they would have no idea whether a particular project were making good use of the resources it consumed, or if it would help the citizens more by shutting down that project and using the freed-up resources to produce more of something else.

Remember that in a market economy, accountants can use market prices to determine if a particular operation is profitable, or if it is suffering a loss. This measure provides a signal showing whether other property owners (implicitly) agree with an entrepreneur's decision to commit scarce resources to the operation. A profit indicates that customers were willing to pay more for the finished product than the entrepreneur needed to spend in order to acquire the inputs. In contrast, a loss indicates that customers were spending more on *other* types of goods, allowing *those* entrepreneurs to bid up the prices of the required inputs and "fining" the original entrepreneur if he continues with his business plan. To sum up, entrepreneurs in a market economy receive constant guidance and feedback from the profit and loss test, which is only possible when all of the various inputs have market prices.

The planners in a socialist system would have no such guidance. Engineers, chemists, and other experts could explain to them the *technological* possibilities for using their stockpile of inputs in order to produce various combinations of finished goods and services. Yet although the planners would know if a project were technologically *feasible*, they wouldn't know if it were *economical*. Without being able to plug in market prices for each unit of input as well as each unit of finished output, the planners couldn't reduce the total inputs and total outputs to a common denominator and see if the operation as a whole created or destroyed wealth. Therefore, even if we set aside the tremendous incentive problems, the socialist planners would also face an insurmountable **calculation problem**.

To grasp the nature of the calculation problem, you should spend a few moments reflecting on the fantastic complexity of a modern economy. On Day One of drawing up their grand economic plan, the socialist leaders would have at their disposal millions of workers with varying skills and endurance; deposits of oil, coal, diamonds, and other minerals; various factories, warehouses, research laboratories, and educational centers; billions of individual tractors, hand tools, and other pieces of equipment, in varying stages of obsolescence; and finally various infrastructures including power lines, telephone and data lines, highways, and bridges. Also remember that to make a coherent economic plan, the socialist leaders would need more than a simple *tabulation* of the various inputs at their disposal. They would also need to know the *location* of the units. For example, if the plan called for a certain mechanic on Tuesday morning to replace the worn-out tires on a tractor trailer, it would need to be the case that the mechanic, new tires, and tractor trailer were all located in the same city by Tuesday morning!

Yet even if the planners could somehow process all of this information—and do it quickly enough to update the economic plan in real-time in response to changing conditions—they still wouldn't be able to overcome the calculation problem. In consultation with experts, they could determine various combinations of different output goods that they could produce with all of the inputs at their disposal. Yet even if they wanted nothing but to make their citizens as happy as possible, *exactly how would they decide what to do*?

Socialist critics of the market economy point to certain "abuses" and think that a group of experts could improve on the decentralized outcomes of a capitalist system. It strikes these critics as outrageous, for example, that some people own 10 sports cars and a yacht, while other people go hungry. But this ethical intuition is *not enough* to design an alternate economic plan. We can concede that the socialist planners would not use society's resources in order to produce huge inequities in the standard of living among the people. Fair enough. That still leaves the question, *what combination of goods and services should each person get*? Even if the planners decide that citizens will have the same number of cars—perhaps adjusted for the number of family members of a certain age range, and the locations of jobs for people in the household—they would still need to decide how many *total* cars to produce, and how fancy to make them. After all, the citizens would like to drive very comfortable, sleek cars with air bags, air conditioning, and high-quality speakers. But to pour more resources into this area would leave fewer resources for *other* things that the citizens would also enjoy, such as more DVD players or bigger houses or more distribution centers (i.e., what would be called "stores" in a market economy).

The Loaded Term "Planning" . . .

The paradox of "planning" is that it cannot plan, because of the absence of economic calculation. What is called a planned economy is no economy at all. It is just a system of groping about in the dark. There is no question of a rational choice of means for the best possible attainment of the ultimate ends sought. What is called conscious planning is precisely the elimination of conscious purposive action.

– Ludwig von Mises, *Human Action*, p. 696

Solving the Calculation Problem?

Naturally, the socialist planners could devise various means of soliciting feedback from the people in order to serve them better. One obvious innovation would be to let the individuals or families have some means of influencing the grand economic plan. It would be obviously wasteful to literally produce the same exact combination of goods and services for each person, since vegetarians wouldn't be interested in beef tips, whereas nonsmokers wouldn't want a ration of cigarettes. Yet to avoid the inequalities of a capitalist system, the planners would still want some way of ensuring that every individual or family had the same "amount" of consumption, however defined.

For example they might assign each person or family a certain quota of voting points each month, which they would use to order different goods and services. Items such as television sets and SUVs would subtract more points from a family's quota than items such as a can of soda or loaf of bread, because it would obviously take "more" resources to produce the former items. (In other words, it wouldn't be fair if one family voted to receive 10 television sets, while another family voted to receive 10 cans of tuna fish. Clearly the former family would be consuming more than the latter.) In order to pick the "correct" number of points for each type of good, the planners would rely on feedback from the managers running the distribution centers. If the shelves were clogged with TVs and the supplies of tuna fish were running low, the planners could reduce the number of points a family needed to deduct to order a TV, while bumping up the number of points it took to order a can of tuna. This would clear out the excess stockpile of TVs and prevent the supplies of tuna from running out.

Unfortunately this type of trick would only deal with excess or deficient supplies *after* they had been produced. Going forward, the planners would still need to tinker with their grand economic plan to decide whether to produce more or fewer TV sets (or cans of tuna) in the *next* period. From the feedback they received from the distribution managers, they would have an idea of how many total TVs would be ordered at various possible point totals assigned to a TV. But that still wouldn't tell them whether the correct decision would be to (a) make more TVs next period and assign them a lower point score or (b) make fewer TVs next period and assign them a higher point score.

To solve *this* question, the planners might try pushing the voting system up a stage. They might give points to the various factory managers, allowing them to order different amounts of workers, gasoline, electricity, and so forth. Just as families were allowed to use their votes to order different combinations of finished goods, the TV producers and tuna producers would use their votes to order different combinations of inputs. That would help ensure that the TV producer didn't "hog" resources unfairly at the expense of the tuna producer.

But this too wouldn't totally solve the calculation problem, as the planners would soon realize. Although it might seem appropriate to force each individual to consume the same "amount" of goods by assigning everyone an equal amount of voting points, it would clearly be nonsensical to insist that each *factory manager* get the same amount of resources for his or her operation. In other words, if the planners each month awarded the same number of voting points to the TV producer as the tuna producer, they would be ensuring that society devoted as many resources to TV production as tuna production. But why in the world would we expect *that* to be the right thing to do, in order to use society's scarce resources to make the citizens as happy as possible?

In order to come up with a coherent and objective way to solve this thorny complication, the planners could award points to each factory manager, proportional to the amount of points that the citizens earmarked for those goods at the distribution centers. In other words, if the citizens used five times as many of their "consumption points" to order television sets as they did to order cans of tuna fish, then in the next period the socialist planners could award five times as many voting points to the TV factory managers as they did to the tuna producers. This rule would allow the citizens to give feedback to the planners not only in terms of stockpiles of already-finished goods, but also in the decision of how many units of each good to produce in future periods.

By now you have probably realized where our discussion is heading. The way the socialist planners can solve the calculation problem is to make their system operate more and more like . . . *capitalism.*

Lesson Recap . . .

- The vision of pure socialism has the government owning all the resources and directing all the workers according to a unified, central plan for the economy. The socialists thought this system would be far more efficient and just than the "anarchic," unorganized market economy.

- Socialism suffers from an incentive problem, because many people are not likely to work as hard when their individual rewards are not tied to personal performance. If the government were to implement the rule "from each according to his ability, to each according to his needs," the total amount of output might shrink drastically.

- Socialism also suffers from a calculation problem. Without market prices for the various resources and labor hours used in a production project, the socialist planners would have no idea if these resources were being used efficiently. It might be possible to shift the resources to other projects in order to produce goods and services that the citizens would prefer, but the planners wouldn't have enough feedback to guide them.

NEW TERMS

Command economy / command-and-control economy / socialism: An institutional arrangement in which the government owns all the major resources, and directs labor, according to a unified central plan.

Economic democracy: An analogy to politics often used by (democratic) socialists to justify socialism. Most people would not like an aristocratic system in which a few elites made all the political decisions, but would instead prefer a democratic "one person, one vote" system. The socialists argue that their program simply applies this logic to the economic arena, taking power away from the small group of wealthy capitalists and showering it on the masses.

Anarchists: People who think there should be no government.

Shirking: Deliberately working less than one's potential.

Calculation problem: The objection Ludwig von Mises raised against socialism, which points out that because socialist planners lack market prices for resources, they can't determine if a particular project uses up more resources than it produces in goods and services. Even if the planners were angels, they would have no idea whether they were using scarce resources in an efficient way to best serve the citizens.

STUDY QUESTIONS

1. Explain the term *command economy*.

2. What is the incentive problem inherent in the slogan, "From each according to his ability, to each according to his needs"?

3. Could a socialist government use punishment to overcome the problem of shirking among workers?

4. What do beer companies and electric utilities have to do with socialism?

5. *Why doesn't a market economy suffer from the same calculation problem that plagues the socialist planners?

LESSON 16

The Failures of Socialism—History

In this lesson you will learn:

- The relevance of historical evidence to economic theory.
- The economic similarity between *communism* and *fascism*.
- The extreme poverty and deaths under many socialist regimes.

Economic Theory and History

Way back in Lesson 2, we explained the difference between economics and the "hard" natural sciences such as physics and chemistry. In economics, basic theory is not developed through a process of hypothesis which is then refuted or confirmed by empirical observation. On the contrary, the basic principles laid out in this book are largely *logical exercises* that simply coach you through particular trains of thought. Basic economic analysis is not a set of relationships discovered in a laboratory or after poring over reams of price data. Rather, the lessons in this book give you a mental framework for *interpreting* price data and other historical evidence.

In this spirit, then, we are not in the present lesson trying to "test" the analysis of socialism that we developed in Lesson 15. Strictly speaking, regardless of the historical record of socialist regimes, the economic arguments we discussed in the previous lesson would still be valid—assuming we didn't make an outright mistake in our reasoning. However, it would always be possible that our results, though valid, were *unimportant*. For example, it could be perfectly true that socialist rulers suffer from the calculation problem in determining the best uses for their country's resources, and it could also be true that workers in a socialist system do not have the same incentives to work as hard as they do under capitalism.

Still, what if these factors only meant that the switch from a pure capitalist system to a pure socialist one, would make the average person 1% poorer? Or worse still, suppose the problems we noted with socialism were correct, but that they were counterbalanced by some *virtues* of socialism that we ignored in our discussion. Then we might wonder whether this *book* made an efficient use of resources by devoting an entire lesson to the topic of socialism, rather than the economics of leaving the toilet seat up.

As we will soon see, the historical record suggests that there is an *enormous* difference between socialist and capitalist countries. To be clear, the evidence is not *conclusive*, in the sense that it can trump economic theory, or even that we can now be sure that the arguments of Lesson 15 must "obviously" be correct. Remember, the basic principles or laws of economics are couched in terms of tendencies; we must hold "other things equal" when discussing how a certain change will impact the economy.

When it comes to the historical record and economic theory, the mere fact that a particular country experienced widespread starvation after implementing socialist policies doesn't prove that socialism is a bad economic system. After all, it's possible that the socialist policies *would have* ushered in unprecedented wealth, except that the workers' revolution occurred coincidentally at exactly the same time as a devastating earthquake or volcanic eruption.

But as you will see, the historical record is far more extensive than simple anecdotes of particular socialist regimes experiencing temporary calamity. The record of the 20th century is quite clear that regimes implementing socialism did not succeed in their promise to provide their people with a higher standard of living in a society free from unfair social privileges. On the contrary, the spread of officially socialist governments went hand in hand with some of the darkest episodes in human history.

Communism versus Fascism

In typical political discussions, the ideology of a regime or its ruler can be placed on a simple spectrum running from left to right. On the extreme left are communists such as Joseph Stalin and Mao Tse-Tung, while on the extreme right are fascists such as Adolf Hitler and Benito Mussolini. According to this standard framework, other ideologies and leaders are much less extreme, and so fall in between these endpoints. For example, Barack Obama would be to the right of Stalin but to the left of Ronald Reagan, who in turn would be a "leftist" compared to Hitler.

Although there are various ways of categorizing political ideologies, this standard left/right spectrum makes little sense *economically*. For although they differ in other important respects, communism and (extreme) fascism are both forms of *socialism*. **Communism** seeks to establish government ownership over the means of production through a revolution of the working class. **Fascism** too seeks to establish absolute government control over the means of production, though the institution of private property is symbolically retained. In practice, however, extreme fascism is socialism, because the government lays down explicit rules governing how owners can use "their" property. Indeed, the term *Nazi* itself stands for *National Socialism*. The term signifies that the difference between the communists and the Nazis wasn't over the sanctity of private property rights, but rather the philosophy that would guide the socialist rulers in their steering of the economy to serve the collective good. The communists tended to be more concerned with international class struggle, whereas the fascists were more concerned with the strength of their individual nations (and the Nazis in particular with the purity of racial bloodlines).

When it comes to evaluating the fruits of various ideologies, therefore, the horrors of both Soviet Russia *and* Nazi Germany can be laid at the feet of socialism. Say what you will about the inequalities and mercilessness of a pure market economy, the Holocaust would not have been possible in a society where private property rights were sacrosanct. Wise political thinkers have always warned that if rulers have the power to do great good, they simultaneously have the power to do great harm. The 20th century experience with both "left" and "right" totalitarianism shows that this was no idle warning.

Socialism's Body Count

In this final section we will very briefly review some of the general statistics concerning the sheer murderousness of various socialist regimes in the 20th century. Now it is true, the governments of capitalist countries participated in their share of mass killing as well, including most famously the United States's atomic bombing of Hiroshima and Nagasaki, but also the Allied conventional bombing of German and Japanese cities which killed hundreds of thousands of civilians. Capitalist countries also participated in great historical injustices such as the African slave trade, extermination of indigenous peoples, and imperialist exploitation of colonies. Naturally the proponent of a pure market economy would point out—quite correctly—that these actions were either (a) necessary measures of self-defense to protect property and lives, and/or (b) deviations from the principle of private property rights and thus not an indictment against capitalism as an institution. But if we are to acquit capitalism of the crimes committed under its banner, then should we not give the same courtesy to socialism? After all, no Marxist academic at Harvard would have wished for the Russian people to suffer the purges of Stalin. He could simply claim that in practice the Soviet rulers didn't implement *true* socialism.

One important difference between the crimes of capitalist regimes versus socialist ones—important at least in terms of evaluating them as economic systems—is that the crimes of capitalist regimes largely concerned *outside* victims, whereas the deaths we document below occurred *among the socialist regime's own populations*. If a particular group of, say, 10 million citizens were deciding whether to embrace the institution of private property on the one hand, or to entrust their fate to a group of experts who would plan the economy on the other, they might be particularly interested to know that if history is any guide, those rulers might very well turn around and slaughter 500,000 of them. It's true, the people might implement safeguards, and cite the experience of democratic socialist regimes in history that did *not* end up killing their own people, but socialism's allowance for this possibility is surely an important thing for the group to ponder before giving their final answer.

Another important difference in the criminal records of various regimes is the sheer quantitative disparity. Many "leftist" thinkers would argue that the Chilean dictator August Pinochet was the capitalist analog to Marxist dictators, as Pinochet overthrew a democratically elected socialist and then implemented "shock therapy" economic reforms with advice from economists trained at the University of Chicago. Yet even if we agree with this comparison, the record is still in favor of capitalism. As brutal and thuggish as Pinochet's regime was, it didn't kill up to *a quarter of the entire population in fewer than four years*, as did the communist Pol Pot's Khmer Rouge regime in Cambodia.

Obviously one single person intentionally killed by a government is one victim too many. The material in this chapter is certainly not offered to excuse or minimize the crimes and atrocities committed by governments claiming to uphold the institutions of private property and free markets. Yet many people have simply never heard the facts, and do not realize that the totalitarian socialist regimes of the 20th century became internal killing machines on a scale that places them in a different category altogether.

The Broad Numbers

You are no doubt familiar with the atrocities committed by the National Socialists in Germany under the leadership of Adolf Hitler. You may not realize that in terms of numbers, communist regimes were actually much worse. *The Black Book of Communism* is a respected collection of essays published by Harvard University Press. Many of the authors were formerly communist historians detailing the new knowledge of the activities of communist regimes after archives were made public with the fall of the U.S.S.R. To give you a quick idea of the contents, we quote three excerpts from the editor's Introduction:

> Having gone beyond individual crimes and small-scale ad-hoc massacres, the Communist regimes, in order to consolidate their grip on power, turned mass crime into a full-blown system of government. After varying periods, ranging from a few years in Eastern Europe to several decades in the U.S.S.R. and China, the terror faded, and the regimes settled into a routine of administering repressive measures on a daily basis, as well as censoring all means of communication, controlling borders, and expelling dissidents.

However, the memory of the terror has continued to preserve the credibility, and thus the effectiveness, of the threat of repression. None of the Communist regimes currently in vogue in the West is an exception to this rule—not the China of the "Great Helmsman," nor the North Korea of Kim Il Sung, nor even the Vietnam of "good old Uncle Ho" or the Cuba of the flamboyant Fidel Castro, flanked by the hard-liner Che Guevara. (pp. 2–3)

[W]e have delimited crimes against civilians as the essence of the phenomenon of terror. These crimes tend to fit a recognizable pattern even if the practices vary to some extent by regime. The pattern includes execution by various means, such as firing squads, hanging, drowning, battering, and, in certain cases, gassing, poisoning, or "car accidents"; destruction of the population by starvation, through man-made famine, the withholding of food, or both; deportation, through which death can occur in transit . . . at one's place of residence, or through forced labor. . . . Periods described as times of "civil war" are more complex—it is not always easy to distinguish between events caused by fighting between rulers and rebels and events that can properly be described only as a massacre of the civilian population.

Nonetheless, we have to start somewhere. The following rough approximation, based on unofficial estimates, gives some sense of the scale and gravity of these crimes:

U.S.S.R.: 20 million deaths

China: 65 million deaths

Vietnam: 1 million deaths

North Korea: 2 million deaths

Cambodia: 2 million deaths

Eastern Europe: 1 million deaths

Latin America: 150,000 deaths

Africa: 1.7 million deaths

Afghanistan: 1.5 million deaths (p. 4)

> [O]ne particular feature of many Communist regimes [was] their systematic use of famine as a weapon. The regime aimed to control the total available food supply and, with immense ingenuity, to distribute food purely on the basis of "merits" and "demerits" earned by individuals. This policy was a recipe for creating famine on a massive scale. Remember that in the period after 1918, only Communist countries experienced such famines, which led to the deaths of hundreds of thousands, and in some cases millions, of people. And again in the 1980s, two African countries that claimed to be Marxist-Leninist, Ethiopa and Mozambique, were the only such countries to suffer these deadly famines. (p. 8)

Close to a Controlled Experiment

As we noted in the disclaimer at the beginning of this lesson, in truth there can be no controlled experiments in the social sciences in general, or in economics in particular. People cannot be completely controlled by the experimenter, so that it is impossible to repeat a particular experiment with the same initial conditions except for one minor tweak.

When it comes to the horrible legacy of communist regimes, some apologists have argued that the crimes were the result of a particularly violent or oppressed people. For example some have argued that after being oppressed by the czars for so long, it is no wonder that the Bolshevik revolutionaries took things too far once they gained power. But if full-blown socialism were implemented in a civilized, democratic society, the socialist could claim, things would be much different.

The closest we can come to testing such a claim is to look at regions that were very similar in all other respects *except* for their institutional framework. One such example would be East versus West Berlin during the Cold War. Since this was a wartime partition of *the same city*, clearly the customs, language, religious views, and so forth were initially quite similar on both sides of the "Iron Curtain." Yet over time, the gap in the standard of living grew substantially, with the capitalist society outpacing its communist mirror. And as many cynics noted during the Cold War era, one telling difference between East and West Berlin was that the guards on the Soviet side of the Wall were there to keep people *in* their ostensible worker's paradise, whereas the border guards of capitalist countries had the job of keeping illegal immigrants *out*.

An even starker illustration of the difference between extreme socialism and moderate capitalism is the case of Korea. (After World War II the Soviet Union was closely associated with communist North Korea, while the American forces stayed in South Korea.) Journalist Barbara Demick provides compelling anecdotal evidence in her book *Nothing to Envy*, based on interviews she conducted with defectors from North Korea. Here is an excerpt from the opening chapter:

> If you look at satellite photographs of the far east by night, you'll see a large splotch curiously lacking in light. This area of darkness is the Democratic People's Republic of Korea.
>
> Next to this mysterious black hole, South Korea, Japan, and now China fairly gleam with prosperity. Even from hundreds of miles above, the billboards, the headlights and streetlights, the neon of the fast-food chains appear as tiny white dots signifying people going about their business as twenty-first-century energy consumers. Then, in the middle of it all, an expanse of blackness nearly as large as England. It is baffling how a nation of 23 million people can appear as vacant as the oceans. North Korea is simply a blank.
>
> North Korea faded to black in the early 1990s. With the collapse of the Soviet Union, which had propped up its old Communist ally with cheap fuel oil, North Korea's creakily inefficient economy collapsed. Power stations rusted into ruin. The lights went out. Hungry people scaled utility poles to pilfer bits of copper wire to swap for food. When the sun drops low in the sky, the landscape fades to gray and the squat little houses are swallowed up by the night. Entire villages vanish into the dusk. Even in parts of the showcase capital of Pyongyang, you can stroll down the middle of a main street at night without being able to see the buildings on either side.

When outsiders stare into the void that is today's North Korea, they think of remote villages of Africa or Southeast Asia where the civilizing hand of electricity has not yet reached. But North Korea is not an undeveloped country; it is a country that has fallen out of the developed world. You can see the evidence of what once was and what has been lost dangling overhead alongside any major North Korean road—the skeletal wires of the rusted electrical grid that once covered the entire country.

North Koreans beyond middle age remember well when they had more electricity (and for that matter food) than their pro-American cousins in South Korea, and that compounds the indignity of spending their nights sitting in the dark. Back in the 1990s, the United States offered to help North Korea with its energy needs if it gave up its nuclear weapons program. But the deal fell apart after the Bush administration accused the North Koreans of reneging on their promises. North Koreans complain bitterly about the darkness, which they still blame on the U.S. sanctions. They can't read at night. They can't watch television. "We have no culture without electricity," a burly North Korean security guard once told me accusingly.

But the dark has advantages of its own. Especially if you are a teenager dating somebody you can't be seen with.

When adults go to bed, sometimes as early as 7:00 P.M. in winter, it is easy enough to slip out of the house. The darkness confers measures of privacy and freedom as hard to come by in North Korea as electricity. Wrapped in a magic cloak of invisibility, you can do what you like without worrying about the prying eyes of parents, neighbors, or secret police.

I met many North Koreans who told me how much they learned to love the darkness, but it was the story of one teenage girl and her boyfriend that impressed me most. She was twelve years old when she met a young man three years older from a neighboring town. Her family

> was low-ranking in the byzantine system of social controls in place in North Korea. To be seen in public together would damage the boy's career prospects as well as her reputation as a virtuous young woman. So their dates consisted entirely of long walks in the dark. There was nothing else to do anyway; by the time they started dating in earnest in the early 1990s, none of the restaurants or cinemas were operating because of the lack of power.[1]

When discussing her book on NPR, Demick relayed the story of a defector who—ironically enough—decided he would leave North Korea after looking at his government's *propaganda* against their southern neighbor. The photo showed striking South Korean workers who were at a protest, and the point of course was to demonstrate the miserable condition of laborers in the exploitative capitalist society. But the North Korean told Demick that three things jumped out at him from the photo, which eventually made him risk his life by fleeing the country.

First, the photo showed that average people in South Korea had cars. This was not the case in North Korea. Second, the photo showed that the striking worker—though clearly enraged with his fist clenched in the air—had a pen in his shirt pocket. This too was unheard-of among the average people of North Korea at the time. Third, the fact of the rally showed that the workers in South Korea *were allowed to protest*. That too was an alien concept to North Koreans.

As the case of North Korea perhaps makes clearer than any other single comparison, socialism has the power to devastate entire economies and literally starve (whether intentionally or accidentally) millions of people. The theoretical concerns we raised in Lesson 15 are very real and very important. It is crucial to know sound economics because civilization itself is at stake.

---

[1]Barbara Demick, *Nothing to Envy: Ordinary Lives in North Korea* (New York: Spiegel & Grau, 2009), pp. 3–5.

The Fatal Conceit

"By the 1980s, Kim Il-sung or [his favored son] Kim Jong-il, who was increasingly assuming his father's duties, offered 'on-the-spot guidance' to address the country's woes. Father and son were experts in absolutely everything, be it geology or farming. 'Kim Jong-il's on-site instructions and his warm benevolence are bringing about a great advance in goat breeding and output of dairy products,' the Korean Central News Agency opined after Kim Jong-il visited a goat farm near Chongjin. One day he would decree that the country should switch from rice to potatoes for its staple food; the next he would decide that raising ostriches was the cure for North Korea's food shortage. The country lurched from one harebrained scheme to another."

—Barbara Demick, *Nothing to Envy: Ordinary Lives in North Korea* (New York: Spiegel & Grau, 2009), p. 65

Lesson Recap . . .

- Historical evidence can't prove or disprove economic laws. However, even though we may have developed an accurate economic law or principle using sound reasoning, in practice its influence might be minor compared to other factors that our reasoning has overlooked. This is why it is useful to supplement our theoretical critique of socialism by looking at real-world examples.

- Standard political theory places communism on the "far left" of the spectrum, at the opposite of the "far right" elements of fascism. Yet from the economic perspective offered in this book, both Nazi Germany and Stalinist Russia were socialist regimes, in which private property rights were subordinated to the will of the dictator.

- During the twentieth century, communist regimes literally killed tens of millions of their *own* people—these figures do not include casualties from foreign wars. Apologists for these regimes might attribute the deaths to famine, but mass starvations did not occur in capitalist countries and there is ample evidence that these "famines" were conscious political tools to consolidate a regime's power. Even when comparing regions that were initially quite similar—such as East vs. West Berlin, and North vs. South Korea—the standard of living diverged sharply after one half fell to communism.

NEW TERMS

Communism: An economic and political ideology that seeks to gain government ownership of the means of production (in the name of the workers) through violent revolution.

Fascism: An economic and political ideology that also seeks extensive government regulation of all resources in the service of the collective good, though fascism (unlike communism) allows private individuals to officially retain ownership of the factories and other capital goods.

STUDY QUESTIONS

1. *Does the historical record *prove* that socialism is a flawed economic system?

2. What is wrong with the conventional "left / right" spectrum on which Stalin is the polar opposite of Hitler?

3. Do governments that officially support capitalism ever kill innocent people?

4. According to the text, which government massacred the largest number of civilians?

5. *Explain this subsection title: "Close to a Controlled Experiment."

Part IV

INTERVENTIONISM: THE MIXED ECONOMY

LESSON 17

Price Controls

In this lesson you will learn:

- The definition of *interventionism*.
- Examples and consequences of *price ceiling*s and *price floors*.
- How to analyze price controls using supply and demand graphs.

The Vision of Interventionism

In Part II of this book, we explained the basic structure and functioning of a pure market economy. In Part III, we surveyed the theoretical problems with pure socialism, and documented some of the horrors of socialist systems in practice.

In this final portion of the book, we will examine some of the most popular components of **interventionism**, which is an approach to economic policy that seeks to avoid the alleged flaws of pure capitalism and pure socialism. An interventionist government will not tolerate the outcomes of a purely free market, but on the other hand it doesn't completely abolish private property. The goal of interventionist policies is to retain the obvious advantages of a free enterprise system, while at the same time moderating the "excesses" of pure capitalism through various corrective measures.

The following lessons will demonstrate that government intervention into the market economy leads to unintended consequences, which very often make the "cure" worse than the disease, even according to the official goals of the interventions. You may be surprised to learn that many of the problems with modern society are either exacerbated or even caused by government intervention. The example of this lesson is **price controls**, in which the government enforces a different price from the market-clearing equilibrium price. We break the discussion up into the treatment of price ceilings and price floors.

Price Ceilings

A **price ceiling** is a legal maximum the government sets on prices in the marketplace for a particular good or service; the idea is that a rising price hits the "ceiling" and is not legally allowed to go any higher. Typically the official rationale for a general price ceiling is that it keeps important items affordable for the poor; a classic example would be **rent control**, in which the government imposes caps on rental rates for certain types of apartments. In specific situations, temporary price ceilings may be imposed to prevent "gouging" of the public in times of distress. For example, after a natural disaster strikes, the local or state government might impose price controls on items such as bottled water, electric generators, and gasoline, in an effort to prevent merchants from "taking advantage of" the situation.

Although the general public applaud such restrictions—if they weren't popular, they wouldn't be so prevalent—our knowledge of how markets work will show that price ceilings actually hurt the very people they are supposed to be helping. The following list isn't exhaustive, but it mentions some of the most damaging consequences of price ceilings:

Immediate Shortages

If it is to have any impact, a price ceiling must be set *below* the market price. But under normal circumstances, the actual market price will tend to be close to the market-clearing price, which (we recall from Lesson 11) is the price at which the quantity supplied equals the quantity demanded. Now if the government forces the price *lower* by imposing a price ceiling, it will cause a *shortage* of the good or service in question. The following diagram illustrates:

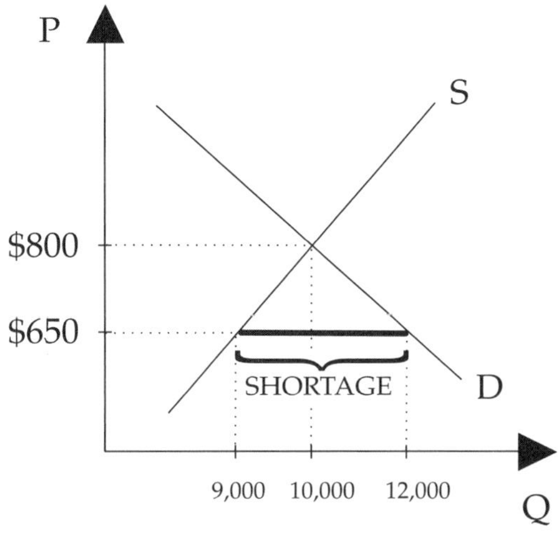

Market for Apartment Units

In the diagram above, the original price of $800 is the equilibrium price to rent an apartment in an urban neighborhood. At that price, consumers want to rent a total of 10,000 apartment units, and owners want to rent out 10,000 apartment units. The market clears and everyone engages in as many transactions as he wants, subject to the high price.

But then the government imposes a price ceiling at $650, claiming that "regular people can't afford" to pay higher rents, and threatening to heavily fine any landlord caught charging more than this amount. At the lower price, the quantity of apartment units demanded rises to 12,000, while the quantity supplied drops to 9,000.[1] There is now a *shortage* of 3,000 units, meaning that 3,000 people in the neighborhood want to rent an apartment at the going price, but can't find any available units.

---

[1]Even though (in the short run) the physical number of apartment units doesn't shrink, the number that owners *put on the market for rent* can definitely drop because of the new rent control law. Most obvious, homeowners who were willing to rent out a spare bedroom to a stranger at $800 per month, might keep it vacant (and available for their kids coming back on college breaks or for other out-of-town guests) if they can only charge $650. Even the owners of dedicated apartment buildings might prefer to rent out only some of the units at the lower price, to a group of tenants who have passed more rigorous background credit checks and so forth.

Shortages are quite serious because they make the good or service unavailable for the very people supposedly helped by the price control. It's true, the 9,000 people who still have an apartment might be thankful that they are saving $150 per month on their rent (though perhaps not if they understand all of the additional points below). However, there are now 1,000 people in the community who would have had an apartment with market pricing but now have *no apartment at all* because of the price ceiling. We know that they would prefer to pay $800 for an apartment rather than having none at all (since the quantity demanded would be 10,000 total at a price of $800), and so they are clearly worse off because of the rent control.[2]

At this first step in the analysis, therefore, we must balance the gains to the 9,000 renters (who save $150 a month) against the presumably much more traumatic loss to the 1,000 renters who have an extra $800 a month, but not an apartment of their own. Even if we completely ignore the fate of the landlords—who are clearly worse off because of the rent control—and focus exclusively on helping tenants, it is not clear that the price ceiling has actually made the group as a whole better off.

The tradeoff is even more striking in other situations of price ceilings. For example, suppose a hurricane strikes a city, knocking out the power and causing flooding that contaminates the drinking water. Left to their own devices, the market prices of bottled water and canned goods would have a tendency to skyrocket because of the sharp increase in demand versus the fixed supply. If the local government passes an ordinance fining merchants who raise their prices on "necessities" in response to the emergency, that won't result in everyone (including the poor) getting access to the items. On the contrary, what will happen is that the first few people to get to the store will clear out the shelves, loading up on bottled water and canned food at the pre-crisis prices. People who get to the store a few hours later will walk away with no water or food at all. For such poor souls, the officially reasonable prices are small consolation. They would much rather

[2]There are also an additional 2,000 people who are frustrated because of the shortage, but in a sense they are not really losing out (except for their headaches and time spent searching fruitlessly for an apartment). If the price were allowed to rise to its market-clearing level, they would have fallen out of the market and not gotten an apartment in that scenario, either.

have paid $5 each for 10 bottles of water, than to have their family drink Coke for a week.

Another illustration is gasoline. People who live on the coast in the path of an oncoming hurricane will try to load the kids up and head inland. Consequently the demand for gasoline in the coastal city will temporarily spike, which normally would cause a sharp rise in prices, say to $7 per gallon. This unusually high price would cause the fleeing residents to only buy enough gasoline to get them onto the interstate where they would search for gas stations charging lower prices. The high market price would have effectively rationed the city's supplies of gasoline on hand (when the news of the impending hurricane hit) among everyone trying to leave town.

However, if the city government threatens the gas station owners with fines or even jail for "price gouging," then the first wave of motorists will fill up their tanks and empty out the gas stations. Subsequent motorists will drive around town but see "No Gas" signs posted at all the stations. They will have to get on the interstate, perhaps with very little gas in their tanks, and possibly break down along the way. If the goal is to get as many people out of the path of the incoming hurricane as smoothly as possible, imposing price ceilings on gasoline is a horrible idea.

Lower Supply in the Long Run

In addition to the immediate drop in the short-run quantity supplied, a price ceiling will also suppress the long-run supply, as entrepreneurs and investors respond to the new realities and shift their efforts and resources to other lines that do not suffer from price controls. For example, if rent control laws are applied in a major urban area, there will be an immediate shortage. However, the problem may become worse over time, as the population grows but investors do not view cheap apartment units as a very lucrative project.

For a different example, merchants who live in a town subject to flooding will not carry as large an inventory of bottled water and other goods, if they know the government will impose price ceilings in situations where they otherwise could have tripled their prices. Thus the expectation of price controls cripples one of the primary features of a market economy—

entrepreneurs can foresee potential crises (water shortages) and know how to ameliorate them (stockpiling more bottles of water in normal times), but they won't act on their foresight because the government takes away the market's usual rewards for such behavior.

Non-price Rationing

One of the functions of the (undisturbed) market price is that it rations the available supply of a good among the competing demands for it. In essence, if someone wants more units of the good, he has to bid more dollars for it. This of course strikes many observers as unfair, since it gives an obvious advantage to the wealthy.

However, by placing a cap on the price, the government doesn't eliminate the fact of scarcity; there are still more people who want to use the good, than there are units of the good to go around. All that happens is that the rationing must occur through *non-price* mechanisms. This actually might end up being more distasteful to the proponents of the price control, than the original price rationing.

For example, under rent control landlords can be much pickier in which tenants they select for their available apartments. They might insist on seeing several months' worth of paycheck stubs, run a background check on the applicant, and require letters of reference from previous landlords. They might also prefer tenants who travel in the same social circles, or come from the same ethnic group, whether from outright bias or because they subconsciously feel more comfortable letting someone move into the building when (say) he goes to the same church. In such an environment, ethnic minorities and recent immigrants—especially if they don't speak the native tongue—will be at a huge disadvantage, and may find it very difficult to find a place to live. This outcome is the exact *opposite* of what most proponents of rent control desire.

Drop in Quality

Another insidious effect of price ceilings is that they reduce the quality of the good or service being regulated. When a price ceiling forces sellers to receive a lower dollar amount per unit sold, they have less incentive to make the good or service desirable.

For example, rent control laws give rise to **slumlords**, the term denoting shady and cruel landlords of low-income apartment units. In a normal market, a merchant who habitually treated his customers with rudeness, and refused to live up to his contractual obligations, would soon go out of business. But under rent control, landlords are under far less competitive pressure to please their customers. Even if the tenant in unit 3-A has had enough and leaves, the landlord knows there is a long line of potential tenants eager to move in.

In essence, price ceilings provide a margin in which the sellers can reduce the quality of the good or service, without hurting their total sales revenues. In the numerical example of rent control diagrammed above, the landlords are in a position to reduce the quality of their units so long as the tenants would still be willing to spend $650 in rent. The landlords might be slow to replace a burnt-out hallway light, they might let the paint crack and peel on the building rather than apply a new coat regularly, and they certainly are not going to get up in the middle of the night to deal with a tenant's broken water heater. Therefore, it wasn't completely accurate to say (in our discussion following the supply and demand graph on page 257) that the 9,000 tenants were better off because they had to pay $650 for an apartment unit that previously was $800. This is because they are not getting the "same" apartment unit in both situations.

Price Floors

A **price floor** is a legal minimum, in which the government does not allow the price of a good or service to fall below the "floor." Buyers caught paying less than the floor price face fines or other forms of punishment. The public justification for price floors is that certain sellers deserve a higher price for their goods or services than what they would receive in a pure market economy.

In modern Western countries labor is the primary recipient of price floors.[3] In particular the government imposes a **minimum wage** making it

[3]Farmers are also beneficiaries of **price supports**, in which the government assures a guaranteed minimum price for certain agricultural products. However,

illegal for an employer to pay a worker less than a certain amount per hour. Because this is the most popular and recognizable example of a price floor, we will concentrate on it for the rest of this lesson.[4] The analysis generally applies to other goods or services.

As with price ceilings, price floors have many unintended consequences, which should make the proponents of the minimum wage reconsider whether they are really helping unskilled workers. The consequences include:

Immediate Surplus (or Glut)

The market-clearing price (wage) for unskilled labor equates the quantity demanded by employers, with the quantity supplied by unskilled workers. If the government sets a floor *above* the market-clearing level, then it will induce a surplus of unskilled labor. There will be a supply glut, meaning more workers are trying to find jobs at the going wage than employers want to hire. This situation is more popularly known as **unemployment**. The following diagram illustrates the effects of a minimum wage law.

---

typically the government establishes this floor by using tax dollars to artificially boost the demand for the privileged items. Rather than punishing people who pay less than $10 per bushel of wheat, the government steps in and buys up wheat (and stores it in silos) whenever the market price would otherwise fall below $10. The analysis of this type of "price floor" is much different from the situation we are analyzing in the text.

[4]Our analysis of a wage floor explicitly enforced by the government largely applies to the case where a union threatens violence or property destruction in order to raise the wages of its members above the market-clearing level. Many economists view this as a form of government intervention, because governments typically do not punish unions for criminal intimidation the way they would punish other attempts (by employers during labor negotiations for example) to disturb voluntary transactions. However in the text we will restrict the discussion to the purer intervention that comes directly from the government.

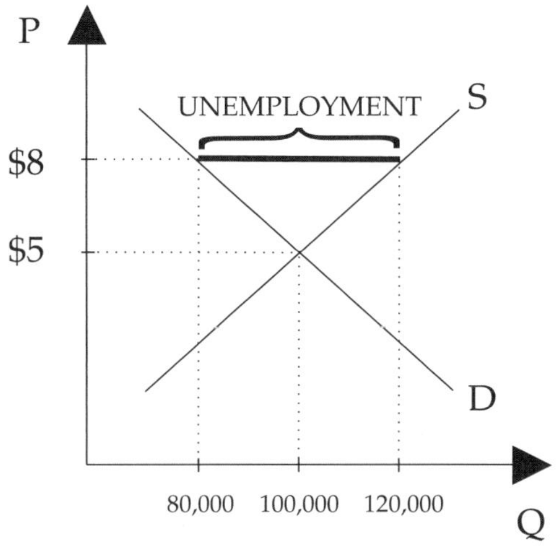

Market for Low-Skill Labor Services

In the diagram, the equilibrium wage is $5 per hour. At this wage, employers want to hire 100,000 workers, and 100,000 people apply for these types of low-skill jobs. When the government comes in and artificially raises the wage rate to $8 an hour, the quantity of workers seeking jobs rises to 120,000, while the quantity demanded falls to 80,000. Thus there is a *shortage* of 40,000 workers. These 40,000 unskilled people are willing to work at the going wage of $8 an hour, but no matter how many applications they fill out, they simply cannot get a job.

Even at this stage, it is not obvious that the minimum wage law is helping unskilled workers. It's true, the 80,000 who retain their jobs now make $3 more per hour, but there are 20,000 people who would have been happy to work at $5 an hour and yet now *can't get a job at all*. In addition, there are 20,000 other workers who are frustrated by the inability to find a job at $8 an hour, but they wouldn't be working in any case since $5 an hour would be unacceptable to them.

It is crucial to realize that the minimum wage law does not compel an employer to *hire* a low-skilled applicant. It simply makes it illegal to hire the applicant for less than the minimum wage. Far from penalizing the rejection of a job application, the minimum wage law actually makes it more burdensome for an employer to give someone a job.

Ruling out cases of philanthropy or other non-commercial contexts, an employer hires a worker because he expects the worker to bring in enough extra revenues to justify the paycheck. (If the employer *didn't* think the employee would do so, he'd be losing money on the deal and would have no incentive to hire.) By artificially raising the bar of the minimum paycheck, the government effectively makes it impossible for people with productivities below a certain level to get a job.

Keep in mind that some unskilled workers simply do not produce $8 worth of extra output for every hour they are on the job. If someone's labor only produces, say, $7 of output per hour, then an $8 minimum wage would force an employer to lose $1 for every hour this person works. If the employer wants to maximize his profits, it would be smarter not to hire this person at all.

Lower Demand in the Long Run

If the government enacts a minimum wage law that takes employers by surprise, they will respond immediately by cutting back on the number of employees.[5] In the longer run (so long as they expect the minimum wage to remain in force) the employers will alter their businesses in ways that will reduce their demand for labor.[6] For example, the employers can install more equipment and better tools to allow each (retained) worker to perform more duties. This raises his or her productivity *on the margin*; a

[5]Or at least, they will desire to do so, just as soon as contractual obligations allow. In practice there might be other constraints, such as the loss of employee morale if the boss lets 10% of the staff go in response to a minimum wage hike. Nonetheless, other things equal a minimum wage increase will reduce the profit-maximizing number of (low-skilled) employees for a given business.

[6]To say that the *demand* (not just the quantity demanded) falls in the long run means two things: First, at the constant minimum wage, the number of workers who can find jobs will fall. Second, even if the government eventually removed the minimum wage, the equilibrium number of workers hired (at that point) would initially be lower than the original number of workers before the imposition of the minimum wage.

given worker can produce more output per hour if his workplace has more machinery.

For example, a modern fast food restaurant can be staffed by a handful of people and still serve hundreds of meals in a single shift, whereas the same feat would have required many more workers at a fast food restaurant in the 1950s. Part of the difference is the tremendous advances in automation in the last 60 years. A well-trained worker can load the soda dispenser with an empty cup and press a button, while using a specialized scoop to dump fries into a carton resting in a specially designed holder, as she listens to a drive-through order on her headset and then punches it onto a keyboard with buttons denoting each value meal. If the customer needs change, the worker might not even have to count it out, as the register automatically shoots out the appropriate combination of quarters, dimes, nickels, and pennies.

Thus rather than having to retain (say) 8 workers at $8 an hour with the old setup, the restaurant owner can spend many thousands of dollars installing the latest equipment and floor design. This investment allows him to achieve the same output but with only 5 workers, thus saving $24 an hour. Over the course of hundreds of shifts, the investment in redesigning the restaurant pays for itself.[7] But after the renovations the restaurant is permanently less dependent on human beings to get the job done.

Non-wage Competition

The "problem" that minimum wage laws seek to fix is that the demand for labor is not high enough so that every willing worker can find a job paying a generous wage. By enacting a minimum wage, the government doesn't alter this underlying reality. Workers still need to compete with each other for every job opening, it's just that the minimum wage takes away one method of bargaining. Ironically this feature of minimum wage

---

[7]Note that at the original wage of $5 per hour, the renovation would only save the owner $15 an hour in reduced labor costs. Depending on the expense of renovation (properly accounting for interest and the depreciation of the new equipment), the minimum wage law could be the difference between designing a restaurant to be run by 8 employees versus 5.

laws hurts precisely those groups that are the most vulnerable and in need of employment.

For example, a 20-year-old immigrant who doesn't speak the native tongue and has no work experience could not possibly compete for a job opening in a factory against middle class suburban college students (home for the summer) who belong to the same gym as the factory owner's family, *if* the two applicants had to receive the same wage. But if the immigrant is allowed to underbid the wage demands of the native college students, he can get the job. The employer might take a chance and hire the immigrant with broken English at, say, $4 an hour, to see if he's a hard worker and can be quickly trained. But if the government requires that all new hires receive $8 an hour from Day One, the immigrant can never get off the ground and establish a (legal) job history, which could allow him to move up the rungs of the wage ladder.

Minimum wage laws take away the ability of low-skilled workers to compete for jobs by lowering their wage demands. Employers will therefore fill the (smaller) pool of job openings according to other criteria. To get a job you "need to know someone," be related to someone already in the company, and so forth. The workers who will fail on these criteria are largely the ones that the proponents of the minimum wage think they are helping.

Drop in Workplace Quality

By forcing employers to pay more per hour, and by ensuring a long line of willing workers ready to replace anyone who quits, minimum wage laws reduce the incentive for employers to make jobs attractive in other dimensions. For example, the employer might reduce break times, stop providing free food in the lunch room, and set the thermostat higher in the summer and lower in the winter. The employer might be slower to replace overhead fluorescent bulbs, and (in an office environment) might spend less money on office furniture. Perhaps the bathrooms will be stocked with very cheap toilet paper and clinical-smelling hand soap.

Perversely, the minimum wage law takes away potential arrangements that would make employers *and* workers happier. Suppose 3,000 people make $8 an hour working at a very hot factory that is cooled only by fans. The owner of the factory surveys the workers and they unanimously agree that they would much rather earn $7.50 an hour, if the employer would install central air conditioning. For her part, the owner of the factory reckons that with 1,000 people working on any given shift, the proposed pay cut would save her $500 per hour in labor costs. She does some research and believes she can install central air and pay the higher utility bills for about $450 an hour, all things considered.

Clearly this sounds like a win-win proposal. The workers take a slight pay cut, it's true, but they would rather have a smaller paycheck without dripping in sweat 8 hours a day. The owner on the other hand would have to shell out thousands of dollars upfront to install the new unit, but over time the lower wage payments would more than compensate for this initial outlay (and the higher utility bills). But if the minimum wage is set at $8 per hour, this sensible proposal will not occur, because it is illegal. Thus the workers toil miserably away in their sweat-soaked clothes, and the factory owner earns $50 less per hour of operations. Although this final example is a bit contrived, it illustrates a major flaw with minimum wage laws: A job is attractive for many reasons, the paycheck being just one. By arbitrarily setting a floor below the wage, the government might perversely cause the other job attributes to decline so that even those workers who *keep* their jobs end up being hurt—let alone those workers who can't get a job at all.

Lesson Recap . . .

- *Interventionism* is a combination of socialism and capitalism. Private individuals retain official ownership over most resources, but the government regulates their use of "their" property.

- Price ceilings lead to shortages, lower long-run supply, non-price rationing, and a reduction in quality. Price floors lead to surpluses, lower long-run demand, non-price competition, and a reduction in the non-monetary qualities of the buyer's offer.

- Supply and demand graphs effectively illustrate the shortages and surpluses caused by price ceilings and floors.

NEW TERMS

Interventionism: The philosophy of the mixed economy, in which the government heavily intervenes in the capitalist system to regulate how individuals can use their private property.

Price controls: Policies that punish people who exchange goods and services at prices different from the acceptable range prescribed by the government.

Price ceiling: A type of price control on a particular good or service that sets a maximum level on the amount a buyer can pay a seller.

Rent control: A price ceiling placed on apartment rents.

Slumlord: The unflattering term applied to a landlord who doesn't maintain the quality of the apartments and who is generally unscrupulous.

Price floor: A type of price control on a particular good or service that sets a minimum level that a buyer must pay a seller.

Minimum wage: A price floor on payments to workers.

Price supports: Government policies that maintain a desired minimum price *not* by threatening buyers who pay too little, but instead by having the government directly buy the good or service whenever its market price would otherwise fall below the floor. (The effects of price supports are different from the effects of price floors.)

Unemployment: A surplus or glut on the labor market, meaning that some workers cannot find jobs even though they are willing to work for the same pay and can perform the jobs just as well as the people who are employed.

STUDY QUESTIONS

1. What is "mixed" in the term *mixed economy*?

2. How can the quantity supplied of apartments fall, even in the short run? Isn't there a fixed number of apartment units at any given time?

3. How might price ceilings on gasoline impede the evacuation of a city in the path of an oncoming hurricane?

4. *How can minimum wage laws reduce the long-run demand (not just short-run quantity demanded) for labor?

5. How can a minimum wage actually hurt even the workers who stay on the job?

LESSON 18

Sales and Income Taxes

In this lesson you will learn:

- The general impact of government spending.
- The three ways government typically pays for its purchases.
- The specific impacts of *sales* and *income taxes*.

Government Spending

One of the most profound ways that the government alters the economy, relative to the free-market outcome, is through its spending programs. In this lesson we will examine some of the ways in which these activities cause economic distortions, in light of our knowledge of how a pure market economy works. Remember to keep in mind that economic analysis *by itself* cannot decide for us whether a government policy is good or bad. However, objective economic analysis *can* show us that the typical justifications for interventionist policies are invalid. This is because the interventions themselves lead to a worse outcome using the very criteria given by those who support the interventions.

Regardless of how the government obtains its funds, when the government *spends* the money it necessarily draws resources out of the private sector and devotes them to lines chosen by the political authorities. For example, if the government spends $100 million building a bridge, we know this is affecting the economy even if we don't know where the $100 million came from. In order to physically construct a bridge, the government must hire workers and buy supplies such as concrete and steel. Once these scarce labor and materials are applied to the bridge construction, they are unavailable to individuals in the private sector. A particular worker is physically incapable of building a factory for a private corporation, during the hours when he is working on the government bridge contract. And obviously concrete and steel that are incorporated into the bridge, cannot be used in other buildings built by private entrepreneurs.

If the political authorities simply declared that they were going to spend government funds in order to make themselves as happy as possible, economics would have nothing more to say. After all, when the owners of Disneyland decide to build a bridge connecting two areas of the theme park, they too are using up resources and making them unavailable to the rest of the economy. So why is there a problem when the government does the same thing?

The crucial difference is that the owners of Disneyland are operating in the voluntary market economy and so are subject to the profit and loss test. If they spend $100 million *not* on personal consumption (such as fancy houses and fast cars) but in an effort to make Disneyland more enjoyable to their customers, they get objective feedback. Their accountants can tell them soon enough whether they are getting more visitors (and hence more revenue) after the installation of a new ride or other investment projects.[1] Remember it is the profit and loss test, relying on market prices, that guides entrepreneurs into careful stewardship of society's scarce resources.

In contrast, the government cannot rely on objective feedback from market prices, because the government operates (at least partially) *outside* of the market. Interventionism is admittedly a mixture of capitalism and socialism, and

---

[1]Strictly speaking, the accountants wouldn't be able to attribute the profitability (or lack thereof) to a specific decision that the management made. For example, suppose that a gambling scandal ruined the good name of Mickey Mouse, just at the same time that Disneyland built a new ride. It's possible that ticket revenue drops by 10% after the new ride opens, when it *would have* dropped 20% had Disneyland not opened the new ride (and partially offset the impact of the scandal involving Mickey). Even so, the accountants can objectively declare whether the business is earning a monetary profit or loss in absolute terms.

it therefore (partially) suffers from the defects of socialism. To the extent that the government *buys* its resources from private owners—rather than simply passing mandates requiring workers to spend time building bridges for no pay, or confiscating concrete and steel for the government's purposes—the government's budget provides a limit to how many resources it siphons out of the private sector. (Under pure socialism, *all* resources in the entire economy are subject to the political rulers' directions.)

However, because the government is not a business, it doesn't raise its funds voluntarily from the "consumers" of its services. Therefore, even though the political authorities in an interventionist economy understand the relative importance of the resources they are using up in their programs—because of the market prices attached to each unit they must purchase—they still don't have any objective measure of how much their citizens benefit from these expenditures. Without such feedback, even if the authorities only want to help their people as much as possible, they are "flying blind" or at best, flying with only one eye.

For example, suppose the government decides to build a public library in order to make books and internet access free to the community. Because the government only has a limited budget, it won't do something ridiculously wasteful such as coating the library with gold, or stocking the shelves with extremely rare first editions of Steinbeck and Hemingway novels. Suppose the government tries to be conscientious,[2] puts out bids to several reputable contractors, and has a modest library constructed for $400,000.

Yet even if outside auditors or investigative journalists could find nothing corrupt or shocking about the process, the question would still remain: Was it *worth it* to spend $400,000 on building this particular library, in this particular location? The crucial point is that we know one thing for certain: *No entrepreneur* thought that he could earn enough revenues from charging for book borrowing to make such an enterprise worthwhile. We know this,

[2]We acknowledge that we are violating are own rule of tying action to the individual: In reality, "the government" doesn't build a library. Instead, certain people make decisions, which sets in motion certain repercussions because of who those decisionmakers are and the obedience they command from other people in the community. But for the sake of brevity we will often say "the government" spends money, raises taxes, etc.

because the library didn't exist until the government used its own funds to build it!

One way to think about government expenditures is that they necessarily call forth the creation of goods and services that people in the private sector did *not* deem worth producing.[3] When the government spends money, it directs resources away from where private spending decisions would have steered them, and into projects that would not be profitable if private entrepreneurs had produced them relying on voluntary funding.[4]

Thus the political authorities in an interventionist economy face one-half of the socialist calculation problem. Even if we dismiss the above considerations on the grounds that "the preferences of rich people over resource usage are irrelevant," the political authorities still have a problem in figuring out the best way to help the poor, disadvantaged, and so forth. For example, is it better to spend the $400,000 on a public library, or would it do "more good" if used to buy free flu shots for every child under the poverty line? In cases such as this, the government in essence is a giant distributor of charitable donations. Even those citizens who welcome the concept should ask themselves: Why do we need to route our donations through the political process? Why not decentralize the decisions and allow each person to donate his or her funds to the various charities that seem most worthy?

To be sure, the proponents of government intervention could offer (somewhat technical) replies to these questions.[5] Even so, at best the case

---

[3]There is a subtlety to this claim: It very often happens that private individuals refrain from investments because they *anticipate* the government will step in. For example, if the government funds the construction of a new sports stadium, people will often say, "This wouldn't have existed without help from the government." It's possible however that the *reason* private investors "needed" government help is that they knew they could shunt some of their expenses onto the shoulders of the taxpayers.

[4]Keep in mind that private-sector organizations can rely on *charitable contributions* and not just revenues from commercial sales. A pure market economy is perfectly consistent with soup kitchens, homeless shelters, and so forth. The crucial difference is that in a pure market economy, the owners of these institutions would need to solicit *voluntary donations* rather than receiving funding from the government, which ultimately was not derived in a purely voluntary manner.

[5]For example, there are situations where private enterprise may be deemed inappropriate, such as the provision of military defense. There are also situations

becomes one of finding the least-bad solution. Regardless of its possible benefits, government spending suffers from the calculation problem afflicting socialism. The system allows a select group of political authorities to override the input of private individuals in how (some of) their property should be used to steer resources into various projects. This is a very serious drawback for anyone who favors interventionism as a way to increase the "general welfare," however defined.

Why Bureaucrats Have Such a Bad Reputation

A bureaucrat differs from a non-bureaucrat precisely because he is working in a field in which it is impossible to appraise the result of a man's effort in terms of money.

— Ludwig von Mises, *Bureaucracy*, p. 53

How Government Finances Its Spending

In addition to the economic distortion (relative to the pure market outcome) caused by government spending per se, additional distortions are introduced depending on the source of the government's revenues. Traditionally there are three main vehicles through which the government raises money: **taxation, budget deficits,** and **inflation**. When the government levies taxes, it decrees that individuals and corporations must pay money to

---

where we can imagine a majority of people agreeing to be "forced" to contribute money to a certain cause, so long as everyone else is similarly forced. For example most residents of a city probably wouldn't view it as "theft" if the local government took $10 a year from everyone in order to maintain "free" garbage cans (placed on busy street corners) and street lights. Because of these types of considerations, many economists who are aware of the flaws with government spending would nonetheless maintain that there is a scope for *some* government purchases.

the government according to certain rules. When the government runs a deficit, it borrows money from individuals, corporations, or other governmental institutions, by selling bonds. The government is legally obligated to pay back these loans with interest. Finally, when the government raises funds through inflation, it creates new money ("out of thin air") and uses it to finance its purchases.

Later in the book we will deal with government deficits and inflation. In the remainder of this lesson, we focus on two of the primary sources of tax revenues for the government: sales taxes and income taxes.

Before proceeding, we should emphasize again that the distortions we discuss below are *in addition to* the distortions caused by transferring resources out of the hands of private entrepreneurs (subject to the profit and loss feedback mechanism) to be directed according to the political process. What we show below is that the government distorts the economy not just when it spends the money, but when it *raises* the funds in the first place through taxation.

To see the difference, imagine an extreme case where the government imposes a 200% income tax, meaning that for every dollar you earn, you are legally required to send the IRS a check for $2! In that ridiculous scenario, it is clear that very few people would work, or at least very few people would work "on the books" and report their incomes to the government at tax time. Consequently, the government would collect very little revenue, and wouldn't be able to spend much money pulling resources away from their most profitable uses. Yet surely it would be wrong to conclude that this hypothetical economy suffered from very little economic distortions due to government interventions. In this scenario, everyone would have quit his or her official job and would be forced to live off the land, or work in **black market** jobs that could be hidden from the authorities. The economy would be plunged into extreme privation because of the punitive tax code, even though it raised very little revenue and the government didn't have a large budget.

In summary, governments distort economies (relative to the pure market outcome) both when they spend money *and* when they collect funds. We now examine the specific distortions caused when the government collects money through sales taxes and income taxes.

Sales Taxes

Under a **sales tax,** the government mandates that a portion of the payment on certain transactions is owed to the government. For example, if there is a 5% sales tax on all restaurant meals, then diners who order $100 worth of food and drinks—according to the prices on the menu—must pay $100 to the restaurant, but then an additional $5 to the government. In practice, the restaurant collects the entire $105 from the diners at the end of the meal, and sets aside the $5 to be sent to the government at periodic intervals.

Sales taxes distort the economy because they force consumers to face incorrect prices. In our example of the restaurant meal, the diners must ultimately pay $105 for the particular combination of food and drinks that they enjoyed, when in reality the restaurant only needed to charge $100 in order to cover the expenses of the labor, raw meat, soda syrup, and other resources used to produce the meal. This distortion is obvious if we consider a case where the government imposes a large sales tax on some items—such as alcoholic drinks—while exempting other items from a sales tax altogether, such as fruits at the grocery store. This imbalance in sales tax rates causes the penalized goods to appear artificially expensive, giving consumers an incentive to purchase less of the penalized goods and more of the exempt goods.

Of course many reformers would say, "That's the whole point! We *want* to discourage people from drinking alcohol." Such a judgment relies on the reformers deciding that their own preferences should be given more say than the preferences of the consumers spending their money in the marketplace. Economic science cannot say whether such **paternalism** is good or bad, but it simply notes that the *consumers themselves* would judge themselves worse off, at least narrowly conceived. The imposition of a high tax rate on liquor only takes away options from consumers. People who want to eat healthy always have the option of spending nothing on liquor, without the government artificially raising its price.

Many practical economists advise governments to adopt *uniform* sales taxes with *low* marginal rates, in order to minimize these types of distortions. For example, rather than levying a sales tax of 10% on half the items in the marketplace, most economists would instead suggest that the government levy a 5% sales tax on *all* the items in the marketplace. This switch would bring in roughly the same amount of revenue to the government,[6] and it would eliminate the arbitrary disadvantages placed on particular sectors of the economy.

However, we should remember that in a pure market economy, *prices mean something*; they are indicators of real scarcity. Consequently, even if the government levies a "fair" single-rate sales tax applied uniformly to all goods and services, nonetheless it will distort the economy, because consumers will still have the incentive to *not earn as much income in the first place*. To see this, let's take a ridiculous example where the government levies a uniform 100% sales tax on every item in the market. Even though every sector is hit with the tax, it's obviously not a "wash." Consumers will end up buying fewer items *in total*, and will allow their monetary incomes to fall by working less (and enjoying more leisure). Besides this obvious impact, there is also the subtle point that it is *impossible* to levy a truly uniform sales tax. For example, a 100% sales tax on chewing gum would make a $1 pack turn into a $2 pack, whereas a $50,000 sports car would turn into a $100,000 car. The sales of chewing gum would probably fall less than the sales of sports cars.

Up until now, we have been assuming that everyone in the society *obeys* the government's tax laws. But in reality, as a sales tax rate becomes higher and applies to more and more items, more merchants and consumers will conduct their operations in the black market, meaning they will engage in

---

[6]Actually the move to "flatten" the sales tax would probably bring in *more* total revenue, because more sales would occur at the lower rates, and because in the original scenario consumers would have shifted their purchases away from the 10%-taxed goods towards the 0%-taxed goods. Therefore, in the new situation (when all goods are taxed uniformly at 5%), the actual number of sales on taxable items would probably more than double relative to the original scenario, which would more than offset the halving of the sales tax rate. (Note that we are just discussing general tendencies; we could invent specific numerical examples where the "flat" 5% sales tax brought in less revenue than a particular 10% sales tax on half the items. For example, if the 10% tax rate originally applied to food and cigarettes, while the 0% tax rate originally applied to yachts and diamond earrings, then switching from that system to a flat 5% sales tax on everything would probably bring in less total tax revenue.)

voluntary transactions without reporting them to the government, or sending in the legally required tax payments. This reaction is yet another distortion caused by sales taxes, because some items (e.g., cartons of cigarettes) are much easier to trade on the black market than others (e.g., cars).

Income Taxes

When the government levies an **income tax**, it requires individuals and corporations to transfer some of their income in a particular period to the government. Income taxes are usually expressed as percentages, and are often **graduated** meaning that different portions of someone's (pre-tax) income are taxed at different rates. For example, suppose an income tax has two **brackets** with a rate of 10% for income up to $10,000, and 20% for income above $10,000. A person with a pre-tax income of $100,000 would thus owe the government (10% x $10,000 + 20% x $90,000) = $1,000 + $18,000 = $19,000.[7]

To the extent that the income tax exempts particular sources of income, it causes distortions between these sectors. For example, the interest income earned from buying municipal bonds (issued by local governments) may be tax exempt, whereas the interest income earned from corporate bonds will be taxed. This causes investors to lend more money to local governments and less to corporations, other things equal, and distorts the allocation of capital funds.

Another example of this type of distortion is related to the problems with health care delivery in the United States. Under the current U.S. income tax code, when employees receive health insurance as part of their job, this benefit doesn't count as taxable income. However, if the employer took the money it otherwise would have spent on the health insurance premium for the employee, and handed this money directly to the employee in the form of a higher paycheck, then it would be taxed—meaning the employee wouldn't get to keep the entire boost in the paycheck. In other words, it's

---

[7]Note that the 20% rate applies *only* to the $90,000 in income falling in the second bracket's range; the higher rate doesn't apply to the whole $100,000 of income. This is why (under normal circumstances) you can't actually see your take-home pay drop after a pay raise that "puts you into a higher tax bracket."

much cheaper (depending on the relevant income tax rate) for the employer to buy health insurance for the employee, than for the employee to buy it him or herself. This is a major reason that health insurance is so intertwined with one's job, whereas people typically use their paychecks to go buy their own auto and fire insurance.

In addition to exempting certain sources of income, another major distortion from income tax codes comes from allowing particular expenses to be *excluded* (or **deducted**) from one's taxable income. For example, homeowners can deduct the interest that they pay on their house mortgages from their federal income tax assessment. So someone with a pre-tax income of $100,000 but who pays $5,000 in interest on the loan that he got from the bank to buy his house, will only report to the IRS that he has $95,000 in **taxable income**. The appropriate bracket tax rates will then be applied to this lower amount, not to the true $100,000 in income. Such a "loophole" in the income tax code arguably brings the economy closer to the market outcome overall (by limiting the applicability of the distortionary income tax), but it clearly causes large distortions between individual sectors, especially if marginal income tax rates are high. In the case of mortgage interest deduction, the distortion gives people an artificial incentive to prolong the length of their mortgage, and to use their money in other investments rather than paying back the bank as quickly as they otherwise would have.[8]

The biggest of all distortions from the income tax code relates to the decision of how much income to earn in the first place. Most obvious, people will work less if the reward for working (i.e., monetary income) is taxed more heavily. College students may prolong their educations, and older workers may retire earlier. In the economy as a whole, the total number

[8]People often say the mortgage interest deduction gives an incentive to buy a home rather than to rent, but prices adjust to eliminate much of this impact. If an entrepreneur buys a house and then rents it to tenants, any interest on borrowed money is a business expense and hence tax deductible too. Competition among entrepreneurs in the housing rental market would tend to lower rents to tenants to reflect this feature of the tax code. At the same time, home prices are probably higher than they otherwise would be, if homeowners weren't able to deduct their mortgage interest payments. So although people often assume that the mortgage deduction gives a huge bias toward homeownership versus renting, the distortion on this decision is not as severe as it may first seem.

of hours worked—particularly "doubletime" hours during holidays—will fall, because of the change in incentives. This will occur both because people will truly work less (and engage in more leisure), but also because they will work "under the table" or "off the books" and not report their earnings to the government. Because some forms of income are easier to hide than others, this encouragement of black market activity will distort the economy too, relative to the pure market outcome.

Finally, we discuss an effect of the income tax code that many analysts overlook. Some people argue that a tax hike, so long as it is modest, won't have a noticeable impact on economic activity, since "people still have to work." For example, suppose the government originally has no income tax at all, but because it needs more revenue it creates a new tax bracket of 20% on all incomes above $80,000. Many observers would think that this would have little effect on the economy, since people who make over $80,000 surely aren't going to stop working because of the new tax!

Yet this analysis ignores the fact that the monetary paycheck is just *one component* of a job's overall appeal to a worker. Suppose someone is the top accountant working for a reputable firm in a sleepy town in the Midwest, making $80,000 per year. He has applied for a job in New York City at a much larger firm where the salary is $140,000 per year. However, the downside is that the man would have to go through the hassle of moving, he would have to pay much higher prices for housing or apartment rental, the job at the large firm would be far more stressful, and the man would spend an extra two hours commuting each day. Before the income tax, the man would have to decide whether the extra $60,000 in salary per year compensated for these drawbacks of the big city job.

After the new income tax goes into effect, the advantage of the New York City position has fallen significantly. Now if the man takes the job, his pretax salary will still jump to $140,000, but he will have to write the government a check for $12,000. Thus his after-tax income will only be $128,000, compared to his $80,000 salary at his current job (which falls just below the tax line). *Now* the man must decide whether an additional $48,000—*not* $60,000—per year compensates for the hassle of moving, more expensive housing, the higher stress, and the longer commute. Even if this particular man decides to move anyway, it is clear that in an economy with millions of workers, a high income tax distorts their decisions about which jobs to accept. Thus the income tax—especially as its top rate grows higher and higher—interferes with the market economy's ability to attract workers into the appropriate channels through higher wages and salaries. The "signal" sent by entrepreneurs bidding more for labor encounters interference from the tax code.

Taxes Discourage Production

"There is a [discouraging] effect when personal incomes are taxed 50, 60 or 70 percent. People begin to ask themselves why they should work six, eight or nine months of the entire year for the government, and only six, four or three months for themselves and their families. If they lose the whole dollar when they lose, but can keep only a fraction of it when they win [because of taxes], they decide that it is foolish to take risks with their capital. In addition, the capital available for risk-taking itself shrinks enormously. It is being taxed away before it can be accumulated. In brief, capital to provide new private jobs is first prevented from coming into existence, and the part that does come into existence is then discouraged from starting new enterprises. The government spenders create the very problem of unemployment that they profess to solve."

—Henry Hazlitt, *Economics in One Lesson*, p. 38

Lesson Recap . . .

- No matter how it is financed, government spending always diverts physical resources away from projects determined in the private sector, and into projects chosen by the political process.

- Government typically pays for its purchases through taxation, borrowing, and inflation.

- All taxes distort the economy, relative to the free-market outcome. Sales taxes favor some goods over others, if the rates are not applied uniformly. Even a uniform sales tax reduces the rewards from working, which artificially encourages people to opt for more leisure. An income tax penalizes work even more directly, and artificially encourages people to choose jobs that feature non-monetary advantages.

NEW TERMS

Taxation: The process in which the government takes ownership of portions of income or other assets from private individuals.

Budget deficits: The excess of government spending over tax receipts. The deficit is the amount the government must borrow to pay its bills in a given period.

Inflation: The creation of more money, which drives up prices.

Black market: The system of illegal transactions that violate government regulations.

Sales tax: A tax that applies to goods and services as they are sold to the customer. Sales taxes are usually applied as percentages of the pre-tax dollar amount.

Paternalism: Overriding the desires of someone else because he or she is not considered competent to make the right decision.

Income tax: A tax that applies to the earnings of an individual or a corporation. Income taxes are usually applied as percentages of the pre-tax dollar income.

Graduated income tax: An income tax that applies higher rates to higher levels of income.

Income Tax Brackets: The thresholds of income that are taxed at various rates. For example, the lowest tax bracket might include incomes ranging from $0 to $10,000, which is taxed at 3%, while the next bracket might include incomes ranging from $10,001 to $20,000, which is taxed at 5%.

Tax Deduction: A provision in the tax code that allows a particular expense (such as medical expenses or the purchase price of a new solar panel) to be subtracted from an individual's taxable income. This means that tax-deductible items are paid for with "pre-tax dollars," which allows an individual to buy more with his income.

Taxable income: The amount of income actually subject to the official tax rates for each bracket. Taxable income is the original income after all deductions and other adjustments have been made.

STUDY QUESTIONS

1. *Does economics conclude that government spending is bad?

2. How do we know that government spending diverts resources from the private sector? Does it matter how the government obtained its funds?

3. **If the government builds a library, do we know that the private sector wouldn't have built a library instead?

4. If the government raises a modest amount of money through taxation, do we know that the tax burden is light?

5. As long as people continue working, does the income tax have little effect on the economy?

LESSON 19

Tariffs and Quotas

In this lesson you will learn:

- The definition of *mercantilism.*
- The general case for *free trade.*
- How *tariffs* and *quotas* make countries poorer.

Mercantilism

M**ercantilism** is an economic philosophy or doctrine which holds that a country grows rich by encouraging **exports** (goods and services sold to foreigners) and discouraging **imports** (goods and services bought from foreigners). According to mercantilism, a **trade surplus** (exporting more than importing) is good for a country's economy, while a **trade deficit** (importing more than exporting) is bad. If mercantilism were correct, countries could succeed only by implementing **beggar-thy-neighbor policies**, because one or more countries can run a trade surplus only if other countries run trade deficits. In other words, it's not possible for *every* country to sell more goods to foreigners than it buys from them.[1] When

[1]Of course, countries per se don't import or export goods; people within a country do. But it is difficult to convey the essence of mercantilism without speaking of various countries as collective units regarding trade.

government officials are motivated by mercantilist ideas, they view other countries as potential threats to their own nation's interests. In such a mindset, international trade is a **zero-sum game**, meaning that the gains of one country must come from losses imposed on other countries.

Mercantilism was the dominant philosophy among the major world powers from the 16th through the 18th centuries. During that period, when countries used gold and silver as the basis of their trading, it seemed intuitive that running trade surpluses made a country richer. After all, by consistently having more exports than imports, a country's stockpile of gold and silver would increase, because "more" or "fewer" exports and imports were measured in terms of gold or silver values.[2] On the surface, it makes perfect sense that the path to national riches is to accumulate increasing amounts of money, especially when the money consists of physical gold and silver.

The British classical economists, notably David Hume and Adam Smith, destroyed the intellectual justification for mercantilist policies with their writings. (We will review some of the problems with mercantilism in the following sections.) You may be surprised to learn that the major powers actually *acted* on this newfound wisdom. During the 19th century, the world enjoyed a period of relatively **free trade**, in which governments substantially rolled back their policies that had previously hindered imports and encouraged exports.

As you may realize, today governments do not support genuinely free trade. Despite signing trade agreements to ostensibly capture the benefits of trade, large barriers still exist to the movement of goods around the globe. Political leaders do not openly advocate mercantilism by name, but they nonetheless support similar **protectionist** policies that favor (certain) domestic industries over their foreign competitors. Because countries no longer use gold and silver as the common money, the rhetorical justification for trade restrictions today rests on "saving jobs" in the protected domestic industries (rather than the accumulation of physical wealth).

---

[2]For example, if France exported 100 gold ounces' worth of wine to Great Britain, while it only imported 80 gold ounces' worth of books from Great Britain, then (if these were the only transactions) there would be a net flow of 20 ounces of gold out of Britain and into France.

The General Case for Free Trade

The British classical economists—most famously Adam Smith in his 1776 *Wealth of Nations*—demolished the ideas of mercantilism, and began building a strong case for free trade. Over the years, economic thinkers have generalized these arguments and have also devised simpler, more intuitive ways of explaining the advantages of free trade among nations. In this section we'll review the basic rationale behind free trade, and in the remaining sections of this lesson we'll explore the specific problems with two types of trade restrictions, namely tariffs and import quotas.

Economically speaking, there is nothing significant about the political boundary separating "foreign" goods from "domestic" goods. Just as an individual American trades with other Americans to obtain his food, clothes, car repair, and medical services, there is nothing "uneconomical" about the United States *in the aggregate* trading with Japan.

In fact, the primary confusion underlying protectionist fallacies (i.e., faulty arguments) is to view "the United States" importing goods from "Japan." In reality, it is *individuals in the United States* who buy goods from *individual sellers* in Japan; talk of "U.S. imports" is just the adding up of all these individual purchases. When we say "the U.S. runs a trade deficit with Japan," all it means is that individuals in the U.S. collectively spent more money buying goods from sellers who were located in Japan, compared to the amount of money that Japanese individuals spent buying goods from sellers who lived in the U.S. There is nothing intrinsically dangerous or unsustainable about this situation, any more than it would be a "problem" if Texans bought more from Floridians than vice versa. Yet we don't ever hear of Texans wringing their hands over a "trade deficit" with Florida.

It is true, there are arguments for protectionist trade barriers that have varying degrees of sophistication. For example, someone might worry about trade deficits with China—whereas not lose a moment's sleep over interstate trade deficits within the borders of the U.S.—because of the specific monetary policies or relatively weak labor laws in China. In this book, we will not address such particular justifications for trade restrictions. We are here only trying to get you to see the general logic behind the case for free trade, and to understand why trade deficits (which is itself a loaded term!) per se are not a problem.

Recall from Lesson 8 the benefits of specialization and the concept of comparative advantage, as they apply among individuals in a pure market economy. The case for free trade among nations is simply an application of these general principles. To restrict the imports of cars from Japan in order to "create jobs" for American workers in Detroit, would be as nonsensical as a man refusing to go to a dentist in order to "create work" for his wife so that she has to be the one to clean his teeth and look for cavities.

In Lesson 8 we explored the commonsense insight that individuals can enjoy a much higher standard of living if they specialize in one or a few activities, and trade their surplus production with others who have specialized in something else. By focusing on his or her (relative) strengths, *each person* in the community can enjoy more goods and services through the benefits of voluntary trade.

The same logic applies to nations. Rather than having to produce everything domestically (i.e., within the geographical borders of the country), the people in each country (on average) are all enriched by the *option* of trading with people from other nations. Because of their different endowments of natural resources—which can include deposits of oil or diamonds, but also things like average rainfall and sunshine—different regions of the world have the comparative advantage in producing different goods, such as barrels of crude oil or bushels of wheat. There are regional differences that arise from less obvious sources as well, besides natural resources. For example, for various historical reasons, New York City and London are major financial hubs, attracting some of the largest financial institutions. *Given* those realities, it is only natural (and efficient) that a large portion of the world's financial transactions flow through these centers—just as it is only natural (and efficient) for Saudi Arabia to sell oil to the rest of the world.

Because of the tremendous differences among regions along natural, historical, and cultural dimensions, total world output (and hence average output per person) is greatest when different regions specialize in their comparative advantages (oil, oranges, wheat, cars, computer chips, etc.) and produce far more of these goods than their own residents want to purchase. The excess is then exported to other regions, which in turn export their own excess goods. Although an individual country can run a trade deficit with another individual country, the world as a whole is always in a trade balance; individual deficits and surpluses necessarily add up to zero.

All the countries in the world (collectively) always buy exactly as many goods and services as all the countries in the world (collectively) sell.[3]

If we imagine an initial situation of worldwide free trade, and then further imagine that an individual country decided to "protect" its domestic industries and "save jobs" by preventing foreign goods from crossing its borders, its residents would become much poorer (on average).[4] This would happen for the same reason that the people living in a particular *house* would be reduced to extreme poverty if the eccentric father suddenly announced that they were no longer allowed to spend money buying things from anyone living outside of the household.

Sometimes people do not see the connection between (a) trade among countries and (b) trade among individuals living within the same country. It's true, restrictions on goods coming into the country would not be nearly as devastating as a father's restrictions on goods coming into a household. But the difference is merely one of degree, not of kind. In a sense, the people living in a country are in a *gigantic* household, and so it's not as crippling when their "father" (i.e., the government) says they can no longer trade with people outside of the house.

Looked at the other way, our hypothetical father has prevented his children from trading with almost the entire population of the earth. In contrast,

---

[3]If you are an advanced reader, we should make the technical point that a given country (such as the United States) can have a trade deficit with one country (such as China) while simultaneously running a trade surplus with another country (such as Australia). However, these deficits and surpluses need not cancel out, for any particular country. The United States, for example, runs a net trade deficit with the-rest-of-the-world. This is possible because people outside the United States can invest in American assets. For example, if a Japanese investor buys a corporate bond issued by IBM, this purchase "returns dollars to the U.S." and helps balance out the net flow of dollars to Japan resulting from the trade deficit in goods and services. (Note that financial assets—such as stocks and bonds—do *not* form part of a country's exports.)

[4]We added the qualifier "(on average)" because technically, imposing a trade barrier can make *some* people in a country better off—namely, the people who compete with the imports that are now being penalized. But as we'll see in the next section in the text, the possible gains to the protected producers are more than offset by the losses to everyone else in the country.

if the U.S. president sealed off the border and outlawed imports, he would only be preventing Americans from trading with people who lived outside of the U.S. The gains from mutual exchange, and specialization and comparative advantage, could still develop among the hundreds of millions of people living inside the U.S. borders. This is why extreme trade restrictions imposed on the country would not be nearly as destructive as those imposed on a single household within the United States. Still, if you can see how it would be incredibly beneficial if the eccentric father allowed his children to trade with other Americans, then you can understand why it would be incredibly beneficial if the U.S. government allowed its citizens to engage in unfettered trade with foreigners.[5]

Before moving on to deal with the specific protectionist measures (namely tariffs and quotas), we should emphasize an important point: *The economic case*[6] *for free trade is unilateral*. In other words, the case for free trade does *not* say, "A country benefits from reducing its trade barriers, but only if other countries follow suit and allow the first country's exports into their own markets." No, as the discussion above should have made clear, when a government erects trade barriers it *takes away options of exchange from its own people*. Therefore, removing those obstacles—giving its citizens more opportunities for beneficial trading—makes them richer (per capita). It would of course be better still if *foreign* governments scrapped their own restrictions so that the foreign consumers had more options to import goods from the original country. But regardless of what foreign governments do with their own trade policies, a particular government can make its own people richer

---

[5]To be clear, we are here focusing on general *economic* arguments for and against free trade. If someone argues that, say, U.S. producers of ballistic missiles shouldn't be allowed to trade with people living in North Korea, that is not a specifically economic argument, but rather a military claim. In the text we are dealing with the very popular—but misguided—belief that trade barriers make a country *richer* by stimulating the domestic economy.

[6]We are calling it the *economic* case for free trade to distinguish it from other types of arguments. For example, someone versed in natural law theory might claim that even if free trade made countries poorer, it would still be the correct policy because the government has no right to restrict how people use their private property.

immediately by removing all trade barriers and enacting a unilateral free trade policy.

It is true that if China maintains its trade barriers against U.S. exports, then this makes Americans poorer. But that is completely irrelevant to the case for the U.S. reducing *its* trade barriers against Chinese (and other) imports. If the U.S. enacted its own free trade policies, Americans would become much richer (per capita), and so would other people around the world (per capita), because they would now have more trading opportunities.[7] This statement is true whether or not other governments followed suit and lifted their own trade restrictions. Unilateral U.S. removal of its own trade barriers would probably provide strong diplomatic pressure for other countries to follow suit, but if this occurred it would simply be gravy for Americans. Having other countries "return the favor" is not needed in the argument for free trade, because lowering American trade barriers is not really a "favor" at all. Yes, it makes foreigners better off, but it makes Americans better off too.

Now that we've outlined the general case for free trade, let's examine the typical ways that governments restrict the flow of goods across borders.

Tariffs

A **tariff** (or a **duty**) is a tax that the government places on foreign imports. Although the government might levy a tariff for the simple purpose of raising more revenue, usually the official justification for a new tariff (or a hike

[7]We have to add the qualifier "(per capita)" because in theory, we can imagine particular individuals being hurt by the removal of trade barriers. We know that if China pursued a free trade policy, total Chinese production and consumption would rise, meaning that *on average* people in China would benefit from the move. But if there were particular producers who benefited from the trade barriers and were put out of business by foreign imports, their individual losses as producers could conceivably be larger than their gains as consumers when they had far more options (and lower prices) in the stores. We stress this point mainly so that you better understand the economic case for free trade. In the real world, a complete move to free trade—rather than removing individual barriers one at a time—would probably make just about everyone better off, especially in the long run.

in an existing tariff) is that it will help domestic producers of the imported good. It is this latter claim—that a tariff on foreign imports helps workers in the protected industry at home—that we will examine in this section.

To make the analysis easier, let's work with a concrete example involving the U.S. and Japan, using unrealistic but nice round numbers. Suppose that initially there is completely free trade between the two countries, and that the equilibrium market price is $10,000 for a no-frills sedan. At that price, American manufacturers can profitably produce some vehicles, but not enough to satisfy the demands of American consumers. The remaining cars are supplied by Japanese producers, so that American consumers can buy exactly as many cars at a price of $10,000 as they want.

U.S. car producers send their lobbyists to Washington. They explain that labor costs are lower in Japan, that the Japanese government provides unfair subsidies to their car companies, etc. etc., and that Washington needs to "level the playing field." If only the federal government would impose a 10% duty on Japanese imports, American producers could profitably expand their operations and provide more jobs for U.S. workers!

The politicians are only too happy to oblige, and they slap a 10% tariff on any Japanese cars entering the U.S. market. This means that if a U.S. consumer wants to buy a Japanese car, he now must pay a total of $11,000 out of pocket: $10,000 goes to the Japanese car manufacturer (as before),[8] and the other $1,000 goes to Washington in the form of tariff revenue. Because U.S. consumers are now being forced to pay $11,000 for Japanese sedans,

[8]A technical note: From the Japanese producers' point of view, American demand for their cars has dropped. That is, at the same (Japanese) price of $10,000 per car, suddenly Americans don't want to buy as many Japanese cars as they did the day before the tariff was erected. To keep things simple, we are assuming that this drop in U.S. demand for imported vehicles doesn't lower the equilibrium price of $10,000 for Japanese cars in the world market. If you go on to study more advanced economics, you will learn that this subtlety can give rise to the theoretical possibility of there being an "optimal tariff" in which a large country such as the U.S. could conceivably gain (while hurting the rest of the world) through the strategic use of low tariffs. In practice this is a slippery argument, if for no other reason than that politicians couldn't be trusted to stick to the "optimal" tariff structure. But if you are going on in economics, you should be aware of this technicality.

it means U.S. producers can raise their own prices too. And lo and behold, the lobbyists were right! At the higher price of $11,000, U.S. producers move along their supply curve, and manufacture more cars built in American plants by American workers. Employment goes up in Detroit and other cities with U.S. car factories, just as the lobbyists predicted. So is the new tariff an economic success?

Most economists would say no. It's true that workers and shareholders in the U.S. car industry benefit from the new tariff, but it's *also* true that U.S. car consumers are hurt by it. After all, Americans who wanted to buy a car could get one for $10,000 before, but now they have to pay $11,000—they are clearly worse off because of this change. Even consumers who faithfully "buy American" are hurt, because American car prices have gone up by $1,000 as well. Under fairly general assumptions, it's easy to show that the benefits to the car producers are more than offset by the losses to the car consumers.[9] On net, therefore, the tariff makes Americans poorer.

In an introductory book such as this, we won't dot every *i* and cross every *t* in the argument. Instead we'll try three intuitive approaches to demonstrate that a new tariff makes the country poorer on average.

Tariffs Are Taxes on Domestic Citizens

Perhaps the most obvious way to realize that tariffs make a country poorer is to realize that *tariffs are taxes on domestic citizens*, not on foreign producers. In our numerical example, it's actually misleading to say, "The U.S. government imposes a tax on Japanese car producers," because the tax is *really* applied to *American car consumers*. Any revenue that the U.S. government collects from the new tariff has come out of the wallets of Americans.[10]

---

[9]The new tariff also hurts some *other* American producers, as we'll see in the text.

[10]In practice, if the new tariff caused the (pre-tax) market price of Japanese cars to fall, then in a sense the payment of tariff revenues would be shared among American consumers and Japanese producers, because the out-of-pocket price of an import to Americans wouldn't rise by the full tariff charge per car. Even

Everything we said about the distorting effects of sales taxes in Lesson 18 applies here, because a tariff is simply a sales tax on goods that happen to be produced abroad. The original market price of $10,000 per car was a signal guiding consumers and producers as to the most efficient way to use resources. The tariff interferes with that signal, and makes Americans act as if the rest of the world is less capable of producing cars than it really is. Those who advocate tariff barriers to "protect" American industry are really saying that raising taxes on Americans is the path to prosperity.

A Tariff Doesn't Increase Employment, It Just Rearranges It

Perhaps the single biggest mistake in the protectionist approach is to believe that a new tariff increases *total* employment. But this belief is wrong, because a new tariff doesn't suddenly create new workers out of thin air. In our example, if the new tariff allows the U.S. auto industry to expand output and hire more workers, other U.S. industries necessarily must *shrink* their output and produce it with *fewer* workers.[11]

People who think tariffs are a good way to boost the economy usually focus narrowly on the jobs that are "created" in the protected sector, and then further take into account all the extra jobs that are "created" when those new workers spend their paychecks at the mall, restaurants, and so forth. And it is undeniable in our example that not only U.S. employment at auto factories, but also at nearby businesses, would increase after the new tariff is erected.

However, what this shortsighted analysis overlooks is that jobs would be *destroyed* in other sectors spread around the country. For one thing, anyone

---

here, though, it's worth stressing that it is U.S. consumers who actually spend the money collected by the tariff.

[11]The one possible exception to this rule is that the unemployment rate could drop. In other words, it's possible for one industry to expand, while others maintain their original levels of employment, if the newly hired workers come from the ranks of the unemployed (or come from sectors which then replenish the lost workers from the ranks of the unemployed). In Lesson 23 we'll explore the business cycle and see that this complication doesn't change the conclusions in the text above.

who buys a new car is out an additional $1,000 compared to the pre-tariff situation. Such a car buyer now has that much less money to spend on restaurants, movie theaters, etc. in her neighborhood, and so the merchants in her area suffer.

The clever protectionist might point out that we are here focusing on the small potatoes, because the (allegedly) *big* bonanza to U.S. industry comes from switching so much business to domestic producers and away from Japanese producers. In other words, rather than focusing on the $1,000 increase in car prices which is a wash—U.S. car consumers are "down" $1,000 per car, whereas U.S. car producers are "up" the same amount[12]—we should be focusing on the fact that for every additional U.S. car produced by American workers, that's $10,000 being kept "in the country" rather than being "sent to Japan." So surely *this* effect is the relevant one, and shows how the country as a whole benefits from the new tariff, right?

Actually no. The analysis of our clever protectionist is still overlooking one enormous effect of the tariff: By penalizing U.S. imports, the tariff simultaneously penalizes U.S. *exports*. Specifically, for every car that U.S. consumers buy from Detroit rather than from Japan, it means Japanese citizens now have $10,000 less to spend on goods made in America. Thus the extra business of U.S. car producers is offset by the drop in sales among American producers of wheat, software, and other exports.

A crucial principle to remember is that *a country ultimately pays for its imports with its exports.* Just as an individual household couldn't (in the long run) continue to buy goods and services from the outside world without *producing* something in return, by the same token an entire country couldn't continue to import cars, electronic goods, sweaters, and all sorts of other goodies from foreigners, unless that country shipped them

---

[12]What about the $1,000 tariff payments sent to the U.S. government for every Japanese car that Americans still decide to purchase? Well, if the government *spends* that money, then this constitutes an additional distortion to the pure-market outcome, for the reasons outlined in Lesson 18. The best case for the protectionist is to assume that the government uses the tariff revenue to reduce other taxes on Americans. In the text we are ignoring this complication because we want to focus on the *other* distortions caused by the new tariff.

goods and services in return.[13] To put it bluntly: The protectionist implicitly assumes that the Japanese car producers are idiots, who are willing to bust their buns and use up scarce resources making beautiful new cars for Americans, all in exchange for green pieces of paper featuring pictures of U.S. presidents.

Before leaving this section, we should emphasize an important point: Focusing on dollar amounts can be misleading, because ultimately it is real goods and services that constitute the standard of living citizens enjoy. In the paragraphs above we "followed the money" just to show what the standard protectionist arguments overlook, and the producers they usually forget. In reality, the significance of a tariff isn't the effect it has on dollar bills—the number of dollar bills isn't changed by a tariff law, and it's ultimately not green pieces of paper that make Americans rich or poor. No, what makes Americans richer or poorer is *how much they can produce* with their own labor and other resources, and *how much they can consume* by either purchasing output from domestic producers or by trading surplus production with foreigners.

A new tariff diverts U.S. labor and other resources out of those industries in which they have the comparative advantage, and into industries in which they do not. It hinders the benefits of specialization among nations. Just as mutually beneficial trades make both parties better off, so too does free trade make all participating nations better off. When a government interferes with this pure-market outcome through the imposition of a new tariff, it hurts not only foreign countries but also the domestic population.

---

[13]We have added the qualifier "in the long run" because an individual household could run up its debt by consuming more than it produces, at least for a while. By the same token, a country as a whole can run a net trade deficit if foreigners are willing to invest in its financial assets (such as buying stocks or bonds from corporations in the country running the trade deficit). But even here, what is really happening is that the country running the trade deficit is effectively borrowing against its future production.

If Tariff Barriers Are Good, Are Naval Blockades Great?

Perhaps the simplest argument to demonstrate the absurdity of tariff barriers was devised by Henry George, who observed that in peacetime nations impose tariffs on themselves in order to keep out foreign goods, while in wartime nations impose naval blockades on other countries in order to prevent them from receiving foreign goods. If the protectionist arguments were correct, wouldn't naval blockades make the enemy country prosper?

Import Quotas

An **import quota** is another popular form of government interference with international trade. In this arrangement, the government doesn't directly interfere with the price of the imported good, but instead sets a limit on how many units can be imported.

For example, rather than imposing a 10% tariff on Japanese cars, while leaving the ultimate determination of total imports up to the (distorted) market, the U.S. government instead could impose a 100,000 vehicle quota. Japanese producers would be allowed to sell 100,000 cars in the U.S. market, and they would receive the (distorted) market price without any of these expenditures flowing into the coffers of the U.S. government. But after the quota had been reached, it would be illegal for any more Japanese cars to cross into the United States for sale.

The primary effects of an import quota are the same as those of a tariff. If U.S. legislators knew in advance how many Japanese vehicles Americans would import after they imposed a 10% tariff, then the legislators could in principle achieve roughly the same outcome on the U.S. economy by simply setting an import quota equal to that number of vehicles. In that case, the major economic effects would be roughly the same, and our analysis in the previous section would apply.

However, in practice import quotas are probably even more dangerous than tariffs, because they seem to burden foreign producers more than domestic citizens, and because it is not as obvious how much damage they cause relative to the pure market outcome. For these reasons, politicians may be more likely to impose an incredibly onerous import quota, rather than an equivalent tariff.

To see this possibility, consider: Under a tariff rate of 50%, it is quite visible how much the government is penalizing foreign producers and rewarding (particular) U.S. producers. People can see what the original import price is, and then realize they are paying 50% more straight to the U.S. government. But if the government simply imposes an import quota, it is not as easy to see how much the distorted pattern of production differs from the pure-market outcome, especially as time passes and conditions change. If the foreign producers came up with innovations that allowed them to slash prices, for example, then American consumers would still benefit if there were a tariff in place, because the post-tariff price would fall. But with a rigid import quota, American consumers would not benefit nearly as much from cost-cutting foreign innovations.

Lesson Recap . . .

- Mercantilism is an economic philosophy that views the accumulation of money as the path to national prosperity. Mercantilism seeks to encourage exports and restrict imports in order to keep money within the country and to provide employment for domestic industry.

- The case for free trade among countries is simply an application of the general case for free markets. A group of people can only benefit when they are given more options. Free trade doesn't *force* people to import goods from foreign producers, it merely removes obstacles. It makes perfect sense for individuals to specialize in particular occupations and trade surplus production with each other, and by the same token it makes perfect sense for different regions of the world to specialize in certain activities and trade surplus output with each other.

- Tariffs and quotas are artificial government restrictions on foreign imports. Contrary to the claims of their supporters, tariffs and quotas make the people in a country poorer, on average. (A tariff or quota might benefit particular individuals in a country, but their gains are smaller than the harms imposed on everyone else.) In the long run, tariffs and quotas don't "create jobs," they simply rearrange workers from more efficient into less efficient industries.

NEW TERMS

Mercantilism: The economic doctrine that views the accumulation of wealth as the path to national prosperity. It encourages exports and discourages imports.

Exports: Goods (and services) that the people of a country sell to foreigners.

Imports: Goods (and services) that the people of a country buy from foreigners.

Trade surplus: The amount by which exports exceed imports, measured in money.

Trade deficit: The amount by which imports exceed imports, measured in money.

Beggar-thy-neighbor policies: Policies (usually involving currencies and trade restrictions) that make other countries poorer, in the attempt to make one's own country richer.

Zero-sum game: A situation in which the gain of one person (or country) corresponds to an equal loss of another person (or country). In a zero-sum game, mutually advantageous, win-win outcomes are not possible. There are winners and losers.

Free trade: An environment in which governments do not impose artificial restrictions on the flow of goods and services between their citizens and foreigners.

Protectionism: The philosophy that uses government trade restrictions in an attempt to help workers within the home country. The rationale is that by restricting foreign imports, the government will encourage consumers to "buy local," providing employment for local workers.

Tariff (duty): A tax levied on foreign imports.

Import quota: A maximum limit on the amount of a particular good that can be imported during a certain time period.

STUDY QUESTIONS

1. *Could every government successfully implement mercantilist policies?

2. What historical role did Adam Smith play with respect to mercantilism?

3. Explain the meaning (not the cause) of this statement: "The U.S. ran a trade deficit with Japan last year."

4. Explain: "The economic case for free trade is unilateral."

5. Explain: "A tariff doesn't increase employment, it just rearranges it."

LESSON 20

The Economics of Drug Prohibition

In this lesson you will learn:

- The definition of *drug prohibition*.
- Why drug prohibition fosters corruption and gang violence.
- Why drug prohibition reduces product safety.

Drug Prohibition

Drug prohibition refers to the severe penalties that governments often impose on the consumption and especially the production and sale of certain drugs. Drug prohibition is qualitatively different from U.S. state and local government's current use of **sin taxes**—very high sales taxes—to discourage people from buying liquor and cigarettes. In the modern American regime of drug prohibition, the possession and especially commercial distribution of drugs such as cocaine and heroin are outright crimes, punishable not only by huge fines but also lengthy prison terms.

As the title states clearly, in this lesson we are going to examine the *economics* of drug prohibition. Using the tools we have developed in this book, we will be able to understand why drug prohibition leads to a familiar pattern of results. In contrast, someone ignorant of economics would be at a loss to explain the pattern. Instead the results of drug prohibition would appear as random occurrences, having nothing to do with the government policies.

We should stress at the outset that economic analysis *by itself* cannot judge whether drug prohibition is a good or a bad policy. Ultimately, citizens and policy makers must incorporate their value judgments before deciding whether it is good or bad for the government to, say, punish convicted cocaine dealers with 25-year prison sentences. However, in order for citizens and policy makers to make *informed* decisions, they must understand the full consequences of drug prohibition.

When it comes to illicit drugs, the question is *not*: "Would it be better to live in a society with or without cocaine?" That particular question is not relevant, because the government is powerless to stamp out cocaine use completely. Rather, the crucial question is this: "Would it be better to live in a society with or without extreme penalties for cocaine use?" In order to imagine what society would be like in one condition versus the other, it is important to learn what economic analysis says about the effects of drug prohibition. Remember that there is a difference between saying something is *immoral* versus saying it should be *illegal*. If someone argues that cheating on one's wife shouldn't carry a jail term, that person isn't thereby condoning adultery.

One final caveat before we plunge into the analysis: In the rest of this lesson we will be focusing on the (usually neglected) negative consequences of drug prohibition. We are doing this because the *positive* consequences of drug prohibition are obvious and visible: Many people believe that the use of certain drugs is personally and socially destructive, and so they conclude that government policies which strongly discourage this behavior are (other things being equal) beneficial. The analysis below is designed to show the ways in which other things are *not* equal when the government engages in drug prohibition. The benefits of reduced and/or stigmatized drug use must be contrasted with the harms of police corruption, gang warfare, and deaths from overdoses—things which most people would *also* deem personally and socially destructive.[1]

---

[1]As with our analysis of other types of government intervention, in this lesson we are interested in *pragmatic* arguments by looking at the *consequences* of drug prohibition. We ignore arguments (for or against) based on a specific code of morality, or a view of property rights and the proper scope of government action.

Drug Prohibition Corrupts Government Officials

In this context, **corruption** refers to government officials who do not execute their legal duties because they are secretly being paid by members of the drug trade whom they are supposedly combating. Most Americans are aware of the widespread corruption in the Mexican and Colombian governments, but many Americans would be shocked to learn that there is a (less severe) problem of corruption plaguing U.S. courts and police departments.

The straightforward explanation for the connection between drug prohibition and corruption is that prohibition leads to huge *monetary* profits in the drug industry, giving drug producers the ability (and of course the motive) to pay enormous bribes to government officials. Simple economic analysis will illustrate why.

Typically, governments try to stamp out the drug trade by inflicting much heavier penalties on suppliers rather than consumers. This emphasis is due to two main reasons: (1) If the goal is to limit total drug consumption, it is a better use of limited police resources to knock out one major supplier rather than the potentially thousands of customers who rely on him, and (2) the public doesn't mind harsh penalties on professional drug dealers, but would balk at draconian punishments of casual consumers. These two factors explain why governments typically enact much higher penalties for those who are obviously drug *dealers*, as opposed to those who are caught with only a smaller quantity of the contraband, intended for personal use.

In addition to the higher official penalties on drug producers versus consumers, we must also consider that the *likelihood of actually being arrested* is much higher for a professional drug dealer, than for a casual customer.[2] After all, the professional drug dealer—especially the larger the operation—must deal with many other members of his industry, be they

---

These viewpoints are definitely important, but they lie outside the scope of a textbook on basic economics.

[2]We should clarify, the likelihood of a professional drug dealer being arrested is much higher than for one of his customers *were it not for bribes ("protection money") regularly paid to the police*. We are trying to understand how drug prohibition alters the original market outcome, and then we will see the scope for corruption.

Police Corruption: It's Not Just a Problem for Mexico

The following excerpts from a 2008 news article about an FBI sting in the Chicago area illustrate the connection between drug enforcement and police corruption:

> Seventeen people—including 15 south suburban police officers—have been charged in a federal probe of allegations that officers provided armed security for large-scale drug deals. The officers apparently thought they were protecting high-rolling drug dealers. It turned out they were actually FBI agents.
>
> All 17 were charged Tuesday with conspiracy to possess and distribute kilogram quantities of cocaine and/or heroin in eight separate criminal complaints unsealed following arrests early Tuesday, according to a release from the U.S. Attorney's office.
>
> Ten sheriff's correctional officers—sworn personnel that worked the jails and lockups—have been charged with criminal conspiracy. The Feds say the sheriff's officers along with four police officers from Harvey and one Chicago cop were caught in an FBI sting.
>
> "An undercover FBI agent was able to deal with not one, not two, but 15 different law enforcement officers who sold out their badge in a greed [sic] for money to help drug dealers do their business," said U.S. Attorney Patrick Fitzgerald.
>
> Prosecutors say the officers took up to $4,000 in payoffs to act as lookouts and protection when what they thought were big drug deals were going down.
>
> Seven of the eight complaints were supported by a single, 61-page FBI affidavit that outlines an undercover investigation that involved such activity as police officers protecting a high-stakes poker game, protecting transportation of large amounts of cash and two law officers actually selling powder cocaine, in addition to the routine activity of providing security for purported narcotics trasactions, the release said.

According to a release, a six-passenger, twin propeller engine aircraft flew on May 13 into west suburban DuPage Airport where three men awaited its arrival. Two of them . . . accompanied someone whom they believed brokered large-scale drug transactions but, in fact, was an undercover FBI agent, the release said. They boarded the aircraft, operated by two other undercover agents, and began counting packages of what was purported to be at least 80 kilograms of cocaine inside four duffel bags.

[The two Cook County correctional officers] and the undercover agent removed the duffels from the plane and took them through the airport lobby to the trunk of the agent's car in the parking lot, the affidavit alleges. [The two officers], in a separate car, followed the agent to a nearby parking lot, where the agent parked and got into the officers' vehicle. Together, the trio watched as yet another undercover agent arrived, removed the duffels and drove away. The FBI agent posing as the drug broker then paid [the officers] $4,000 each—allegedly their most profitable payday in the corrupt relationship they began with the undercover agent at least a year earlier.

Of the 17 defendants, 10 are Cook County Sheriff's correctional officers, four are Harvey police officers and one is a Chicago police officer. They allegedly accepted between $400 and $4,000 each on one or more occasions to serve as lookouts and be ready to intervene if real police or rival drug dealers attempted to interfere with transfers of cocaine and heroin, according to the affidavit.

"Ideally, it should be hard to find one corrupt police officer and it should never be easy to find 15 who allegedly used their guns and badges to protect people they believed were dealing drugs instead of arresting them," U.S. Atty. Patrick Fitzgerald said in the release. "And the involvement of some in off-loading and delivering what they thought were large shipments of drugs flown in by plane is particularly shocking."

Source: CBS 2, "15 Cops Charged in FBI Sting, Drug Dealing Probe," December 2, 2008 at: http://cbs2chicago.com/local/harvey.police.raid.2.877798.html.

higher-level suppliers or lower-level retailers. For example, one member of the drug trade might run an operation where he buys cocaine from Colombian "wholesalers," hires Mexican truck drivers to smuggle it across the U.S. border, and then sells fractions of what gets through to the heads of regional drug gangs in California. If Colombian, Mexican, or U.S. anti-drug forces should penetrate any portion of this extensive operation, the particular dealer would be vulnerable to arrest. His entire workday involves the habitual violation of anti-drug laws. In contrast, the casual customer is really only at risk when he needs to purchase more product, and he only interacts with other "small fish" such as a neighborhood dealer. There is much less chance of his life being ruined by government punishment for his involvement in the drug industry.

Because of these disparities in the effective penalties facing drug producers versus consumers, the supply of illegal drugs falls much more than the demand, relative to an initially unregulated market. This pushes up the new equilibrium price of illegal drugs, meaning that the monetary "markup"—the difference between the monetary expenses to produce the product, versus the actual payment that the end users give in exchange—becomes quite high. The following diagram illustrates the hypothetical unregulated, versus prohibited, market for cocaine.

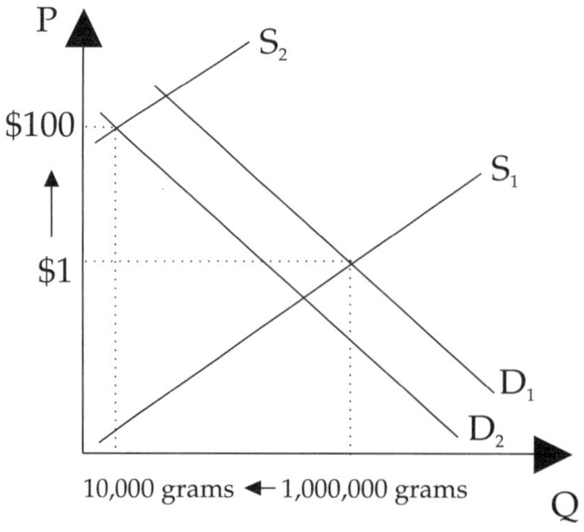

Market for Cocaine

In the previous diagram, we see that the unregulated market price of cocaine is initially $1 per gram. At that price, producers want to sell 1 million grams of cocaine, and consumers want to buy 1 million grams.

After the imposition of strict drug laws, the supply and demand curves for cocaine both shift to the left. That is, for a given dollar-price of a gram of cocaine, producers are willing to offer much less than before (since they now risk going to jail), *and* consumers are not willing to buy as many grams either. However, the quantitative shift is much greater on the supply side than the demand side. That is why the new (prohibition) equilibrium has a market price of $100 per gram, where producers want to supply 10,000 grams and consumers want to buy the same amount.

A crucial point is that the monetary *profit* will remain high, even years after the drug prohibition has gone into effect. The supply curve in the diagram above shifted to the left because of the *non-monetary* risks associated with remaining in the cocaine business. The higher price paid by customers will therefore not translate into higher prices paid to the farmers in Colombia who harvest coca. No, the huge markup must remain, in order to make it worthwhile (in the eyes of some) to remain cocaine producers even in the face of significant penalties.

In the new equilibrium, it's not true to say that "it's now more attractive than before to become a cocaine dealer." People choose occupations based on many factors, only one of which is how much money they will typically earn. It's more accurate to say that because of the new government penalties (and presumably the corresponding social stigma), the "salaries" of drug dealers had to skyrocket in order to compensate for the new downsides of the profession. This principle is not unique to illegal drugs—coal miners and taxi drivers (who are often robbed) receive an implicit form of **hazard pay** as well. The difference is that with illegal drug dealers, the hazard comes not from nature or muggers, but the government judicial system.

The Significance of "Victimless Crimes"

It is important to note that the scope for government corruption due to drug prohibition is much larger than for more traditional crimes such as homicide and robbery. Indeed in the United States, to talk of a "dirty cop" is almost synonymous with one who takes drug money; no one would think that the term might refer to a police officer who is regularly paid off by contract hit men so that they can murder with impunity 6 days a week. Yet criminal gangs *do* routinely pay off police and other government officials in order to run major drug operations with official (though of course discreet) protection.

To understand this disparity, we need to reflect on the common remark that illegal drug transactions are "victimless crimes." Naturally the supporters of drug laws would reject this phrase as an inaccurate cliché, since children are certainly victims if their father loses his job and becomes abusive due to addiction. But there *is* a definite sense in which the production and consumption of drugs is qualitatively less victimizing than traditional crimes such as homicide, rape, and robbery. The difference is that in a "victimless crime"—which in the United States includes not only drug transactions but activities such as gambling and prostitution—*all parties to the transaction are voluntary participants*. This feature has two major implications, both of which help explain the connection between drug prohibition and corruption.

First, there is the simple fact that police officers, judges, and other government officials won't feel as bad "looking the other way" for someone who supplies desired products to willingly paying customers, as they would for ignoring their official responsibilities to prevent nonconsensual crimes against person or property.

Second, the drug trade is after all a *business*. There are many millions of people in the United States who willingly spend their money on illegal drugs on a regular basis. According to the Office of National Drug Control Policy, a 2007 survey showed 6% of young adults reported using cocaine within the previous year, and 2% had used cocaine within the past *month*.[3] There is quite simply much more money in the drug business, than in the hit man or even bank robbery "businesses." Because it is victimless in the

[3]See http://www.whitehousedrugpolicy.gov/drugfact/cocaine/cocaineff.html#extentofuse. Regarding marijuana, a survey conducted between 2006 and 2007 found that more than 10% of the U.S. respondents reported using the drug within the last year. See http://economix.blogs.nytimes.com/2009/08/11/drug-use-across-the-united-states-or-rhode-island-needs-more-rehab/.

important sense defined above, the drug trade can be much more easily kept quiet than crimes with explicit victims who would call the police—and might get someone who *wasn't* on the criminals' payroll—or, failing that, could go to the media and complain.

We mention these differences to deal with a standard defense of drug prohibition which says, "Well if we should legalize drugs because of corruption, why not legalize murder too?" As we have shown above, the scope for corruption due to drug prohibition is far larger than for traditional crimes, and the difference stems from the "victimless" nature of drug crimes. This difference by itself doesn't prove that drugs should be legalized, but it *does* show a problem of drug prohibition that is not nearly as rampant with other crimes.

Corruption as Cause and Consequence

Most people abhor systemic government corruption because it breaks down traditional respect for the law and makes citizens more likely to commit crime. However in the context of drug prohibition there is a much more specific dynamic at work. Government corruption is both a consequence *and* a cause of illegal drug trafficking.

Here's how the feedback cycle works: We have already seen that drug prohibition typically raises the market price of (newly illegal) drugs, because the supply curve shifts left far more than the demand curve. This skyrocketing price allows entrepreneurs to earn millions of dollars annually, giving them the wherewithal to bribe government officials who otherwise could arrest them. This is the sense in which corruption is a consequence of illegal drug trafficking.

However, it's also true that corruption is a necessary component of illegal drug trafficking, and in that sense is a cause of it. In truly oppressive regimes—such as Afghanistan under Taliban rule—the drug trade can be snuffed out by the government. If the penalties were high enough *and consistently enforced,* then supply and demand could be reduced so much that the new equilibrium quantity of, say, cocaine production and consumption would be *zero*. Yet in practice this rarely happens, because the government *itself* can't police its own employees, when they might be offered literally hundreds of thousands of dollars per year to shirk their official duties.

Widespread corruption allows drug criminals to escape the huge official punishments that the law books require, and thus the supply curve for illegal drugs does not shift as much as it would in the absence of corruption. To put it succinctly, under drug prohibition in relatively free societies, the supply curve shifts left until the new market-clearing price is high enough for the remaining producers to afford adding narcotics officers and judges to their payrolls.

Drug Prohibition Fosters Violence

Everyone knows that the illegal drug trade is plagued by excessive violence, often in the form of gang warfare. Worse still, innocent bystanders are often killed as collateral damage from turf battles between rival drug dealers. The casual observer might conclude that drugs such as cocaine and heroin are intrinsically bad, and go hand-in-hand with violence. Yet this explanation is wrong. Both economic theory and American history demonstrate that drug *prohibition* causes violence, not drugs per se.

Alcohol Prohibition in the United States

The historical evidence is clear enough in the case of alcohol Prohibition. From 1920 to 1933, under the Eighteenth Amendment to the Constitution,[4] the sale, manufacture, and transportation of alcohol (for purposes of consumption) was illegal in the United States. Yet despite the official illegality, alcohol was still produced and distributed by **bootleggers**, and drinkers could still gather socially at **speakeasies**.

Although Prohibition didn't eliminate alcohol use, it *did* place the industry under the control of organized crime. During the Prohibition period—often called the "Noble Experiment"—mobsters such as Al Capone (based in Chicago) derived significant revenues from the illicit alcohol trade,

---

[4]The Eighteenth Amendment was actually ratified in 1919, but alcohol Prohibition did not take effect until 1920.

money that they used to bribe government officials and hire "soldiers" and other henchmen for their criminal networks.

For our purposes, the important feature of alcohol Prohibition was that the alcohol trade could be as violent as the heroin or cocaine trade is today. The infamous St. Valentine's Day Massacre was a 1929 gangland hit in which Al Capone arranged for the murder of seven members of rival Bugs Moran's operation. Historians cite various motivations for the slayings, but all agree that Capone and Moran were enemies due in part to rivalry in the bootleg market.

If you have seen movies or read true crime accounts dealing with Prohibition-era gangsters, these historical events are familiar and do not cause any puzzlement. Yet on the surface it should be shocking that rival entrepreneurs would try to kill each other over *alcohol*. Can you imagine turning on the television tomorrow and learning that the distributors of Budweiser had ordered a hit on the distributors of Heineken? That would be inconceivable.

Alcohol is no longer controlled by organized criminals, but instead by legitimate businessmen and women. Now that alcohol is legal, its producers try to gain market share by improving the product quality or cutting its price. It wouldn't even occur to them to use violence to gain more customers.

On the other hand, what activities *do* we see in the hands of criminal organizations? They include drugs such as heroin and cocaine, prostitution, gambling, and **loan sharking**.[5] In short, all areas that are still (unlike alcohol since the repeal of Prohibition) either prohibited or heavily regulated by the government.

The historical episode of alcohol Prohibition provides very compelling evidence that the violence we currently associate with illegal drugs is due to government's prohibition, not to the nature of the products themselves. In the remainder of this section we'll explain this undeniable connection using economic reasoning.

---

[5]A *loan shark* refers to someone who makes short-term loans at very high interest rates (which may violate **usury laws**) and popularly resorts to physical punishments in order to ensure repayment.

Drug Prohibition Raises the Marginal Benefits of Violence

We have already seen how prohibition raises the monetary earnings of drug dealers. Among its other consequences, this increase in price translates into a much greater benefit from boosting sales and controlling a greater share of the retail market.

In a regular, legal market, competition tends to drive down the price until the monetary returns are comparable to that of other projects. Because there is usually such a small "markup" from the production expenses compared to the retail price, most legitimate business owners don't see significant increases in their monetary profits by "stealing" a few customers away from their competitors.

In contrast, a cocaine dealer sees an enormous increase in his total monetary earnings if he can add a handful of regular users to his customer base. This is because the expenses in his business are largely **fixed**, meaning they are the same whether he sells 10 grams of cocaine per day or 100 grams. And note that this feature is greatly amplified by prohibition itself, because when cocaine distribution is illegal, the primary "business expenses" are mental ones, namely the risks of going to prison or being killed by a rival dealer.

Because it makes individual customers so much more lucrative, drug prohibition increases the benefits (on the margin) from using violence to intimidate or actually kill competitors. This is one of the major explanations for why prohibited industries tend to be rife with violence, whereas legitimate businesspeople almost never resort to violence as a means of competing.

In a typical treatment of the economics of drug prohibition, the writer will often explain that producers in prohibited industries cannot rely on police protection and contract enforcement, and so must resort to private violence to protect their merchandise. Explanations of this sort often cast the drug industry as one suffering from "government neglect," and into this anarchy violent gangsters flow.

Such explanations have things backward. There are plenty of commercial relations in everyday life that are not protected by government courts. Using eBay, Amazon, and other mechanisms, Americans spend billions of dollars per year buying items—often of high value—from perfect strangers who might live across the country. In principle someone could file a lawsuit in the event of fraud, but in practice these transactions are largely "self-policing" through the private-sector hosts and the sometimes elaborate system of reputation that they develop.[6]

It is completely inverted to view prohibited industries as suffering from a lack of police and judicial oversight. On the contrary, it is precisely these industries that receive the *most* government attention! It is simply not true that the police ignore drug dealers, even in inner city projects. If it *were* true, then the market price of drugs in these areas would fall to (nearly) the monetary production costs, and young teenagers would find being a drug dealer to be no more lucrative than becoming a paper boy. The police are not viewed as friendly servants of the public in certain drug-ridden neighborhoods, but they definitely enforce drug laws, if only sporadically—that's why the market price stays high, allowing drug dealers to buy fancy cars and expensive jewelry.

It is true that *given* the prevalence of violent drug dealers, anyone with the temerity to enter the industry and try to earn significant amounts of money must *himself* become heavily armed and gain a reputation for ruthlessness, because he can't look to the police for protection. But again, this observation is surely only incidental. It doesn't explain why the drug industry is *rife with violence in the first place.* The average dry cleaner doesn't worry about a rival from across town spraying his shop with machine gun

---

[6]Indeed, if drug dealers could conduct major transactions using electronic payments routed through a universally respected third party, the number of violent drug deals "gone bad" would plummet. Rather than bringing suitcases of cash (along with heavily armed bodyguards) to parking garages in the dead of night, a cocaine retailer could deposit $1 million with a reputable financial institution, which would agree to transfer the funds to a Colombian wholesaler once the retailer had received his goods. (The process could unfold in stages if the Colombians wanted to make sure *they* weren't double-crossed.) The reason drug dealers currently can't operate in this fashion *isn't* that they fear a bank will steal their money and then the drug dealers won't be able to call the police. The first time that happened, nobody—even people unconnected with the drug trade—would use that bank again. In reality drug dealers can't use the simple mechanism we've described because of the risk that the *government* would seize their funds as "drug money." So we see that it is not government neglect, but government enforcement of drug laws, that makes violence more appealing in the drug trade.

fire, and his confidence in this regard is *not* simply that he could call government detectives who would find and punish the drive-by shooters after the fact.

No, the real reason that dry cleaners don't compete using violence is that *it wouldn't be worth it*. In contrast, drug prohibition makes it "worth it" for cocaine producers to kill each other.

Drug Prohibition Lowers the Marginal Costs of Violence

Another aspect to the connection between violence and drug prohibition is that on the margin, prohibition lowers the cost of an individual violent act. Consider this: Part of the reason that a major Budweiser distributor wouldn't take out a contract on the life of his Heineken rival is that such a move would completely transform his own life. As a legitimate businessman, he could travel in respectable social circles, and assuming he had paid his taxes properly, he would be under no threat of going to jail for the rest of his life. In this situation, committing the heinous crime of paying to have someone murdered would be incredibly risky.

In contrast, the head of a cocaine distribution network has *already* committed more than enough crimes to go to jail for life if he should ever fall out of the good graces of the police on his payroll, or become the target of higher-level government officials whom he cannot bribe. Because he must associate with other habitual lawbreakers, he does not worry nearly as much that violent acts will ruin his social standing in respectable circles—he forfeited that option when he decided to become a large-scale drug dealer.

Another important consideration is that the illegal drug dealer must develop a network of relationships with criminals, allowing him to much more easily recruit "soldiers" or arrange for professional hit men to carry out violent attacks on his rivals. In contrast, the legitimate businessperson would probably have no idea how to have someone murdered with little chance of being caught; it's not as if he would trust the top hit when searching Google for "contract killer."

Finally, the nature of the black market makes violence a much more practical option. If cocaine and other drugs could be sold legally, then retail shops could operate safely even in the toughest of neighborhoods using security measures such as bulletproof partitions separating customers from employees. In contrast, with drug prohibition the "employees" of drug operations often operate on the streets, making it less costly for their competitors to attempt to wipe them out.

The Feedback Loop of Violence

As with corruption, there is a dynamic at work in which violence begets violence in the (prohibited) drug trade. By discussing the changing benefits and costs of engaging in violence, we may have made it seem as if the *same people* would sell drugs with or without drug prohibition, and that it was the change in government policy that transformed mild-mannered executives into ruthless crime bosses.

Obviously this is not the real story. In practice what happens is that drug prohibition chases away honest and nonviolent people from the industry. As more and more of them leave, the supply of (illegal) drugs shrinks further and further, driving up the price. Yet this creates an opportunity for new entrepreneurs to enter the market. They are not necessarily the best businessmen, conventionally defined; they probably couldn't compete in a normal market and rise to the top. Yet what they *are* good at is outwitting and outmuscling their competitors, and at corrupting government officials. In the prohibited drug industry, these are indispensable skills. People who in other walks of life would have been unemployable suddenly have an opportunity to use their "talents" to earn millions of dollars.

Because the prohibited drug trade attracts violent individuals who think of immediate payoffs and disregard long-term consequences, it should come as no surprise that over many years, prohibition fosters a subculture of gang warfare.

Violence From the Consumer

Thus far we have focused on the violence coming from producers in the drug trade. But it is also worth noting that violence from drug *consumers* will also tend to rise because of prohibition, simply because of the huge price increase. When there are addicts willing to do just about anything to get their next fix, citizens should think twice before recommending government policies that make cocaine up to 1,000 times more expensive than it would otherwise be.

Drug Prohibition Reduces Product Safety

Yet another unintended consequence of drug prohibition is the increase in injury or death from product impurities or consumer mistakes. For example, in 1920—the year alcohol Prohibition was introduced in the United States—the national death toll from liquor poisoning was 1,064. Five years later, deaths from liquor poisoning had quadrupled to 4,154. Such results led Will Rogers to quip that "governments used to murder by the bullet only. Now it's by the quart."[7]

The economic explanation for this pattern is straightforward. Under prohibition, relative amateurs make the product, often in their homes (depending on the drug). This makes quality control difficult and reduces product purity. Another problem is that illegal drugs are typically transported in generic packaging. There is nothing like a sealed bottle with "Tylenol" stamped on it to vouch for the safety of the contents and to clearly explain the proper dosage. Because of the difficulty in building up name-brand recognition, the truly safe (illegal) drug producers cannot capture as much of the market as they would without prohibition. Consumers consequently have to take their chances and hope that what they buy won't end up killing them.

Another factor to explain the rise in overdoses is that the consumers of illegal drugs tend to seek out more potent forms to get their fix. In order to minimize the number of illegal purchases, as well as to make concealment easier, a drinker during Prohibition might switch to whiskey rather than beer. This effect also operates—and probably much more heavily—on the production side. For example, someone growing marijuana in his closet only has so much space to work with. He will tend to grow those strains that have the highest potency and hence the highest market price

[7]Death statistics and Will Rogers quotation from Mark Thornton, "Alcohol Prohibition Was a Failure," *Cato Institute Policy Analysis* No. 157, July 17, 1991, at: http://www.cato.org/pubs/pas/pa157.pdf.

per weight. For an analogy, if the government decided to prohibit the sale and consumption of shrimp, the proportion of "jumbo" to normal-sized shrimp would probably increase in the black market, compared to their proportions in a legal market where retailers could store their shrimp in large refrigerators.

Unintended Consequences of Alcohol Prohibition

Irving Fisher was a famous University of Chicago economist who was a very strong *supporter* of alcohol Prohibition. Yet Fisher himself reported: "I am credibly informed that a very conservative reckoning would set the poisonous effects of bootleg beverages as compared with medicinal liquors at ten to one; that is, it requires only a tenth as much bootleg liquor as of pre-prohibition liquor to produce a given degree of drunkenness. The reason, of course, is that bootleg liquor is so concentrated and almost invariably contains other and more deadly poisons than mere ethyl alcohol."

—Irving Fisher, quoted in Mark Thornton, "Alcohol Prohibition Was a Failure," *Cato Institute Policy Analysis* No. 157, July 17, 1991

Lesson Recap . . .

- There is an important distinction between activities that are immoral and those that are illegal. In the case of illicit drugs, it is a coherent position to support legalization while personally condemning drug use. (Someone could think infidelity shouldn't carry a jail term, without thereby condoning adultery.)

- Prohibition raises the market price of the drugs, leading to huge monetary (accounting) profits. Because the illegal drug trade is so lucrative, and because it is a "victimless crime," prohibition leads to police corruption.

- Drug prohibition raises the marginal benefits and reduces the marginal costs to drug dealers of using violence against their competitors. In addition, the incentives of prohibition lead producers and consumers to shift to "harder" drugs, which leads to more overdoses and other health problems.

NEW TERMS

Drug prohibition: Severe penalties that the government imposes on the consumption and especially the production and sale of certain drugs.

Sin taxes: High sales taxes on goods such as cigarettes and liquor that are imposed not merely to raise revenue, but also to encourage people to reduce their purchases of these dubious items.

Corruption: In the context of the drug trade, the failure of police and other government officials to execute their duties, either because they are accepting bribes from drug dealers or because they themselves are trafficking in prohibited substances. In some cases police officers have simply robbed drug dealers (of cash) at gunpoint, knowing that they had no recourse.

Hazard pay: The higher earnings necessary to attract workers into an industry that is more dangerous than others.

Loan sharking: The practice of lending money at high interest rates and using illegal methods to obtain repayment.

Usury laws: Price ceilings on interest rates.

Fixed costs: Monetary expenses that do not increase when a business expands output. For example, a barber shop's monthly water bill will be roughly the same whether it provides 1 haircut or 100 haircuts per day, and so this is a fixed cost.

STUDY QUESTIONS

1. What role does economic science play in the analysis of drug prohibition?

2. In what sense do cocaine dealers (under drug prohibition) earn hazard pay?

3. *What is the connection between corruption and a "victimless crime" such as cocaine distribution?

4. How does drug prohibition raise the marginal benefits of using violence for drug dealers?

5. How might drug prohibition contribute to fatal overdoses?

LESSON 21

Inflation

In this lesson you will learn:

- The difference between *monetary inflation* and *price inflation.*
- How government intervention makes prices rise.
- The harmful effects of price inflation.

Money Inflation versus Price Inflation

People use the term *inflation* all the time, and yet they don't always agree on what the term means. Historically, the term **inflation** referred to an increase in the amount of *money* in the economy.[1] However, over the course of the 20th century the term gradually came to signify the general increase in *prices* of goods and services in the economy. To avoid confusion, in this chapter we will use the more specific terms **monetary inflation** and **price inflation.**

[1]Some economists would say that the term *inflation* refers to an expansion of the amount of money *and credit* in the economy. This is a very technical issue having to do with the fact that banks are legally allowed to grant more loans than they actually have cash in the vault. This arrangement is described as a *fractional reserve banking system*. We will ignore this complication.

The Old Switcheroo

The word 'inflation' originally applied solely to the quantity of money. It meant that the volume of money was *inflated*, blown up, overextended. It is not mere pedantry to insist that the word should be used only in its original meaning. To use it to mean 'a rise in prices' is to deflect attention away from the real cause of inflation and the real cure for it.

—Henry Hazlitt, *What You Should Know About Inflation*
(New York: D. Van Nostrand, 1965), p. 2

The two phenomena—a rising stock of money[2] and a general rise in prices—typically go hand in hand. In fact, after documenting the very tight historical correlations—across the centuries and across the world—the economist Milton Friedman famously summarized his research by declaring, "Inflation is always and everywhere a monetary phenomenon."

What Friedman was saying is that whenever and wherever he had found long-term and rapid price rises in his research, he also found a rapidly increasing stock of money. People often blame price inflation on greedy companies, aggressive labor unions, or a government running up its debt. But what Friedman had established was that historically, lasting price inflation could only happen if the amount of money in the economy grew as well.

In the next section we will go over the basic economics of price inflation, in order to make sense of the correlations Friedman (and others) have found between (a) growth in the money stock and (b) growth in the prices of most

[2]Throughout this chapter, we will use the term **stock of money** rather than the more usual *money supply*, in order to avoid confusion. When people are comparing money to prices, they almost always mean how many *actual units of money* are in the economy; they are *not* referring to the "supply curve of money," a concept that would actually be difficult to even *define* in modern economies where the government has intervened so heavily in the area of money.

goods and services. We should stress that *there is not a precise one-to-one connection between money and prices.* For example, if the amount of money goes up by 10 percent in one year, we can't automatically assume that the prices of all (or even most) goods and services will rise by a comparable amount. We are making the weaker claim that across history and across countries, whenever there has been a period of long-term price rises, there has also been long-term expansions in the amount of money in that economy.

The following chart shows the relationship between money and prices in the United States over a 50-year period:

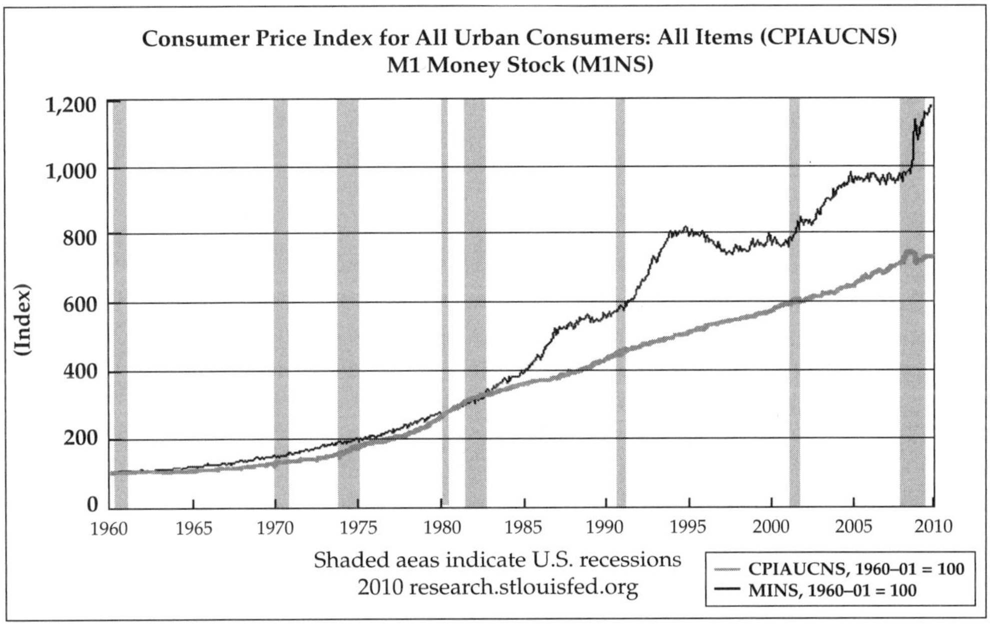

In the chart above, CPI (the gray line) refers to the **Consumer Price Index** which is a standard index used to gauge movements in prices. The CPI takes an average of the prices of typical items in the United States that consumers purchase (such as food, gasoline, etc.) in order to come up with a rough comparison between "the price level" in different years. The black line in the chart is **M1**, which is a particular measurement of the money supply that includes actual paper currency as well as the total amount of checking account balances held by everyone in the United States.

The units of the vertical axis of the chart are an index, set to 100 for the first point on the chart, namely the values of CPI and M1 on January 1960. The chart shows that for the first 24 years (from 1960 through 1984) CPI and M1 grew at similar proportions. The money stock grew a bit more quickly—it had doubled from its initial 1960 value by the end of 1975, whereas prices hadn't doubled until early 1977—but the connection seems quite strong between the two series.

Notice in particular that the rapid price inflation of the late 1970s was matched with a comparable increase in the money stock. To be specific, from January 1975 through January 1980, CPI rose 49%, while M1 rose 40%. To make sure you understand what these numbers mean, we are saying that in general, something that cost $10 in early 1975 would cost about $15 just five years later, for an average yearly rate of price inflation of more than 8% for five years in a row.[3]

Now picture an economist who was an expert on the history of U.S. money (as measured by M1) and prices in the year 1983. At that point, going all the way back to 1960, he would have believed there was a very tight connection between M1 and CPI. Sure, sometimes one series would rise faster than the other, but the different growth rates tended to balance out so that after 23 years had passed, the two series had increased by almost the exact same proportion. Someone who thought economics was all about careful measurements and statistical correlations might think he had discovered the economic equivalent of the charge on an electron.

However, the chart shows what happened. Since the mid-1980s, the stock of money—at least as gauged by the particular measure M1—has risen far more quickly (in percentage terms) than prices, at least as gauged by the CPI. And of course, the connection between the two series utterly breaks during the financial crisis of 2008, when M1 shot up sharply while CPI declined.

---

[3]If you are a math whiz, we point out that we have calculated the average compounded annualized growth rates. In other words we didn't simply take the total percentage growth and divide by 5, but rather we accounted for the exponential growth involved (multiplying percentages by percentages).

We are discussing the chart above to make sure you understand the lessons *and limitations* of the empirical work on monetary and price inflation. Throughout history, whenever there has been significant price inflation—especially **hyperinflation** when prices rise at inconceivable rates, such as one million percent (or more!) per year—we always find that the money stock rises significantly during the same period.

Yet as the chart on page 327 shows only too well, there is not a mechanical rule connecting prices with the stock of money. Everything in the economy ultimately occurs because of *individual human actions* which are guided by people's *subjective values and beliefs*. If people's values and beliefs about certain things remain roughly constant over a period of years, then statisticians might discover apparent "laws" connecting various measures of economic activity. Yet those laws can be shattered in an instant when the actual human beings change their preferences or their beliefs about the future.

In an introductory book such as this, we will not try to explain the exact patterns in the chart above. However, in the next section you will learn how basic economic tools can be applied to money and prices, which will at least provide the framework for a fuller understanding.

How Governments Make Prices Rise

In Lesson 7 we laid out the general explanation of money in a pure market economy. We saw that the same principles of economics applied to goods such as gold and silver when they became money, i.e., widely accepted media of exchange.

You will probably not be surprised to learn that historically, government rulers did not leave the "money market" alone. Instead governments throughout the ages have systematically **debased** the currency—meaning they reduced the market value of each unit of money—while enriching themselves.

For example, the Caesars of ancient Rome would engage in the following process: They would take the gold coins that were paid as tax tribute, and would melt them down. Then they would add in some baser metal, and have their mints produce more coins than the original number, and yet keep the official markings of the coin the same. Over time, this process ensured that the "gold" coins that were used in commerce actually had progressively smaller amounts of actual gold in them.[4] Merchants became aware of this and would adjust their prices accordingly, so that what used to cost "one gold coin" would eventually cost several "gold coins."

The point of this procedure, of course, was that at least initially—before the merchants realized the full extent of the debasement—the Roman government could afford to buy more things than without debasing the currency. For example, if the government originally collected 1,000 gold coins in taxes, without resorting to debasement they could afford to buy…1,000 gold coins' worth of goods. But through the trick described above, if the government took the original coins and transformed them into 1,100 coins that superficially appeared to be the same as the original batch, then obviously the government could obtain more goods and services from producers in the community.

Once the merchants began to catch on to this scam, an arms race of sorts developed. The merchants could raise their prices *expecting* further debasement, but there was nothing to stop the Roman government from accelerating the pace of the metal dilution. The inevitable result was that prices in the Roman Empire grew quite rapidly.

The Rise of Fiat Money

As you probably realize, governments around the world gradually moved away from monetary systems anchored on precious metals. Today all major economies are based on **fiat money** which refers to government-sponsored money that is not "backed up" by any goods from the market. For example, in the United States the official money is the U.S. dollar. The U.S. government and the central bank, the **Federal Reserve**, strictly control the number of green pieces of paper of varying denominations and (to a lesser extent) the total deposits in all checking accounts that are measured in U.S. dollars. But there is nothing to "guarantee" the value of the dollar.

[4]Note that even without debasement, gold coins would not be *pure* gold, because they would be too malleable. Some amount of baser metal would be added to keep the coins durable and useful as money.

The U.S. dollar is simply the U.S. dollar. The dollar doesn't *entitle* the holder to anything else—it's not a legally binding contract or a claim on the U.S. government in any way. If you walk up to the U.S. Treasury or a Federal Reserve Bank, hand in a $20 bill, and say, "Now what do I get?" they will tell you, "Either two tens, four fives, or twenty singles. Which do you want?"

This is a very strange arrangement when you think about it. People are willing to work grueling hours in a hot factory, rob banks, and even kill each other, all in order to get their hands on more of these green pieces of paper that are intrinsically useless. That is, even a $100 bill *by itself* isn't good for very much besides being a bookmark—and even then, a very germy bookmark at that. So on the surface, it's extremely odd that these little pieces of green paper are some of the most coveted things on the planet.

Of course, the reason workers are willing to give up their leisure for dollars, and that merchants are willing to sell their goods for dollars, is simply that...they expect other people will do the same in the future. In other words, the reason a man will spend 40 hours a week taking orders from a guy he can't stand, is that he will get a pile of dollars in exchange for these services. Then, he thinks other people will take orders *from him* because of his stockpile. He'll walk into a building and people will snap to attention, cleaning off a table just for him, and then bring him all sorts of delicious food and tasty beverages. One person will prostrate herself so much as to introduce herself by name and say she will be *serving* the man. The man will say, "Bring me some eggs," and lo and behold, the people in the building will obey him. Possession of the green pieces of paper enables him to be the boss, and for the same reason that he himself took orders from the loudmouth at his own job.

Clearly whoever is in charge of *creating* these green pieces of paper has a very nifty operation. It's extremely easy for the U.S. government to print up more dollars; the cost is just a few pennies to buy the paper and ink necessary, and the government can print bills with more zeroes on them to achieve any amount of new money at a negligible expense. This is an awesome amount of power to be vested in the hands of a single group, and it's interesting to see how things came to this.

Although modern economies are all based on fiat money, it was not always so. In Lesson 7 we learned how market commodities (such as gold and silver) could emerge spontaneously from an initial barter economy and eventually become money. In such a situation, it's true that *part* of the reason people would work hard for an ounce of gold was simply that *others* would work hard for that same ounce of gold in the future. But beyond that, gold, silver, and other commodity monies were in themselves *actual goods in the market* that people subjectively valued even before they had achieved their status as money. In a pure market economy, there is no single agency in charge of "the money." No, various people could own gold mines, for example, and thus the total amount of money in the economy was determined in the open market through supply and demand, in the same way that the total amount of bicycles isn't set by a government agency.

Historically, governments took over control of the money by first issuing paper currency that was *linked* to gold and/or silver. For example, from 1834 through 1933 (with very minor exceptions), Americans knew that $20.67 in U.S. currency would entitle them to one ounce of gold. This wasn't merely a prediction or a hope on their part; the government was *legally obligated* to hand over physical gold to people who presented it with paper dollars. Thus the paper dollars themselves weren't the true money, but rather were *certificates* that entitled the holder to get the *real* money, namely gold.[5]

In 1933 after his inauguration in the depths of the Great Depression, President Franklin D. Roosevelt formally ended the government's promise to redeem dollars for gold. For the next several decades, other governments (and their central banks) could still hand in U.S. dollars for gold, but Richard Nixon closed even this avenue by officially severing the dollar from gold in 1971. From that point onward, the U.S. dollar has been a true fiat money, backed up by nothing. Because at that point all of the other major currencies were themselves tied *to the U.S. dollar*, it meant that the entire world economy was now subject to fiat monies.

In terms of the basic economics, the significance of a fiat versus a commodity money is that it's so much easier to increase the amount of fiat

---

[5]The history of gold and silver legislation in the early United States is quite complicated and lies outside the scope of this introductory book. The important point is that even before the Constitution was written, the colonists were using gold and silver coins as money. Americans began using pieces of paper connected to the U.S. government only because originally these were *claim tickets* on the pre-existing commodity monies.

money in the economy. Large and rapid price inflation would be extremely unlikely, for example, if everyone used actual gold as the money good, for the practical reason that it is difficult to dig up more gold. On the other hand, with fiat money governments have the ability to increase the amount of money a millionfold in very short order—indeed, they can do it with a few presses of a button with modern electronic banking. All of the historical examples of hyperinflation—where a money was destroyed because it lost its value so quickly—occurred because governments fell into a vicious cycle where prices kept rising, and so governments kept printing more and more money to pay their bills.

Standard debates over proper "monetary policy" overlook this rather important feature of our world since 1971: The people in charge of their country's respective currencies literally have the power to destroy them overnight. Of course this doesn't happen in practice because government officials presumably have no *interest* in wrecking their own economies (though you might not know it from their decisions). But most people would not give one or a handful of people the ability to, say, wipe out a country's entire collection of books, or the complete contents of its hard drives, simply by pressing a few buttons. Yet this is the current state of our world with respect to perhaps the single most important good: money.

The Price of Money Set By Supply and Demand

Whether we have a commodity money such as gold, or a fiat money such as today's U.S. dollar, its market price is set by supply and demand. Of course with a commodity money, the market supply consists of the individual supplies of all the different producers in the private sector. In contrast, with modern fiat money, governments (or their designated agencies) determine the quantities of dollars, euros, pesos, and so forth.[6] Despite this

[6]Strictly speaking, the U.S. government and the Federal Reserve don't have *complete* control over the quantity of U.S. dollars, if we include checking account balances as part of the total. The willingness of commercial banks to grant loans, and of private individuals to borrow money, plays a role here as well. But for all practical purposes, the U.S. government and its agency, the Federal Reserve, control the "dollar supply curve."

difference, the same tools of supply and demand can explain the price of ounces of gold as well as the price of rectangular green portraits of Benjamin Franklin.

The one major hitch in using supply and demand analysis in this lesson is that the "price" of money behaves in the opposite way of how you are used to thinking about other prices. For example, suppose we are analyzing the car market for a certain city. With the original supply and demand, imagine the equilibrium price is $20,000 and the equilibrium quantity is 1,000 cars. Then there is a new dealership that opens up, so that the supply curve for cars shifts to the right. In the new equilibrium, the price has dropped to $15,000 and the quantity of cars has doubled to 2,000 vehicles. This is all basic review.

Now what happens if we analyze this same market, but from the point of view of the money? After all, even fiat money is an economic good, so we should be able to use our tools of analysis. The problem here is when we want to mark the "price" of dollars. In terms of the car market, we could say that initially, the price of a $1 bill was 1/20,000th of a car, but that after the new dealership opened up, the price of a $1 bill *increased* to 1/15,000th of a car.

So we see that the movement in the price of money was in the *opposite* direction of the price of the cars. In other words, if it takes fewer dollar bills to buy a car, that's the same thing as saying it takes more of a car to buy a dollar bill. That language might strike you as strange at first, but essentially the car dealer is *selling cars* in order to *buy U.S. dollars*. His customers are on the other side of the transaction; they are *selling dollars* in order to *buy cars*.

If dollar bills and cars were the only goods in the economy, we would be done. However, the whole *point* of having money is that it stands on one side of every transaction involving many thousands of different types of goods. So it's not really true to say that *the* price of money is 1/20,000th or 1/15,000th of a car. We also have to think about how many dollar bills exchange for packs of gum, gallons of gasoline, hours of carpentry, and so on.

For example, suppose that a gumball originally costs 25 cents, but then the price doubles to 50 cents for one gumball. An equivalent expression would be to say that the price of a $1 bill was originally 4 gumballs and then *fell in half* to 2 gumballs. This is a crucial point: *When the price (measured in dollars) of a regular good or service goes up, that is the same thing as saying the market value of the dollar goes down.* When the "price of money" falls, it means that the dollar-prices of other goods are going *up*.

In the real world, prices of various goods and services do not all rise to the same degree, and in fact some prices rise while other prices fall. That's why it's very controversial to even define what we mean by "the price of money." Economists have devised various "baskets" of goods to provide a rough idea, of which the Consumer Price Index (CPI) is one such measure. For our purposes, the important point is that you understand that rising prices (measured in money) *are the same thing* as a falling value or "purchasing power" of money.

Once we understand the connection between regular prices and the "price" of money, it's easy to see what causes price inflation: anything that causes the price of money to go *down*. Using our standard tools, that means there can be two causes for a general rise in the prices of goods and services in the economy: (1) The supply of money has increased, and/or (2) the demand for money has fallen.

With this insight, we can return to some of the points mentioned earlier in this lesson. For example, the complete collapse of some currencies—where the purchasing power or price of the money fell to virtually zero very quickly—happened when the respective governments began creating incredible amounts of new currency (i.e., the supply increased). Once this process began, the public became doubtful about the currency's ability to buy goods and services in the future, and so they didn't want to hold it; hence the demand for the currency began falling. The process snowballed until the price of the currency was virtually zero, meaning that units of it (such as the German mark) could fetch nothing in the marketplace.

On the other hand, we can also explain what happened in the United States in the mid-1980s. As the graph earlier in this lesson illustrated, the stock of money (as measured by the statistic M1) grew very quickly even though prices (as measured by the CPI) did not rise nearly as much. In other words, from the mid-1980s onward the U.S. saw a large increase in the quantity of money but a much smaller fall in its price. The broad explanation of this pattern is simple: The supply of dollars increased but *so did the demand.* The specific reasons for the increase in demand—which probably include the strong U.S. economy, and the success in bringing down price inflation rates from the dangerous levels of the late 1970s—are beyond the scope of our discussion. The important point is that you cannot look at the number of dollar bills and mechanically calculate what will happen to prices, because the market value of money is set by supply *and* demand.

The Danger of Government Price Inflation

Price inflation is not the sole product of government intervention. Even in a pure market economy using gold, a huge influx of gold (from newly discovered mines or from newly discovered foreign lands) can cause the prices of most goods and services (measured in gold ounces) to rise. In theory, if the medieval alchemists had been successful and figured out a way to turn lead into gold, then the market price of gold would have fallen until the returns to alchemists were the same as in other industries. In other words (depending on the exact alchemic process) the price of gold would probably fall until it was close to the price of lead. In this fanciful scenario, people in a pure market economy would probably switch to another form of money, for the same reason that historically people never used lead as a commodity money.[7]

In practice, however, the great threat to price stability has come not from market-based commodity money, but from government-controlled money, and in particular fiat money.[8] For example, when the U.S. dollar was firmly

---

[7]Even here, the "collapse" of the gold money would be a mixed blessing, not an unmitigated disaster. It's true that it would be very disruptive to the world economy if its money—gold—all of a sudden saw its value fall quite sharply because of the alchemists' discovery. On the other hand, it would be *wonderful* if the alchemists made such a discovery, because of all the new gold. Besides the fall in prices for beautiful jewelry, consumers would benefit from much cheaper dental work (gold fillings etc.) and arthritis treatments (which inject gold into the body), as well as the industrial applications. Unlike a fiat currency, a market-based commodity money is actually *useful* for reasons other than its status as a medium of exchange, and so sudden increases in supply are beneficial in that respect.

[8]We should point out that technically, economists have imagined a fiat money even in a pure market economy, and have written books and articles describing the mechanics of such a system. In the text above we will ignore this complication and assume that fiat money is always the result of government intervention in

linked to gold at $20.67 an ounce the purchasing power of the dollar was fairly constant over long stretches of time. It might fall during a war and rise during an economic crisis, but generally speaking dollars could buy the same amount of goods in one year as they would have in previous decades. During arguably the most prosperous decade in U.S. history, for example, the CPI was virtually flat from 1922 through 1929. American shoppers did not see significant movements in the prices of milk, eggs, and meat throughout this period, even though the economy was booming.

This is no longer the case. Especially since Richard Nixon "closed the gold window" in 1971 and formally severed the dollar's tie to gold, there has been a steady and virtually uninterrupted fall in the purchasing power of the dollar. In other words, prices of goods and services in the U.S. have constantly risen as the economy moved away from a commodity money (gold) and toward a fiat money. Nowadays young people must tolerate their parents and grandparents' boring discussions of how cheap things were "when I was growing up." What these young people—and possibly even their parents and grandparents—don't realize is that this steady erosion of the dollar *is not a fact of nature*. It is the result of the government's intervention into the economy, through its monopolization of the money stock and its decision to continually pump new dollars into the economy.

Besides generating boring stories from grandpa, the harm of persistent price inflation is that it partially defeats the purpose of using money in the first place. Remember that the great contribution of having a money is that it helps people make plans and coordinate their activities in the market. Entrepreneurs can tell if they're running a successful business by adding up the money prices of the inputs they buy, and comparing this grand total to the sum of the money prices of the things they sell to their customers. Workers can make an informed decision about whether to take a new job across the country, by looking at the typical prices of important goods (such as food and housing) in the new area compared to the typical prices in their current location, and do the same for the salary differences in the two locations. Retired couples who are planning a luxurious European vacation can avoid starving twenty years later by consulting with a financial planner

---

the market economy. Whether this is true even in theory is a controversial issue among economists, but the connection between governments and fiat money is certainly correct in practice.

to make sure they've set aside enough investments to support them later on. Having a **sound money**—meaning a money for which the value doesn't bounce around erratically, and doesn't lose its purchasing power over time—makes all of these activities much more orderly. Having an unsound fiat money is (usually) still better than nothing, but in the extreme governments can render their monies so useless that the public literally abandons the currency and adopts other items as media of exchange.

One of the official duties of the Federal Reserve—the government-established central bank of the United States—is to maintain price stability. Since the Federal Reserve's founding in 1913, the U.S. dollar has lost about 95% of its purchasing power. To see it another way, things that cost $1 in the market in 1913 cost about $22 today. But beyond this sustained drop in the "price" of the U.S. dollar (compared to most goods and services), is the fact that the drop has been incredibly *volatile*. Prices rose very quickly during World War I, then they collapsed in 1920 and 1921, then were steady again through the 1920s, then collapsed again during the early years of the Great Depression. Since the end of World War II, U.S. prices have risen steadily, but the pace of the increase has been irregular. In particular, prices rose very quickly at the end of the 1970s, before slowing to much lower growth rates in the 1980s.

Currently (2010), U.S. investors are divided in their forecasts about future price inflation. Some expect a collapse in prices, comparable to the early period of the Great Depression. Others expect a surge in prices, comparable to (though not as extreme as) the recent case of Zimbabwe.[9] Because of this uncertainty over a very important aspect of the future—namely the purchasing power of the U.S. dollar—Americans and indeed people all over the world are distracted from building their businesses, playing with their

[9]Things became so absurd in Zimbabwe that its central bank eventually issued 100 trillion dollar bills. At a conference in the spring of 2010, someone humorously gave the author of this textbook a "tip" which was a "FIFTY TRILLION DOLLARS" note issued by the Reserve Bank of Zimbabwe. The jokester had acquired this piece of currency—which has a "5" followed by 13 zeroes printed on it—very cheaply on eBay. According to Steve Hanke, by November 2008 Zimbabwe was suffering from a *monthly* price inflation rate of 79.6 *billion* %. At this inconceivable rate, prices in Zimbabwe were doubling every 25 hours! (See http://www.cato.org/zimbabwe)

kids, and watching kung fu movies because they have to do research on Federal Reserve meetings and constantly tinker with their financial portfolios to include more gold or more bonds. All of this activity makes sense at an individual level, *given* the poor track record of the Federal Reserve in its official mission of price stability. But in terms of the whole economic system, it is very wasteful. In a pure market economy with a sound money, people could focus on the more important things in life (such as kung fu movies).

Price Inflation Contained Through Proper Forecasts?

Some people pooh pooh the harmful effects of price inflation. They will concede that if the rising prices took everyone by surprise, *then* there would be a problem. But by this point, some would argue, everybody knows that the U.S. dollar (and other fiat currencies) will shed their purchasing power over time. When businesses borrow money, and older workers decide on retirement, they take this phenomenon into account. What's more, in modern economies sophisticated financial instruments allow investors to protect themselves against price inflation through various means. In short, people in the mixed economy aren't sitting ducks when the government intervenes in the supply of money. They respond and protect themselves using other aspects of the market economy.

This is all true, but notice that we could say the same thing if the government randomly injected people with viruses or set their houses on fire. People wouldn't sit still and passively accept the new reality; instead they would take active countermeasures (vaccines, more smoke alarms, etc.) and would buy more financial protection through medical and fire insurance policies. But it would be nonsense to say that these defensive measures completely neutralized the harmful effects of our hypothetical government virus-injectors and arsonists.

The same principle applies to government price inflation. It's true that the harm can be mitigated through the market's defensive reactions. But the society still ends up poorer compared to the situation where the government left money to the private sector.

No matter what, government *monetary* inflation must distort the economy relative to the pure market outcome. This is because the government and central bank invariably use the new money to *buy things*, whether tangible goods (like tanks and bombers during a war) or financial assets (like a mortgage-backed security in the wake of the 2008 financial panic).

We have already seen in Lesson 18 that government distorts the economy when it takes resources out of the control of private hands and places them under the discretion of government officials. This harmful process necessarily occurs whenever the government creates new money, i.e., engages in *monetary* inflation.

No matter what the public does in response, it cannot prevent the government from siphoning away actual goods and assets (barrels of oil, corporate bonds, etc.) when the government controls the printing press. Under a fiat money system, the government's newly printed $100 bills are legal tender just as much as the money already in the wallets and purses of average citizens. For this reason, even if a particular episode of *monetary* inflation doesn't lead to immediate *price* inflation,[10] the government intervention still distorts the economy relative to the pure market outcome.

[10]Keep in mind that the government's injection of new money might prop up prices that would otherwise have fallen. For example, the government might print up new money and buy goods for which the (private sector) demand had fallen. In this case, the monetary inflation still causes price inflation, but from a lower starting point, as it were. Thus the observed prices might not rise, but it would be wrong to conclude that the monetary inflation had no effect on prices.

Lesson Recap . . .

- *Monetary inflation* refers to the expansion of money; in our economy the term refers to an increase in the total number of dollars. *Price inflation* refers to a general increase in the prices of goods and services, as measured in units of money.

- Government intervention leads to systematic inflation. All major governments have used various means to force their people to stop using market-based commodity monies (such as gold and silver) and to instead use paper fiat currencies. It is much easier to expand the amount of fiat money, versus digging up more gold and silver.

- Large-scale and persistent price inflation can devastate an economy. When money's purchasing power erodes quickly and erratically, it limits the benefits of having a money in the first place and pushes society back towards a situation of barter. Without a sound currency, people have less incentive to save and make long-term investment decisions.

NEW TERMS

Inflation: A term that originally referred to monetary inflation, but nowadays tends to refer to price inflation.

Monetary inflation: An expansion in the total amount of money in the economy.

Price inflation: A general increase in the prices of goods and services, quoted in units money. Price inflation is the same thing as a fall in the purchasing power of money.

Stock of money: The total amount of money in the economy at a particular time.

Consumer Price Index (CPI): The Bureau of Labor Statistics' gauge of the "price level" affecting regular households. The CPI is an average (weighted by their relative importance) of the prices of gasoline, food, and other common items.

M1: A popular measure of the total amount of money in an economy. M1 includes the actual currency held by the public (in their wallets, purses, and cashiers' drawers) but also the total amount of checking account balances. (Because of the fractional reserve banking system, M1 is larger than the number of dollars printed on green pieces of paper. If everyone tried to withdraw his or her checking account from the banks at the same time, there wouldn't be enough currency to go around. This is why M1 indicates more total money than just the amount of paper currency.)

Hyperinflation: Very severe inflation. There is no precise boundary between inflation and hyperinflation, but in a hyperinflation people begin buying anything at all in order to unload their money holdings which are losing value by the hour.

Debasement: Government policies that weaken the money. When coins were valued because of their precious metal content, debasement meant melting the coins and re-minting them with baser (less valuable) metals added to the mixture. Under fiat money, debasement involves the rapid creation of new money, which reduces the value of a single unit of money.

Fiat money: Paper money that is not "backed" by anything. The only reason people accept fiat money in trade, is that they expect it to have purchasing power in the future.

Federal Reserve: The central bank of the United States, founded in 1913. The "Fed" is responsible for U.S. monetary policy, and has the dual mandate of providing stable economic growth (which implies full employment) and low price inflation.

STUDY QUESTIONS

1. What are the two meanings of the term *inflation*?

2. Is there a strict connection between money growth and price increases?

3. Why do workers sell their labor hours in exchange for intrinsically useless pieces of fiat money?

4. If the stock of money increases, what happens to the "price of money," other things equal? What does this imply for the prices of goods and services?

5. What is the harm of government price inflation?

ADVANCED LESSON 22

Government Debt

In this lesson you will learn:

- The difference between government deficits and debt.
- The connection between government debt and inflation.
- How government debt makes future generations poorer.

Government Deficits and Debt

Like a private company, the government takes in revenues which it uses to pay its expenses. Just as a private company can sometimes have periods where its expenses are higher than its revenues, so too for the government. In any particular budget period, the government may want to spend more total money on social programs, the military, and so forth than the government has collected in taxes, fees for the use of public parks, etc. When the government spends more than it takes in, it runs a *budget deficit.*

In most financial reports and commentary, government deficits are measured on an annual basis. For example, a critic of Ronald Reagan might say, "The U.S. federal budget deficit almost tripled during the 1980s, rising from about $74 billion in 1980 to $221 billion in 1990."[1] Strictly speaking, this sentence only tells us about the federal government's finances in

[1]The finances of the U.S. federal government are usually recorded by *fiscal years,* which do not coincide with calendar years. For example, Fiscal Year 1990 ran from

two different years; the budget deficit in 1980 was the difference between receipts and expenditures in that year, and the deficit in 1990 was the gap ten years later.

Sometimes reporters use sloppy language when reporting on a new government program. For example they might say, "Because the new health reform legislation will raise federal spending by $900 billion while increasing taxes by only $800 billion, it will add $100 billion to the deficit over the next ten years." But since most people use *deficit* to mean a single-year mismatch between receipts and spending, our reporter's sentence is confusing. It would be as if a baseball announcer said that the big hitter at the plate had a batting average of 3,000 in his first ten years in the major leagues.

The government deficit measures the difference between spending and receipts during a particular slice of time; it is a **flow variable** that happens over a period (such as one year). In contrast, the government *debt* refers to the total amount of money that the government owes to other organizations or individuals.[2] The debt is a **stock variable** meaning that its value is defined at any point in time. For example, it makes sense to ask, "What was the total government debt as of Monday at noon?" But it wouldn't make sense to ask, "What was the federal budget deficit as of Monday at noon?" unless you implicitly had a previous *starting point* in mind, so that you were really asking, "How much has the government spent between the start point and Monday at noon, versus how much has it collected in taxes during the same period?"

October 1, 1989 through September 30, 1990. The $221 billion deficit thus refers to the mismatch between federal receipts and expenditures during these two dates.

[2]There are different items that could be included in this figure, which would make the "federal debt" greater or smaller. For example, a smaller figure of the debt might refer exclusively to the actual bonds issued by the U.S. Treasury. A much broader figure would include not just the bonds, but also the federal government's expected future liabilities in programs such as Social Security, in which the expected payouts will at some point exceed the "contributions" from workers and will thus constitute a drain on general tax revenue, contributing to the government's overall indebtedness.

When the government runs a deficit, it covers the shortfall just as a corporation can: it issues debt, meaning that the government sells Treasury bonds to outside investors.[3]

Interest on the "National Debt"

When the government borrows money from lenders by selling them government bonds, it must pay them interest. Specifically what happens is that the investors pay less for the bond than the **face value**,[4] with the difference giving rise to the implicit interest return (or yield) on the bond. For example, if an investor buys an IOU from the U.S. federal government promising to pay him $10,000 in exactly one year, but the investor only has to pay (roughly) $9,524 for it, he earns a return of 5% on his money, because $9,524 x 1.05 = $10,000 (roughly).

As the federal budget deficit grows, the interest payments to service that debt (typically) grow as well.[5] When people talk of the enormous **national debt**—by which they almost always mean the U.S. federal government's debt—they might complain that interest payments are one of the largest spending categories, leaving less money available for other government programs.

The table on page 348 illustrates a hypothetical government's finances for a three-year period. By walking through the table you will have a much better understanding of government deficits, debt, and interest payments.

---

[3]The U.S. Treasury is the financial arm of the federal government. The Treasury collects taxes and disburses funds. When the federal government runs a deficit, it borrows money from lenders by having the Treasury sell bonds.

[4]In the text we are restricting our attention to "zero coupon" bonds, which apply to Treasury debt that is one year or shorter in maturity. If the government (or another entity) issues long-term debt, it will often involve periodic interest payments ("coupons"). In this case, the lender hands over the full face amount of the bond upfront, because the interest earnings are handled separately. (But for bonds that carry no coupon payments, the investor must earn his interest through a discount initially paid for the bond.)

[5]If interest rates fall then the government could enjoy lower interest payments even as its debt grows.

2010		2011		2012	
Tax Rev:	$1 trillion	Tax Rev:	$1 trillion	Tax Rev:	$1 trillion
Expenditures:	$1.1 trillion	Expenditures:	$1 trillion	Expenditures:	$975 billion
Deficit:	$100 billion	Deficit:	$0	Surplus:	**$25 billion**
Debt at start:	$0	Debt at start:	$100 billion	Debt at start:	$100 billion
Debt at end:	**$100 billion**	Debt at end:	$100 billion	Debt at end:	**$75 billion**
EXPENDITURES		**EXPENDITURES**		**EXPENDITURES**	
Military:	$300 billion	Military:	$280 billion	Military:	$270 billion
Social:	$800 billion	Social:	$715 billion	Social:	$700 billion
Interest:	$0	Interest:	$5 billion	Interest:	$5 billion
FINANCING		**FINANCING**		**FINANCING**	
(Gov't has no outstanding bonds to retire from previous years.)		Gov't must redeem the 10,500,000 bonds at their $10,000 face value, paying out $105 billion.		Gov't must redeem the 10,500,000 bonds at their $10,000 face value, paying out $105 billion.	
Gov't sells (*issues*) 10,500,000 bonds ($10,000 face value) at $9,523.81 each, to raise **$100 billion.**		Gov't *reissues* 10,500,000 bonds at $9,523.81 each, to raise $100 billion.		Gov't *reissues* 7,875,000 bonds at $9,523.81 each, to raise **$75 billion**. It *retires* **$25 billion of debt.**	

The table above contains a lot of information, but if you spend a few minutes to learn how it works, you will have a good grasp of the mechanics of government debt financing. Here are some general points:

- In any given year (each vertical column), the Tax Revenue is $1 trillion while the Expenditures vary. However, the Expenditures always equal the sum of that year's spending on Military, Social programs, and Interest on the debt.
- If Tax Revenue is higher than Expenditures, there is a Surplus. If revenues are lower, there is a deficit. If they are equal, the budget is balanced.
- The government debt changes during the course of the year based on that year's surplus or deficit.
- When the government carries a debt, part of its tax revenues must go to paying interest on the debt. Even if the government balances its budget in a particular year, it has less money available for the military and social programs if it is carrying a debt from earlier years.
- It is not counted as an expense of government when it simply reissues or rolls over debt that is maturing. In the table this happens in the year 2011. The government has a balanced budget, even though technically it must pay out a grand total of $1.1 trillion while tax revenues are only $1 trillion. Of the $105 billion that the government must pay to the bondholders (who purchased bonds in 2010), only $5 billion is considered a government expense—namely an interest expense—for the year 2011. The other $100 billion is simply rolled over by reissuing the same amount of debt in new one-year bonds.
- At any given time, the outstanding government debt is simply the *present market value* of the government bonds held by the public. This number is lower than the summation of the face value of all the outstanding bonds, because the government is not obligated to pay the full face value until the actual time of maturity. When that event is still in the future, the government's contractual obligation is discounted by the interest rate (5% in our example).

In our example, the government's debt always consists entirely in one-year bonds. In the real world the government spreads its debt among bonds of varying maturities (1-month, 3-months, 6-months, 1-year, 5-years, etc.). This allows the government to plan its finances more accurately by "locking in" interest rates for longer than one year when it borrows money.

Government Debt and Inflation

It is very common among the lay public and even sophisticated financial analysts to associate government debt with rising prices. Whenever the U.S. government runs a particularly high budget deficit, for example, many people will say, "This will hurt the dollar and cause [price] inflation."

There is certainly an element of truth to this popular association, and there is also a decent (though far from tight) historical correlation between the U.S. federal debt and the CPI:

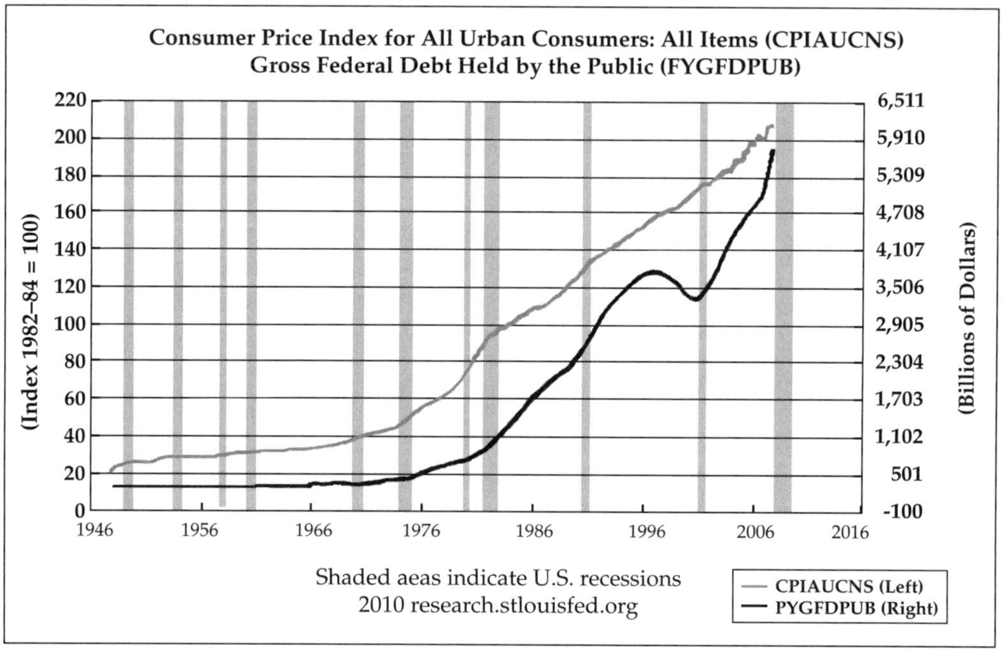

Yet even though there is apparently a general connection between government debt and rising prices, it's important to use sound economic theory to understand *why* this should occur. The first important point is that *a*

government budget deficit by itself is NOT inflationary. When the government runs a deficit and borrows money by issuing new bonds, it does *not* create new money in the economy. On the contrary, if the government runs a deficit of (say) $200 billion, it means that other people in the economy have that much less money in their possession. They hand $200 billion in money to the government, in exchange for IOUs issued by the Treasury. U.S. government bonds are very liquid (marketable) financial assets, but they are *not* the same thing as U.S. dollars—they are not money. In this narrow respect, a federal budget deficit is no more inflationary than a private corporation's decision to borrow money from the public.

But there is more to the story. All we have really established is that *by itself* a government budget deficit doesn't create new dollars, and therefore should not have any direct influence on the prices of goods and services in the United States. In practice, however, government budget deficits provide a strong incentive for the Federal Reserve to create more U.S. dollars. In the first place, price inflation tends to lighten the "real" burden of debt. By raising prices throughout the economy—including wages and salaries—through the creation of new dollars, the Federal Reserve can indirectly boost tax revenues for the federal government. This makes it easier to afford the fixed dollar payments on debt, especially long-term debt that was originally issued many years earlier.[6]

The more basic connection between government debt and inflation is simple: When the government wants to spend an incredible amount of money—such as during a world war—it can only raise so much through taxes. Then it can only raise so much more through borrowing. At that point, if the government *still* wants to spend more money, it turns to the printing press.

Suppose the government wants to spend $6 trillion, and only has tax revenues of $2 trillion. The government in principle could borrow the remaining

---

[6]It's true that investors will take this dynamic into account when lending money to the government; they will insist on a higher yield (interest rate) knowing that the purchasing power of the dollar will likely fall over time. Even so, it is still true that when the Federal Reserve causes inflation, it makes it easier for the federal government to service its pre-existing debt. If the Federal Reserve were to suddenly stop inflating altogether, it would be *harder* for the government to service its debt compared to the expected scenario.

$4 trillion, but investors would become nervous at such a large sum and might demand a much higher than normal interest rate. Furthermore, the public might balk at such a huge deficit (as a fraction of the total budget) and insist that the government slash its spending. In this pickle, then, the government might only borrow $1 trillion, and then literally create the extra $3 trillion in new money, in order to pay its bills. The government would be employing its position as the money monopolist in the exact same way that a private sector counterfeiter behaves.

Now in the United States financial system, the government actually doesn't behave this blatantly. Instead, if the government wants to use its control of the printing press to help cover a deficit, it goes through a very complicated process: First, the Treasury issues enough new debt to buyers in the private sector to completely cover the official budget deficit. However, the private bond dealers are happy to oblige the Treasury with very low interest rates on these massive loans, because the Federal Reserve quickly steps in and buys the newly-issued Treasury bonds from the private dealers. The Federal Reserve pays for the bonds not out of its past savings, but rather through creating new dollars out of thin air.

When all is said and done, the Federal Reserve ends up holding the new Treasury bonds on its books, while the private bond dealers are back to their original position (plus a little money for commissions on the trades). If we step back and ignore the middlemen (i.e., the private bond dealers), what happens in the grand scheme is that the Federal Reserve creates new dollars and lends them to the Treasury, which then spends them on its various programs.[7] So although the process is convoluted, the government's

[7]If you are a sharp reader you might think that this isn't truly printing up new money just to close a budget shortfall, because the federal government still owes interest and the return of principal to the holder of the bonds it issued. But guess what? The Federal Reserve is the recipient of these payments (since the Federal Reserve bought the bonds from the private dealers), and as standard operating procedure the Federal Reserve remits all of its excess earnings back to the Treasury. In other words, after the Federal Reserve pays it electric bill, employees, and so forth, any extra money it has, it sends back to the Treasury. So even though technically speaking the Treasury didn't get those new dollars with no strings attached, for all practical purposes it did, since its interest payments on the debt held by the Federal Reserve will (largely) come right back to the Treasury, and because the

control of the monetary and banking systems gives it the option of creating new dollars in order to close a budget shortfall. This is one important mechanism through which government deficits can lead to monetary inflation and ultimately higher prices.

Government Debt and Future Generations

In popular discussions, opponents of government deficits often claim that they represent theft from unborn generations. The idea is that if the government spends an extra $100 billion to make voters happy but without "paying for it" through raising taxes, then the present generation has gotten to enjoy an extra $100 billion whereas future taxpayers will have to bear the cost. Is this typical claim really right?

As with the popular association of government debt and inflation, the answer is nuanced: *Yes* government deficits do impoverish future generations, but *no* they don't do so for the superficial reason that most people believe.

When thinking about any debt, be it government or private, keep in mind that *all goods are produced out of present resources*. There is no time machine by which people today can steal pizzas and DVDs out of the hands of people 50 years in the future. If the government spends an extra $100 billion to mail every voter a lump sum payment to go spend at the mall, it doesn't matter whether the expenditure is financed through tax hikes or borrowing. Either way, it is the *present generation* (collectively) who pays for it.

Now of course, in practice there is a difference in how this burden is *shared* among the present generation, and that's the whole reason that it's popular to run budget deficits. If the government raised everyone's taxes in order

---

Federal Reserve will likely roll over the principal on its outstanding holdings of Treasury debt. For an analogy, if you could always borrow money from your parents (at a contractual interest rate) when you spent more than your job's paycheck, *and* if you knew you never had to pay back the principal, *and* if you knew your parents would always increase your birthday and Christmas gifts to give you all the "interest payments" on these loans right back to you, then the process of signing a loan contract with them would be a farce. You would spend with reckless abandon, which is exactly what the D.C. politicians have done and continue to do.

to send them all the money back in a check, that would be pointless. But if instead the government borrows $100 billion from a small group of investors and *then* mails this money out to everybody else, the average voter feels richer.

One way to see the fallacy in the standard "we're living at the expense of our children" analysis is to realize that today's investors bequeath their government bonds to their children. It is certainly true that higher government deficits today, mean that future Americans will suffer higher taxes (necessary to service and pay off the new government bonds). But by the same token, higher deficits today mean that future Americans will inherit more financial assets (those very same government bonds!) from their parents, which entitle them to streams of interest and principal payments.[8]

So what does all this mean? Are massive government deficits really just a wash? No, they're not. The critics are right: Government deficits *do* make future generations poorer. But the reasons are subtler than the obvious fact that higher debts today lead to higher interest payments in the future, since (as we just explained) those interest payments go right into the pockets of people in the future generations. So here are two main reasons that government deficits make the country poorer in the long run:

- *Crowding out.* When the government runs a budget deficit, the total demand for loanable funds shifts to the right. This pushes up the market interest rate, which causes some people to save more (moving along the supply curve of loanable funds) but also means that other borrowers end up with less.[9] In effect, the government competes with

[8]Things get more complicated if we consider that foreign investors might be the ones financing the U.S. government's debt. In that case, present Americans would indeed be living above their means and in the process force future Americans to live below their means. But if we take "the present generation" to mean all humans, and "future generations" to mean all future humans, then we're back to the analysis in the text above.

[9]Some economists would argue that in the grand scheme, government deficits are largely irrelevant, because rational taxpayers will realize that they need to set aside more money to pay for future debt service. In other words, these economists say that when the government shifts out the demand for loanable funds, people

other potential borrowers for the scarce funds available. Economists say the government borrowing **crowds out** private investment. At the higher interest rate, entrepreneurs invest fewer resources into making new factories, buying more equipment, etc. So long as we make the very plausible assumption that the government will not use the borrowed money as productively as private borrowers would have, it means that future generations inherit an economy with fewer factories, less equipment, and so on. *This* is a major factor in explaining why government deficits translate into a poorer future.

- *Government transfers are a negative-sum game.* Another way that government debt makes future generations poorer is through the harmful *incentive effects* of the future taxes needed to service the debt. For example, if the government runs a deficit today, and needs to pay back $100 billion to creditors in 30 years, that does indeed make the country poorer at that time. But the problem is not the $100 billion payment per se—that comes out of the pockets of taxpayers, and goes into the pockets of the people who inherited the government bonds. Rather, the problem is that in order to *raise* the $100 billion, the government would probably raise taxes (rather than cut its spending), and this action would cause dislocations to the economy over and above the simple extraction of revenue.[10]

---

in the private sector rationally respond by shifting out the supply curve as well. Thus the market interest rate stays the same, and what the government hands out to taxpayers with its right hand, it borrows back from them with its left hand. However, in practice this view can't be right, because otherwise deficit spending wouldn't be as popular as it is.

[10]Recall our thought experiment from Lesson 18: If the government enacted ridiculously high income and sales tax rates, virtually all economic activity would go underground and the government would take in virtually no tax revenue. But clearly these policies would be very harmful to the economy, despite the apparently low "burden" as measured by tax receipts. This principle explains how the true damage of an extra $100 billion in taxes (needed to pay down the government

- *The option of borrowing leads to higher spending.* Yet another danger of government deficits is that they tempt the government into spending more than it otherwise would. Recall from Lesson 18 that *all* government spending, no matter how it is financed, siphons scarce resources away from entrepreneurs and directs them into channels picked by government officials. Because the public typically resists new government spending less vigorously when it is paid for through higher deficits, the possibility of issuing government bonds leads to higher government spending (and hence more resource misallocation, compared to the pure market outcome) than would occur if the government were forced to always run a balanced budget.

So we see that government deficits really *do* make everyone poorer (on average), but the mechanisms are subtler than the simple increase in the amount of money the federal government owes to various creditors. But as the bullet points above indicate, the way to alleviate these problems of deficits is to *cut spending*, not to raise taxes on the *present* generation! In other words, if the real problems of government deficits are that they take resources out of the present capital markets, and make it more likely that the government will hike tax rates in the future, then it would be no "solution" to close a budget deficit through tax hikes in the present. That would be a cure worse than the disease.

---

debt) is greater than the simple extraction of that amount of money from taxpayers.

Lesson Recap . . .

- A government budget deficit is the amount by which it spends more than it collects in tax receipts *over the course of a certain period* (such as the year 2010). The overall debt is the total amount the government owes lenders *at a certain time* (such as May 14, 2010). The debt is the cumulative result of all previous deficits and surpluses.

- Government deficits *by themselves* do not create new money, and do not directly contribute to rising prices. However, in a very subtle process, government deficits allow the Federal Reserve to purchase more Treasury bonds, a practice that *is* inflationary.

- Government deficits do not impoverish future generations in the simple way that many people believe. If the government borrows $50 billion to build tanks today, those resources (steel, computer chips, labor hours, etc.) are provided by the *present* generation; they are not "paid for by our grandchildren" through a time machine. However, government deficits divert real resources away from private-sector investment, and result in a smaller inheritance for future generations. In that respect today's deficits make future generations poorer than they otherwise would be.

NEW TERMS

Flow variable: A concept that is measured over a period of time. For example, the flow rate of an irrigation pipe could be 100 gallons *per minute*. This measurement wouldn't refer to the total amount of gallons contained in the entire pipe, but instead would refer to how many gallons passed through a particular section of the pipe every 60 seconds.

Stock variable: A concept that is measured at a specific point in time. For example, a man's weight at 9 a.m. on May 11, 2010 could be 150 pounds. This measurement wouldn't refer to the number of pounds the man had recently gained or lost, but instead would refer to his weight at that very moment.

Face value of a bond: The amount of money the bond issuer promises to pay to the holder of the bond at the maturity date.

National debt / public debt: Usually refers to the total outstanding value of bonds issued by the U.S. Treasury. As of May 2010, the "public debt" was almost $13 trillion, but much of this consists of Treasury bonds held by other government agencies (such as the Social Security Administration's "trust fund"). When economists compare the levels of debt owed by various governments, they usually net out the "intragovernmental holdings" and report only the government debt *held by the public*. As of May 2010, this figure for the U.S. Treasury was almost $8.5 trillion. (See http://www.treasurydirect.gov/govt/reports/pd/mspd/2010/opds052010.pdf)

Crowding out: The reduction in private-sector investment that results from government deficit spending. The government's borrowing increases the demand for loanable funds, which makes the equilibrium interest rate higher than it otherwise would be. At the higher interest rate, private-sector businesses borrow less to fund investment spending.

STUDY QUESTIONS

1. *Explain: "The government deficit is a *flow variable*, while the debt is a *stock variable*."

2. When the government spends more than it collects in tax revenues, what can we say about the budget?

3. *Is it possible for the government to sell new bonds in a given year, even if the budget is in surplus?

4. Are government budget deficits *directly* inflationary?

5. *Does it help future generations by raising taxes now to close a budget deficit?

ADVANCED LESSON 23

The Business Cycle

In this lesson you will learn:

- The typical elements of the *business cycle*.
- How government intervention causes the business cycle.
- The causes of mass unemployment.

The Business Cycle

The **business cycle**, also known as the **boom-bust cycle**, refers to the periodic rhythm that seems to plague market economies. Rather than enjoying uninterrupted growth, for some reason the people living in capitalistic economies experience alternating stages of prosperity and recession. On the upswing of the business cycle, businesses expand and hire workers, wages and prices rise, the stock market soars, and there is a general feeling of euphoria. However, for some reason the economy always starts to sputter, eventually giving in to a downturn in which workers lose their jobs, business sales and wages plummet, and the stock market falls or even crashes.

Most people, including even many fans of capitalism, believe that business cycles are an inherent property of the pure-market economy. Indeed because of this widespread perception, it is very popular for the government to engage in **countercyclical policies**, through which the alleged extremes of the market can be tamed. For example, many analysts would say that social welfare programs and progressive income taxes, beyond their other possible merits, also serve to "dampen" the ups and downs of the unregulated business cycle. During the boom period, people are pushed into higher tax brackets (because of rising incomes) and thus the government takes in extra revenue, which helps build up a cushion for the down times, and also helps "cool off" an "overheated" economy.[1]

Then when the bust occurs, government programs such as unemployment benefits and food stamps automatically kick in to provide needed income to people who have lost their jobs. In this way—according to the popular understanding—the slump in business activity doesn't fall into a vicious downward spiral, where one round of layoffs leads to less money for consumers to spend, which in turn hurts business sales even further, and so on. The concept of countercyclical policies reflects one of the guiding themes in conventional discussions of economic policy, namely that the government (and Federal Reserve) should use their various powers to navigate the economy through the choppy waters of prosperity and recession. In this popular view, the goal or duty of the government and Federal Reserve is to give citizens a steady and smooth increase in living standards, without the wild swings that would allegedly occur in a purely free market.

By this point in the book, you should be skeptical of these typical claims of the ability of government intervention to "fix" things in the economy. We have already seen several examples where it was not the free market, but instead government intervention, that caused certain social problems—these included slumlords, drug gang violence, and apartment shortages in big cities.

Indeed, when it comes to **macroeconomics**—which is the study of the whole economy, rather than individual product or labor markets—there is an alternative viewpoint that blames business cycles on *government intervention*. According to this school of thought,[2] the government causes a period of *false prosperity* when it artificially pushes down interest rates below their

[1]In this common analogy, the economy is likened to an engine, where "overheating" means high price inflation and apparently irrational increases in stock prices and other assets.

2 If you are curious in reading further, we are here presenting the basics of the so-called "Austrian business cycle theory," developed by economist Ludwig von Mises and elaborated by Friedrich Hayek.

proper free-market levels. But the illusion cannot last forever, and at some point the economic house of cards collapses, leading to all of the things we associate with "recession."

In an introductory book we can only provide you a sketch of this explanation for business cycles. We have saved this discussion for the final lesson because it will draw on several concepts from earlier lessons. Although some of the remaining material may be a bit too advanced for you, we urge you to digest as much as possible because it is crucial for citizens to understand the causes of the business cycle. If the theory presented in the following pages is correct, it means that governments not only *create* business cycles, but that the "medicine" they give during the recession phase is actually *poison*.

How Governments Cause the Business Cycle

In order to understand how government intervention could possibly be the cause of the familiar ups-and-downs of the business cycle, let's first review what happens in a pure market economy when consumers decide to increase their saving.

Sustainable, Market-Driven Economic Growth

In Lesson 4 we explained how poor Robinson Crusoe, all alone on his tropical island, could improve his standard of living through discipline and foresight. By *saving* (rather than *consuming*) some of the coconuts he collected with his bare hands every day, Crusoe could build up a stockpile so that eventually he could begin *investing* his time and other island resources into building *capital goods* such as a long pole. With the pole and other capital goods, Crusoe's labor would be vastly augmented in the future, so that he could enjoy more coconuts, fish, shelter, and leisure, compared to his situation when he first landed on the island.

In Lesson 10 we took these basic insights about Crusoe's world and applied them to a modern market economy. In this setting it is also possible for people to cut back on their present consumption, in order to save and invest which allows them to enjoy a permanently higher standard of living in the future.

Recall the specific role that interest rates play in this process: When most people in the economy decide that they want to cut down their present spending in order to provide for their retirement (or to provide a bigger inheritance for their heirs), their decision causes interest rates to fall.[3] The lower interest rates provide a signal for entrepreneurs to borrow more and invest in longer-term projects. This is because a given investment project—which has a certain number of years of money "going in" before the finished product can be sold and money can be "taken out"—will seem more or less profitable depending on the interest rates used to evaluate the timing of its expenses and revenues. As the market interest rate falls, the longer-term projects are penalized less and less, as it were, and entrepreneurs are given the green light to hire workers and buy raw materials to begin these projects.

The crucial thing to remember is that in a sustainable, market-driven expansion—where the interest rate falls because people are consuming less and saving more—the extra resources flowing into the new investment projects are coming from the sectors which are seeing a drop in sales. For example, if consumers are cutting back on restaurant dining and purchases of DVDs, in order to contribute more to their savings accounts every month, then restaurants will have to lay off waiters and waitresses, and some of the factories producing DVDs may have to shut down. These workers and other resources are then "freed up" to be absorbed into the expanding sectors, namely those industries that are growing because of the lower interest rate.

What actually happens in a sustainable, market-driven expansion is that workers and other resources are *redeployed* away from present consumption goods and into capital goods. It is the analog of Crusoe devoting some of his labor hours *not* on coconut gathering, but rather on pole construction. In both cases the ultimate objective, of course, is to enjoy a greater amount of consumer goods. But because of scarcity, there is a short-term *tradeoff* in which consumption actually *drops* in the present, in order to fund the construction

[3]In terms of diagrams, the supply curve of loanable funds shifts to the right, pushing down the equilibrium interest rate.

of more capital goods. Eventually this abstinence more than pays for itself, but it's important to remember that sustainable prosperity and economic growth rely on discipline and patience. Absent a new technological invention, or the discovery of new supplies of natural resources, there is no magical way to increase the productivity of labor so that everyone can consume more *immediately and permanently*.

Unsustainable, Government-Driven Economic Growth

Now let's suppose that government officials do not have the patience that sustainable economic growth requires; they want the benefits of more investment without the pain of higher saving (i.e., reduced consumption). To this end, the central bank (the Federal Reserve in the United States) pushes down interest rates below their free-market level. The specific mechanism that the Federal Reserve uses is rather technical, but for our purposes you can simply imagine that it prints up new $100 bills and enters the loan market, offering to lend the new money at lower interest rates than the prevailing market rate. In effect, the Federal Reserve becomes a new supplier of loanable funds (which come from the printing press), and moves the supply curve to the right.

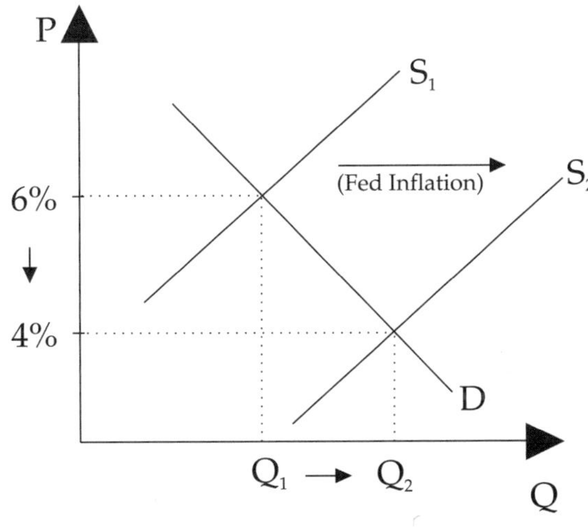

Market for Loanable Funds

Superficially, the results of this operation resemble a market-driven expansion. At the lower interest rate, entrepreneurs are given the green light to start longer-term projects. They hire workers and buy raw materials for enterprises that appeared unprofitable at the original market interest rate, but which now make sense given the "cheap credit" supplied by the Federal Reserve.

However, unlike the market-driven expansion, in the government-driven version there is no corresponding drop in consumer spending on restaurants, DVDs, and other retail sectors. On the contrary, these businesses are enjoying an *increase* in sales, because at the lower interest rate, people have less of an incentive to save and so they spend more on present enjoyments. In other words, while the entrepreneurs who make capital goods are seeing their businesses boom, *so are the consumer sectors*. It therefore seems that *every* sector is enjoying growth. The competition to hire new workers leads to increasing wage rates, which further contributes to the general feeling of prosperity.

But we know that this perception of euphoria must be an illusion. The government didn't come up with a new scientific formula or stumble upon an unknown oil field; all it did was print up green pieces of paper and hand them out to entrepreneurs. This action by itself doesn't alter the underlying facts of scarcity. It is physically impossible for the economy to produce more tractors *and* more television sets with the same amount of workers, raw materials, and equipment. In a market-driven expansion, consumers had to cut back on television sets (and other consumer goods) in order to allow for more tractors. Yet in the government-driven expansion, initially it seems as if the economy can have its cake and eat it too—that it can produce more capital goods *and* more consumer goods, without any waiting period. What's going on?

The answer is that the government's distortion of the interest rate has misled entrepreneurs. Remember that one of the functions of free-market prices is that they provide signals which help coordinate economic activity. By making it artificially cheap to borrow capital funds, the government has (loosely speaking) fooled investors into behaving as if there were more savings than actually exist. Therefore what the entrepreneurs in one part of the economy are trying to do with resources, does not mesh with what entrepreneurs in other parts are trying to do, and no one's plans match up with how consumers expect to spend their paychecks.

You might think that such confusion and divorce from the actual economic facts would immediately reveal itself. After all, if NASA builds a rocket using false "laws" of physics or engineering, they realize their mistake pretty quickly. But when it comes to the false prosperity of a government-induced boom, it can sometimes take years before reality rears its head.

This delayed reaction is made possible by **capital consumption**. In other words, it actually *is* possible for the economy to suddenly produce more capital goods[4] (tractors, drill presses, two-by-fours) and more consumer goods (TVs, iPods, bicycles) simultaneously—at least for a while. The tradeoff can be temporarily postponed if entrepreneurs *ignore the wearing out of the existing capital stock.*

In order to make *anything*—whether a consumer or a capital good—entrepreneurs must use existing tools and equipment. Regular usage results in depreciation, the wearing away or using up of these items. Even after Robinson Crusoe's initial saving and investment have paid off, he still must periodically attend to maintenance on his pole, or to the gradual construction of a new pole to replace the old one when it becomes too tattered. The

[4]Strictly speaking, if the false boom allows for an increase in consumption, then total investment—correctly measured—must drop, since the printing press doesn't give society the ability to create more goods and services. However, "total investment" is a subtle concept that requires market prices to be calculated. During the artificial and unsustainable boom, the producers of many types of capital goods can see their output increase, even though the economy as a whole is not investing enough in its capital structure to offset depreciation. For example, a factory owner may defer his normal practice of stopping production every month in order to lubricate the machinery etc., because "on paper" he is making more profits by cranking out orders for his customers. Yet in a few months, when his equipment is worn down from the hard usage and he needs to buy replacement units, he finds to his shock that equipment prices have skyrocketed. Up until that point, the factory owner would have thought he was increasing his wealth and hence his "stock of capital," but in reality he was consuming capital because his increased output of capital goods (the product of his factory) wasn't enough to offset his failure to engage in maintenance on his equipment.

same is true for a modern market economy. In order to simply maintain the current standard of living, at least some output every year must go toward replacing the capital goods used up in that year's production.

Now you should be able to understand the general outlines of how a false, government-driven expansion or boom is at least possible. The false prices (caused by printing up new money and injecting it into the financial markets) can mislead entrepreneurs, so that they unwittingly begin long-term projects for which there are not enough actual savings. The charade can continue for years, with everyone seeming to enjoy a higher standard of living, through "eating the seedcorn" and not plowing enough resources back into maintaining the existing economic structure. Of course the vast majority of people don't realize this is occurring—on paper the business-people are making record profits, and are increasing the value of their enterprises. But once the bust occurs, and market prices quickly change to more realistic numbers, everyone will realize that they behaved foolishly during the boom period.

The Inevitable Bust Following an Artificial Boom

In the typical business cycle, the period of (apparent) prosperity tapers off once rising price inflation causes the central bank to raise interest rates. Recall that in Lesson 21 we learned that monetary inflation (other things equal) causes price inflation. This cause-and-effect relationship still holds, regardless of the *purpose* for the new money creation. When the central bank (the Federal Reserve in the United States) creates new money in order to increase the supply of loanable funds, there are two major distortions: (1) An artificial boom created by the lower interest rate which (falsely) signals an increased availability of savings, and (2) rising prices.

As the boom progresses, the central bank generally has to continue pumping ever increasing amounts of new money into the loan market, if it wishes to keep the "stimulus" going. In the first place, a simple one-shot injection of new money—a burst of, say, $1 billion over the course of a week—would quickly work its way through the loan market and into the broader economy. Interest rates would drop, but only temporarily. In order to *keep* the interest rate below the free-market level, the central bank needs to continually feed in new money.

However, even a continuous yet *stable* stream of new money might quickly lose its ability to fuel an economic boom, because entrepreneurs would adjust to the new condition and largely offset its impacts in their calculations. There is also the obvious fact that a given dollar amount—for example $1 billion a week in newly injected money—would have less and less impact, as the money stock grew over time. Finally and perhaps most significant, as the "real" problems of the unsustainable expansion began to appear, ever greater amounts of monetary inflation would be necessary to hide the growing imbalances in the structure of production.

For all these reasons, the central bank typically needs to pump in ever increasing amounts of new money, the longer it wants to sustain the apparent economic prosperity. But this eventually leads to worrying spikes in various prices, perhaps first hitting financial and commodity markets, but eventually showing up in prices at the grocery store. As the price inflation becomes progressively higher, more and more analysts and even the general public begin to question the central bank's "easy money" and "cheap credit" policies.

At some point, therefore—and perhaps several years after the start of the monetary expansion—the central bank chickens out and at least slows the injection of new money into the loanable funds market. Interest rates begin to rise, closer to their true free-market level. As market prices become more accurate, many entrepreneurs realize they have behaved foolishly, and are overseeing half-finished, grandiose projects that clearly should never have been started. These entrepreneurs do what they can to salvage a bad situation. Some need to shut down immediately, lay off all their workers, and sell their equipment and inventory off to the highest bidders, to be incorporated into businesses that were not so completely taken in by the false reality of the boom period. Other businesses can afford to stay in business, but they suffer large losses and experience a period of belt-tightening.

The Causes of Mass Unemployment

The single most significant aspect of the business cycle—in both political and human terms—is the mass unemployment that occurs during the bust or recession phase. Yet ironically—and perversely—the very government policies that most people recommend to "help" the plight of the unemployed actually prolong the recession and sow the seeds for the next unsustainable boom.

The artificial prosperity of the boom period was fueled by the government's interventions pushing down the interest rate. The "false" price of borrowing credit led entrepreneurs to borrow more than there was true savings available. Remember from Lesson 12 that the pure market interest rate serves to ration the available savings among all the competing borrowers, and that the process isn't simply about money. There are real, physical resources involved as well. If workers and materials are devoted to building a new car factory that will take two years to complete, then those resources are "locked up" in the project for at least two years until they begin to "bear fruit" in the form of new cars.

During the artificial boom, too many of these long-term projects are started, because the false interest rate is too permissive. But the mere printing up of new money hasn't actually created more workers or other resources to go around. It's still the case that if work begins on a new car factory, it absorbs resources that could have been used elsewhere. If, during the early stages of the boom, too many projects are started, then it is *physically impossible* for them all to reach completion. The sooner the central bank chickens out and lets interest rates return to their appropriate level, the better, because then the entrepreneurs catch their mistakes sooner and stop digging themselves deeper into their mistaken projects.

When the boom collapses and turns into a bust, there is a period of confusion where everyone in the market needs to reevaluate his or her situation, in light of the shocking realization that the plans made during the boom were mistaken—and in some cases, very badly mistaken. If we step back and think about the adjustment process, during which the economy returns to a sustainable growth path, it must go something like this: Those resources that were drawn into unprofitable projects or sectors during the boom period, now need to be *redirected* elsewhere. And that requirement includes labor resources, meaning that people who happen to be working at extremely unprofitable businesses (but which seemed profitable during the boom) need to *lose their jobs* once the bust occurs.

For example, if six months' work has been done on a new car factory that will take another 18 months to complete, but for which (in light of the new information) there won't be enough car buyers to support its operations, then obviously the correct thing to do is to *stop building it immediately*. From the point of view of the whole economy, it's not "compassionate" for the government to, say, use tax dollars to subsidize the company that owns the factory, in order to prevent the construction workers from being laid off, and to "create" jobs in the factory making cars that no one wants to buy. No, the correct thing to do is allow those workers and other resources (which can be salvaged) to flow into other projects or sectors that are actually profitable.

The problem with this "tough love" recommendation, of course, is that it takes *time* for the economy to rebalance itself after an artificial boom, especially if the boom has lasted years. Consequently, there could be a period of months or even longer for some of the displaced workers, where they can't find a productive niche in the streamlined economy, in the wake of the bust. Rather than waiting for the "laissez-faire medicine" to work, many people would far prefer the government to step in and provide immediate relief.

Yet even here, it's important to realize the actual *function* that a prolonged spell of large-scale unemployment serves. Remember the critical flaw with outright central planning, i.e., pure socialism: Without market prices and the profit-and-loss test, the central planner wouldn't know how to make *efficient* use of the resources at his disposal. In the modern United States, for example, a would-be central planner would have no idea how many people "should" be brain surgeons, or construction workers, or school teachers, and let alone how many people within each of these broad totals should live in each particular city in the United States.

By the very same token, then, no person or even group of experts could possibly know the "right" way for the economy to adjust, in light of a collapsing boom. For example, consider the construction workers who built houses in Las Vegas during the great housing boom from the early 2000s through 2006. Clearly there were too many workers (and other resources such as lumber and nails) going into the Las Vegas housing industry during these years, and the "correct" thing to do would be for them to do something else with their labor time.

But what, specifically? Each construction worker in the Las Vegas area was a unique individual, with different skills, interests, and personal circumstances. The "correct" response of one worker may have been to get on a bus to Texas to take a job at an oil refinery. The correct response of another may have been to go back to graduate school and finish his Ph.D. in literature. And perhaps the correct response of a third worker would have been to take a huge pay cut flipping burgers in Vegas, waiting for the housing market to recover, because his wife held a great job as a personal assistant to a successful Vegas attorney.

Now that we have some idea of the scope of the problem, we see that *the pure market economy is the best way to solve it.* After the boom collapses, many workers realize that they can't earn the same paychecks they had become accustomed to. That's what it means to say the prosperity of the boom years was *illusory*—people really weren't as rich as they thought. What happens then is that laid off workers begin looking for work, hoping to find a new job that offers a salary and other features comparable to their old job, and which doesn't require them to move or (at least) to move to an area they detest.

It takes *time* for people to search for new positions. The longer an unemployed person searches, the better his new job is likely to be. However, the drawback of longer searches is that the unemployed person isn't contributing anything directly to the economic system; he must live off of the output of others during his search.

Notice that all of these issues are given their due weight in the pure market economy. Each displaced worker is allowed the freedom to choose his or her new job, based on all the factors *relevant to the individual*; no government official decides where the worker "ought to go now." At the same time, individuals bear the brunt of their delay in finding new work, because there are no government unemployment programs that (to put it bluntly) pay people not to find a new job.

As we have stressed throughout this book, economic analysis per se cannot decide which government policies are good and which are bad. But it can shed light on the *results* of particular policies, so that citizens and government officials can make informed decisions. In the case of mass unemployment, the issue is not simply a matter of cruelty versus compassion. By establishing a system of unemployment compensation, for example, the government reduces the earnings of employed workers, and makes it less attractive for profitable businesses to expand at the onset of the recession.

The government doesn't *create* resources or wealth, it simply redistributes them. If there were no formal government scheme for unemployment insurance, individuals and businesses would still have the option of using their larger paychecks and profits (which would no longer be subject to contributions to the unemployment fund) to build up their savings in order to provide a cushion during times of economic hardship. Perhaps this free market cushion would in practice be smaller than the duration of unemployment checks established by the government, but again, what economics shows us is that there is a *tradeoff* involved. It is not a fact of engineering or chemistry to say how long unemployment relief *should* last; that is clearly an economic question.

For example, it would clearly be wasteful if the government established a rule saying that anyone laid off from his job could collect checks equal to 95% of his former salary, for up to 20 years, until he finds a new job. Even the most zealous advocates for the unemployed would admit that *that* hypothetical policy would be disastrous, and would in fact hurt workers (all things considered). But once we admit that there can be such a thing as unemployment benefits that are *too* "generous," our knowledge of basic economics makes it hard to justify the government's decision to provide benefits in excess of what would have occurred in a voluntary pure-market economy.

Finally, if the government were *really* interested in helping the unemployed, it would stop using the central bank to artificially suppress interest rates. If the government and public could resist the urge to meddle during a recession, and simply let the correct market prices redirect workers and resources to sustainable niches, there would be no need for further dislocations. Unfortunately, in practice the central bank often "cures" a recession simply by fueling the upswing of another unsustainable boom.

Lesson Recap . . .

- The *business cycle* is the regular pattern in market economies where there are a few years of a "boom" characterized by low unemployment, rising wages and corporate earnings, and the expansion of many businesses. After the boom there is a "bust" or recession, characterized by high unemployment, stagnant or even falling wages and corporate earnings, and the liquidation of many businesses.

- The government, acting through the central bank, causes the boom-bust cycle by interfering with the market interest rate. When the central bank creates new money and releases it into the credit markets, this artificially lowers the interest rate, giving a false signal to entrepreneurs to expand their operations and invest in long-term projects. People feel richer during the boom, but the prosperity is an illusion, because it is not based on genuine saving but instead on inflation. The inevitable crash is actually the market's *desirable* readjustment to the underlying realities.

- During an unsustainable boom (generated by inflation in the credit markets), many workers and other resources are channeled into the wrong industries. After the recession sets in, the market must reallocate them to their proper niches. This shuffling of workers can take time, and appears as high rates of unemployment. Government efforts to "help"—such as sending checks to people without a job—prolong the period of high unemployment.

NEW TERMS

Business cycle / boom-bust cycle: The regular pattern in market economies where a "boom" period—characterized by low unemployment and prosperity—is followed by a "bust" or recession period—characterized by high unemployment and business failures.

Countercyclical policies: Standard government and Federal Reserve policies that are supposed to counteract the movements of the free market. For example, Keynesian economists would justify government deficits during a recession as a way to stimulate total spending and to boost employment.

Macroeconomics: The subdivision of economics that focuses on economy-wide issues such as price inflation and the business cycle.

Capital consumption: Achieving a higher standard of living (temporarily) by failing to invest enough in the maintenance of capital goods. "Eating the seedcorn," metaphorically speaking.

STUDY QUESTIONS

1. Why is the business cycle sometimes called the *boom-bust cycle?*

2. Explain: "[I]n a sustainable, market-driven expansion—where the interest rate falls because people are consuming less and saving more—the extra resources flowing into the new investment projects are coming from the sectors which are seeing a drop in sales."

3. *Do central banks typically lower interest rates by imposing a price ceiling (analogous to rent control)?

4. *How does capital consumption give the illusion that an economy can have its cake and eat it too?

5. How does an unsustainable boom lead to mass unemployment?

Glossary

Absolute advantage: Occurs when a person can produce more units per hour in a particular task, compared to someone else. (Lesson 8)

Anarchists: People who think there should be no government. (Lesson 15)

Arbitrage opportunity: The ability to earn a "sure profit" when the same good sells at different prices at the same time. (Lesson 7)

Austrian economics: A school of thought (inspired by Carl Menger and others who happened to be Austrian) that blames recessions on government interference with the economy, and recommends tax and spending cuts to help the economy during a recession. (Lesson 2)

Axioms: The starting assumptions or foundations in a deductive system. For example, the method of constructing a straight line between two points could be an axiom in a geometry textbook. Axioms are not proved, but are assumed to be true in order to prove other, less obvious, statements. (Lesson 2)

Bank: A common credit intermediary, which takes deposits from many different lenders and makes loans to many different borrowers. (Lesson 12)

Bankrupt: The situation that occurs when a business has liabilities greater than its assets. (Lesson 14)

Barter: A situation where people exchange goods and services directly, rather than using money in an intermediary transaction. (Lesson 1)

Beggar-thy-neighbor policies: Policies (usually involving currencies and trade restrictions) that make other countries poorer, in the attempt to make one's own country richer. (Lesson 19)

Benefits: The subjective enjoyments flowing from a course of action. (Lesson 4)

Black market: The system of illegal transactions that violate government regulations. (Lesson 18)

Bond: A corporation's IOU, which is a legally binding promise to repay borrowed money plus interest. The buyer of a bond gives money to the corporation today, in the hopes of receiving back the principal plus interest in the future. (Lesson 12)

Borrowing / dissaving: The amount by which consumption spending is greater than income. (Lesson 10)

Budget deficits: The excess of government spending over tax receipts. The deficit is the amount the government must borrow to pay its bills in a given period. (Lessons 2, 18)

Business cycle / boom-bust cycle: The regular pattern in market economies where a "boom" period—characterized by low unemployment and prosperity—is followed by a "bust" or recession period—characterized by high unemployment and business failures. (Lesson 23)

Callable bonds: Bonds that the issuer (borrower) has the right to pay off ahead of schedule. (Lesson 14)

Calculation problem: The objection Ludwig von Mises raised against socialism, which points out that because socialist planners lack market prices for resources, they can't determine if a particular project uses up more resources than it produces in goods and services. Even if the planners were angels, they would have no idea whether they were using scarce resources in an efficient way to best serve the citizens. (Lesson 15)

Capital consumption: Achieving a higher standard of living (temporarily) by failing to invest enough in the maintenance of capital goods. "Eating the seedcorn," metaphorically speaking. (Lesson 23)

Capital goods: Producer goods that are produced by human beings; they are not direct gifts from nature. (Lesson 4)

Capitalism: A economic system relying on private property and free enterprise. No single person or group controls the system as a whole. (Lesson 5)

Capitalists: The people in a capitalist society who control (large amounts of) financial wealth. The very wealthy capitalists exercise a large degree of control over businesses. (Lesson 5)

Collateral: An asset that a borrower "puts up" when applying for a loan. If the borrower defaults, the lender may take possession of the collateral as compensation. (For example, if a borrower wants money to buy a house or a car, these items themselves can serve as the collateral, meaning that if the borrower fails to make his or her payments on schedule, the lender can take control of the house or car.) (Lesson 12)

Command economy / command-and-control economy / socialism: An institutional arrangement in which the government owns all the major resources, and directs labor, according to a unified central plan. (Lesson 15)

Communism: An economic and political ideology that seeks to gain government ownership of the means of production (in the name of the workers) through violent revolution. (Lesson 16)

Comparative advantage: Occurs when a person has the relative superiority in a particular task, when taking all other tasks into account. (Jim can have a comparative advantage in a certain task, even if Mary has the absolute advantage, because Mary might have an absolute advantage that's even *greater* in something else.) (Lesson 8)

Competition: The rivalry that exists between entrepreneurs who have the option of hiring the same workers and buying the same resources, in order to produce goods and services to be sold to the same customers. (Lesson 9)

Complements: Goods (or services) that consumers use together. For example, hot dogs and mustard might be complements if someone goes to the store in preparation for a cookout. A change in the price of one good tends to cause a change in the opposite direction in the demand for a complement. (A reduction in the price of hot dogs will probably cause an increase in the demand for mustard.) (Lesson 11)

Consumer goods and services: Scarce physical items or services that directly satisfy a person's preferences. (Lesson 4)

Consumer Price Index (CPI): The Bureau of Labor Statistics' gauge of the "price level" affecting regular households. The CPI is an average (weighted by their relative importance) of the prices of gasoline, food, and other common items. (Lesson 21)

Corporate stock: Partial ownership claims to a corporation. If there are 100,000 total shares of stock in a corporation, someone who buys 5,000 shares owns 5% of the corporation itself. (Lesson 14)

Corruption: In the context of the drug trade, the failure of police and other government officials to execute their duties, either because they are accepting bribes from drug dealers or because they themselves are trafficking in prohibited substances. In some cases police officers have simply robbed drug dealers (of cash) at gunpoint, knowing that they had no recourse. (Lesson 20)

Countercyclical policies: Standard government and Federal Reserve policies that are supposed to counteract the movements of the free market. For example, Keynesian economists would justify government deficits during a recession as a way to stimulate total spending and to boost employment. (Lesson 23)

Credit card: A device that allows the borrower to achieve virtually instant loans from the credit card company when making purchases. (Lesson 12)

Credit history: A person's record of borrowing and repayment behavior. (Lesson 12)

Credit limit: The maximum amount of money that a person can borrow from a pre-approved source (such as a credit card). (Lesson 12)

Credit intermediary: A person or organization that is the "middleman" between lenders and borrowers. (Lesson 12)

Credit risk: The likelihood that a borrower will be unable to pay back a loan. (Lesson 12)

Credit score: A number that an agency will assign to a person based on his or her credit history, which helps potential lenders decide on the riskiness of lending money to the person. (Lesson 12)

Crowding out: The reduction in private-sector investment that results from government deficit spending. The government's borrowing increases the demand for loanable funds, which makes the equilibrium interest rate higher than it otherwise would be. At the higher interest rate, private-sector businesses borrow less to fund investment spending. (Lesson 22)

Credit Transaction: An exchange where one person gives up something (such as money) today, while the other person promises to give up something (such as money) in the future. (Lesson 12)

Debasement: Government policies that weaken the money. When coins were valued because of their precious metal content, debasement meant melting the coins and re-minting them with baser (less valuable) metals added to the mixture. Under fiat money, debasement involves the rapid creation of new money, which reduces the value of a single unit of money. (Lesson 21)

Default: A situation when a borrower stops making repayments on a loan. (Lesson 12)

Delinquencies: Cases where borrowers are not in good standing with the lender (such as a bank), because they have not been keeping up with their required payments. (Lesson 12)

Demand: The relationship between the price of a good (or service), and the number of units that consumers want to purchase at each hypothetical price. (Lesson 11)

Demand curve: A graphical illustration of the demand relationship, with price placed on the vertical axis and quantity on the horizontal axis. Sometimes a generic demand curve is drawn as a smooth, curved line or even as a simple straight line. Demand curves are "downward sloping," meaning that they start in the upper left and move down and to the right. (Lesson 11)

Demand schedule: A table that illustrates the demand relationship either for an individual or a group. (Lesson 11)

Depositors: People who give their money to a bank. (Lesson 12)

Depreciation: The wearing away or "using up" of capital goods during the course of production. (Lesson 4)

Direct exchange / barter: Trading that occurs when people swap goods that they directly value. (Lesson 6)

Discount: The percentage by which the value of a unit of money is reduced, because it will not be received until the future. (Lesson 12)

Disequilibrium: An unstable situation in which at least two people stand to benefit from an additional trade. (Lesson 6)

Disutility of labor: Economists' term to describe the fact that people prefer leisure to labor. People only engage in labor because of its indirect rewards. (Lesson 4)

Dividend: A disbursement of a portion of a corporation's net earnings to the stockholders. (Lesson 14)

Division of labor / specialization: The situation where each person works on one or a few tasks, and then trades to obtain the things produced by others. (Lesson 8)

Drug prohibition: Severe penalties that the government imposes on the consumption and especially the production and sale of certain drugs. (Lesson 20)

Economic democracy: An analogy to politics often used by (democratic) socialists to justify socialism. Most people would not like an aristocratic system in which a few elites made all the political decisions, but would instead prefer a democratic "one person, one vote" system. The socialists argue that their program simply applies this logic to the economic arena, taking power away from the small group of wealthy capitalists and showering it on the masses. (Lesson 15)

Economic problem: How to allocate society's scarce resources (including labor) in order to produce the combination of goods and services that best satisfies people's preferences. (Lesson 13)

Economies of scale: A condition in which output will increase more than proportionally as inputs are increased. For example, there are economies of scale if doubling the amount of inputs leads to a tripling in output. (Lesson 8)

Economize: The act of treating a resource with care because it is scarce and can only satisfy a limited number of goals or preferences. (Lesson 4)

Entrepreneur: The person in a market economy who hires workers and buys resources in order to produce goods and services. (Lesson 9)

Equilibrium: A stable situation after all disturbances or changes have worked themselves out. (Lesson 4)

Equilibrium position: A stable situation in which there are no further gains from trade. (Lesson 6)

Equilibrium price / market-clearing price: The price at which producers want to sell exactly the number of units that consumers want to purchase. On a graph, the equilibrium price occurs at the intersection of the supply and demand curves. (Lesson 11)

Equilibrium quantity: The number of units that producers want to sell, and consumers want to buy, at the equilibrium price. On a graph, the equilibrium quantity occurs at the intersection of the supply and demand curves. (Lesson 11)

Exchange rate: The "price" of one currency in terms of another, or how many units of one currency will trade for one unit of another currency. (Lesson 12)

Expectations: An individual's forecasts of the future, which involve his or her understanding of "how the world works" and therefore guide current actions. (Lesson 4)

Expenses: The amount of money an entrepreneur spends on labor, raw materials, and other inputs during a period of time. (Lesson 9)

Exports: Goods (and services) that the people of a country sell to foreigners. (Lesson 19)

Face value of a bond: The amount of money the bond issuer promises to pay to the holder of the bond at the maturity date. (Lesson 22)

Fascism: An economic and political ideology that also seeks extensive government regulation of all resources in the service of the collective good, though fascism (unlike communism) allows private individuals to officially retain ownership of the factories and other capital goods. (Lesson 16)

Federal Reserve: The central bank of the United States, founded in 1913. The "Fed" is responsible for U.S. monetary policy, and has the dual mandate of providing stable economic growth (which implies full employment) and low price inflation. (Lesson 21)

Fiat money: Paper money that is not "backed" by anything. The only reason people accept fiat money in trade, is that they expect it to have purchasing power in the future. (Lesson 21)

Fixed costs: Monetary expenses that do not increase when a business expands output. For example, a barber shop's monthly water bill will be roughly the same whether it provides 1 haircut or 100 haircuts per day, and so this is a fixed cost. (Lesson 20)

Flow variable: A concept that is measured over a period of time. For example, the flow rate of an irrigation pipe could be 100 gallons *per minute*. This measurement wouldn't refer to the total amount of gallons contained in the entire pipe, but instead would refer to how many gallons passed through a particular section of the pipe every 60 seconds. (Lesson 22)

Fractional Reserve Banking: The typical practice where banks do not keep all of their customers' deposits in the vault. In other words, all of the bank's customers have more money on deposit, than the bank has cash in the vault. (Lesson 12)

Free enterprise: A system in which individuals can choose their own occupations and are free to start whatever business they wish. They don't need special permission from anyone to enter an industry. (Lesson 5)

Free trade: An environment in which governments do not impose artificial restrictions on the flow of goods and services between their citizens and foreigners. (Lesson 19)

Gains from trade: A situation in which two people can both gain (subjective) benefits from swapping their property with each other. (Lesson 6)

Going public: Allowing the general public to buy shares of stock in a corporation, as opposed to restricting ownership to those specifically invited by the owners. (Lesson 14)

Goods: Scarce physical items that an individual values because they can help to satisfy his preferences. (Lesson 3)

Graduated income tax: An income tax that applies higher rates to higher levels of income. (Lesson 18)

Gross profit / accounting profit: The excess of revenues over out-of-pocket expenses. This is what newspapers mean when they report on a corporation's "profits" for a given time period. (Lesson 13)

Guilds: The organization of occupations in the medieval period, before the capitalist era. A person who wanted to become a blacksmith or a carpenter would first need to be accepted by other members of the guild. (Lesson 5)

Hazard pay: The higher earnings necessary to attract workers into an industry that is more dangerous than others. (Lesson 20)

Hyperinflation: Very severe inflation. There is no precise boundary between inflation and hyperinflation, but in a hyperinflation people begin buying anything at all in order to unload their money holdings which are losing value by the hour. (Lesson 21)

Import quota: A maximum limit on the amount of a particular good that can be imported during a certain time period. (Lesson 19)

Imports: Goods (and services) that the people of a country buy from foreigners. (Lesson 19)

Income: The flow of consumer goods and services that a person has the potential to enjoy during a specific period of time. (Lesson 4)

Income / earnings (business): Revenues minus expenses. (Lesson 10)

Income (individual): The amount of money that can be spent on consumption goods in a certain period, from the sale of labor and the earnings of other assets (such as stocks). (Lesson 10)

Income tax: A tax that applies to the earnings of an individual or a corporation. Income taxes are usually applied as percentages of the pre-tax dollar income. (Lesson 18)

Income Tax Brackets: The thresholds of income that are taxed at various rates. For example, the lowest tax bracket might include incomes ranging from $0 to $10,000, which is taxed at 3%, while the next bracket might include incomes ranging from $10,001 to $20,000, which is taxed at 5%. (Lesson 18)

Incorporation: Transforming a business into a corporation, so that its ownership is allotted by shares of stock. (Lesson 14)

Indirect exchange: Trading that occurs when at least one of the parties accepts an item that he or she does not intend to use personally, but instead will trade it away in the future to get something else. (Lesson 6)

Inflation: A term that originally referred to the creation of new money, but nowadays often means an increase in prices. (Lessons 18, 21)

Initial public offering (IPO): The auction of shares to the general public when a corporation first decides to go public. (Lesson 14)

Institutions: Social relationships and practices that allow people to interact with each other. Institutions provide a framework of predictability in society. (Lesson 5)

Interest: The income earned during a period of time from lending savings to others. Interest is usually quoted as a percentage of the principal (the amount of money originally lent) earned per year. For example, if someone lends $1,000 today and is paid back $1,050 twelve months later, then the principal is $1,000, the interest earned is $50, and the interest rate is 5%. (Lesson 10)

Interest rate risk: The risk bondholders face because rising interest rates will reduce the market value of their bonds. (Lesson 14)

Interventionism: The philosophy of the mixed economy, in which the government heavily intervenes in the capitalist system to regulate how individuals can use their private property. (Lesson 17)

Investment: Diverting resources or savings into projects that are expected to increase future income. (Lessons 4, 10)

Issuing debt: Raising funds by selling bonds to lenders. (Lesson 14)

Issuing stock / issuing equity: Raising funds by selling stock shares to investors. (Lesson 14)

Keynesian economics: A school of thought (inspired by John Maynard Keynes) that prescribes government budget deficits as a way to lift the economy out of recession and restore full employment. (Lesson 2)

Labor: The contribution to production flowing from a person's body. (Lesson 4)

Land / natural resources: Factors of production that are gifts of nature. (Lesson 4)

Law of Demand: If other influences stay the same, then a lower price will lead consumers to buy more units of a good (or service), while a higher price will lead them to buy fewer units. (Lesson 11)

Law of Supply: If other influences stay the same, then a higher price will lead producers to sell more units of a good (or service), while a lower price will lead producers to sell fewer units. (Lesson 11)

Leisure: A special type of consumer good that results from using one's body (and time) to directly satisfy preferences, as opposed to engaging in labor. (Lesson 4)

Leverage: Enhancing the potential returns from an investment by using borrowed money. (Lesson 14)

Loan sharking: The practice of lending money at high interest rates and using illegal methods to obtain repayment. (Lesson 20)

Loanable funds market: The market in which lenders give money to borrowers at an agreed-upon interest rate. (Lesson 12)

Logical deduction: A form of reasoning that starts from one or more axioms and moves step-by-step to reach a conclusion. (Lesson 2)

M1: A popular measure of the total amount of money in an economy. M1 includes the actual currency held by the public (in their wallets, purses, and cashiers' drawers) but also the total amount of checking account balances. (Because of the fractional reserve banking system, M1 is larger than the number of dollars printed on green pieces of paper. If everyone tried to withdraw his or her checking account from the banks at the same time, there wouldn't be enough currency to go around. This is why M1 indicates more total money than just the amount of paper currency.) (Lesson 21)

Macroeconomics: The subdivision of economics that focuses on economy-wide issues such as price inflation and the business cycle. (Lesson 23)

Marginal productivity: The increased revenues that result from hiring an extra worker. (Lesson 9)

Marginal utility: A technical economics term referring to the subjective enjoyments of one additional unit of a good or service. (Lesson 4)

Market economy: Can be a synonym for *capitalism*. It also refers to the collection of voluntary exchanges that occur in a capitalist system. (Lesson 5)

Maturity: The time duration of a specific loan, and the interest rate that applies to it. (Loans and their corresponding bonds can have shorter or longer maturities.) (Lesson 12)

Medium of exchange: An object that is accepted in a trade, not because the person receiving it wants to directly use it, but because he or she wants to trade it away in the future to acquire something else. Every indirect exchange requires a medium of exchange, which is the good through which the ultimate trade occurs. (Likewise, sound waves require a *medium* to travel through, in order to reach your ears. When it comes to sound waves, the medium will usually be the air, but it can also be water if you are in a pool with your head below the surface.) (Lesson 7)

Mercantilism: The economic doctrine that views the accumulation of wealth as the path to national prosperity. It encourages exports and discourages imports. (Lesson 19)

Minimum wage: A price floor on payments to workers. (Lesson 17)

Mixed economy: A system that allows private citizens to legally own resources, but in which government officials lay down rules that limit the choices the legal owners can make with their property. (Lesson 5)

Monetary inflation: An expansion in the total amount of money in the economy. (Lesson 21)

Monetary profit: The amount by which revenues are greater than expenses. (Lesson 9)

Monetary loss: The amount by which expenses are greater than revenues. (Lesson 9)

Money: A good that is accepted by everyone in the economy on one side of every trade. In economics jargon, it is a widely (or universally) accepted medium of exchange. (Lessons 6, 7)

Mortgage: A special type of loan in which the borrower buys a house (or other real estate) with the funds. Usually the property serves as collateral for the mortgage. (Lesson 12)

National debt / public debt: Usually refers to the total outstanding value of bonds issued by the U.S. Treasury. As of May 2010, the "public debt" was almost $13 trillion, but much of this consists of Treasury bonds held by other government agencies (such as the Social Security Administration's "trust fund"). When economists compare the levels of debt owed by various governments, they usually net out the "intragovernmental holdings" and report only the government debt *held by the public.* As of May 2010, this figure for the U.S. Treasury was almost $8.5 trillion. (See http://www.treasurydirect.gov/govt/reports/pd/mspd/2010/opds052010.pdf.) (Lesson 22)

Net profit / economic profit: The portion of gross profits over and above the normal interest return on the invested capital. (Lesson 13)

(Opportunity) cost: The benefits of the *next-best alternative* to a given action. (Lesson 4)

Owner: The person who has legal authority to decide how a particular unit of a resource or good shall be used. The owner can usually transfer ownership to another person. (Lesson 5)

Paternalism: Overriding the desires of someone else because he or she is not considered competent to make the right decision. (Lesson 18)

Preferences: An individual's goals or desires. Economists interpret a person's actions as attempts to satisfy his or her preferences. (Lesson 3)

Price: The terms of a trade, meaning how many units of one item are given up to acquire a unit of a different item. (Lesson 6)

Price ceiling: A type of price control on a particular good or service that sets a maximum level on the amount a buyer can pay a seller. (Lesson 17)

Price controls: Policies that punish people who exchange goods and services at prices different from the acceptable range prescribed by the government. (Lesson 17)

Price floor: A type of price control on a particular good or service that sets a minimum level that a buyer must pay a seller. (Lesson 17)

Price inflation: A general increase in the prices of goods and services, quoted in units money. Price inflation is the same thing as a fall in the purchasing power of money. (Lesson 21)

Price supports: Government policies that maintain a desired minimum price *not* by threatening buyers who pay too little, but instead by having the government directly buy the good or service whenever its market price would otherwise fall below the floor. (The effects of price supports are different from the effects of price floors.) (Lesson 17)

Private property: A system in which resources are owned by people outside of the government. (Lesson 5)

Private sector: The portion of an economy that is controlled by people outside of the government. (For example, a grocery store is in the private sector.) (Lesson 5)

Producer goods / factors of production / means of production: Scarce physical items or services that *indirectly* satisfy preferences, because they can be used to produce consumer goods and services. (Lesson 4)

Productive debt: Debt used to finance investments. Ideally, the extra income from the investment spending will allow the borrower to make the interest payments resulting from the increase in debt, so that the extra borrowing "pays for itself." (Lesson 12)

Productivity: The amount of output produced by a factor of production in a period of time, often used in reference to labor. (Lesson 4)

Productivity of labor: The amount of output a worker can produce in a certain period of time. (Lesson 8)

Progressive income taxation: A system that taxes individuals or corporations at higher rates based on the level of income. (Lesson 3)

Protectionism: The philosophy that uses government trade restrictions in an attempt to help workers within the home country. The rationale is that by restricting foreign imports, the government will encourage consumers to "buy local," providing employment for local workers. (Lesson 19)

Public sector: The portion of an economy that is controlled by the government. (For example, the local police station is in the public sector.) (Lesson 5)

Purposeful action: An activity undertaken for a conscious reason; behavior that has a goal. (Lesson 2)

Raise capital: The process of obtaining funds for a growing business by selling partial ownership of the business to outside investors. (Lesson 14)

Reduction in demand / leftward shift in the demand curve: A situation in which a change *besides* the price of a good (or service) causes consumers to reduce the number of units they want to purchase, at various possible prices. On a graph, this change causes the demand curve itself to move to the left. (Lesson 11)

Reduction in supply / leftward shift in the supply curve: A situation in which a change *besides* the price of a good (or service) causes producers to reduce the number of units they want to sell, at various possible prices. On a graph, this change causes the supply curve itself to move to the left. (In a similar way, an *increase* in supply or a *rightward* shift in the supply curve, occurs when a change causes producers to *increase* the number of units they want to sell, at various possible prices.) (Lesson 11)

Refinancing (a mortgage): The situation that occurs when a homeowner gets a new mortgage from the bank (perhaps at a lower interest rate or with lower monthly payments) and uses it to pay off the current mortgage. (Lesson 14)

Rent control: A price ceiling placed on apartment rents. (Lesson 17)

Residual claimants: Refers to stockholders, who are entitled to the earnings of a corporation only after the other creditors have first been paid. (Lesson 14)

Revenues: The amount of money customers spend on an entrepreneur's output during a period of time. (Lesson 9)

Rolling over debt: Paying off an old set of bondholders by issuing new bonds. (Lesson 14)

Sales tax: A tax that applies to goods and services as they are sold to the customer. Sales taxes are usually applied as percentages of the pre-tax dollar amount. (Lesson 18)

Saving: Consuming less than one's income would allow; living below one's means. (Lesson 4)

Savings: The amount by which income is greater than spending on consumption. (Lesson 10)

Scarcity: The condition of desires exceeding the available resources to satisfy them. Scarcity is a universal fact requiring people to make exchanges. (Lesson 1)

Service: A person's performance of a task that another person values because it helps to satisfy preferences. Services are the "goods" that people create through their labor power. (Lesson 3)

Secured loan: A loan that has an asset (such as a house, car, etc.) pledged as collateral, in case the borrower defaults. The advantage to the borrower is that the interest rate is lower than it would be for a comparable unsecured loan. (Lesson 12)

Shirking: Deliberately working less than one's potential. (Lesson 15)

Short sale: A transaction in which a person borrows an asset (such as a share of stock) from an existing owner, in order to sell it at the current price. The person eventually must buy back the asset to return it to the original owner. (Lesson 14)

Shortage: A situation where consumers want to buy more units than producers want to sell. This occurs when the actual price is below the market-clearing price. (Lesson 11)

Sin taxes: High sales taxes on goods such as cigarettes and liquor that are imposed not merely to raise revenue, but also to encourage people to reduce their purchases of these dubious items. (Lesson 20)

Slavery: A system in which some human beings are considered the legal property of others. (Lesson 5)

Slumlord: The unflattering term applied to a landlord who doesn't maintain the quality of the apartments and who is generally unscrupulous. (Lesson 17)

Socialism: An economic system in which government officials decide how society's resources shall be used to produce particular goods and services. (Lesson 5)

Sole proprietorship: A business owned by a single person. (Lesson 14)

Speculator: A person who buys an asset (such as a corporate stock) thinking its price will rise, or who sells an asset thinking its price will fall. (Lesson 14)

Spontaneous order: A predictable pattern that is not planned by any one person. Examples would include the rules of grammar in the English language, the style of clothing that characterized the 1970s disco clubs, and the use of money. (Lesson 7)

Spread: The difference between the interest rate that a credit intermediary (such as a bank) earns from its borrowers, compared to the interest rate it pays to its lenders or depositors. A positive spread allows the credit intermediary to earn income from its activities, so long as it has correctly estimated the likelihood of default by its borrowers. (Lesson 12)

Stock brokerages: Companies that help individuals buy and sell stocks. The broker will act on behalf of the client and execute his or her orders to buy and sell shares. (Lesson 14)

Stock exchanges: Particular locations or venues where stocks are traded. The most famous example is the New York Stock Exchange, located on Wall Street. (Lesson 14)

Stock of money: The total amount of money in the economy at a particular time. (Lesson 21)

Stock market: A special type of market in which buyers and sellers exchange shares of corporate stock. (Lesson 14)

Stock variable: A concept that is measured at a specific point in time. For example, a man's weight at 9 a.m. on May 11, 2010 could be 150 pounds. This measurement wouldn't refer to the number of pounds the man had recently gained or lost, but instead would refer to his weight at that very moment. (Lesson 22)

Subjective: Unique to each individual; "in the eye of the beholder." (Lesson 3)

Substitutes: Goods (or services) that consumers use for similar purposes. For example, Coke and Pepsi might be substitutes if someone goes to the store looking to buy soda. A change in the price of one good tends to cause a change in the same direction in the demand for a substitute. (A reduction in the price of Coke will probably cause a reduction in the demand for Pepsi.) (Lesson 11)

Supply: The relationship between the price of a good (or service), and the number of units that producers want to sell at each hypothetical price. (Lesson 11)

Supply curve: A graphical illustration of the supply relationship, with price placed on the vertical axis and quantity on the horizontal axis. Sometimes a generic supply curve is drawn as a smooth, curved line or even as a simple straight line. Supply curves are "upward sloping," meaning that they start in the bottom left and move up and to the right. (Lesson 11)

Supply schedule: A table illustrating the supply relationship, either for an individual or group of producers. (Lesson 11)

Surplus / glut: A situation where producers want to sell more units of a good (or service) than consumers want to purchase. This occurs when the actual price is higher than the market-clearing price. (Lesson 11)

Tariff (duty): A tax levied on foreign imports. (Lesson 19)

Tax Deduction: A provision in the tax code that allows a particular expense (such as medical expenses or the purchase price of a new solar panel) to be subtracted from an individual's taxable income. This means that tax-deductible items are paid for with "pre-tax dollars," which allows an individual to buy more with his income. (Lesson 18)

Taxable income: The amount of income actually subject to the official tax rates for each bracket. Taxable income is the original income after all deductions and other adjustments have been made. (Lesson 18)

Taxation: The process in which the government takes ownership of portions of income or other assets from private individuals. (Lesson 18)

Time preference: The degree to which people prefer to consume sooner rather than later; a gauge of people's impatience to receive enjoyments. (Lesson 12)

Trade deficit: The amount by which imports exceed imports, measured in money. (Lesson 19)

Trade surplus: The amount by which exports exceed imports, measured in money. (Lesson 19)

Tradeoffs: The unfortunate fact (caused by scarcity) that making one choice means that other choices become unavailable. (Lesson 1)

Unemployment: A surplus or glut on the labor market, meaning that some workers cannot find jobs even though they are willing to work for the same pay and can perform the jobs just as well as the people who are employed. (Lesson 17)

Unsecured loan: A loan that has no collateral serving as a backup. If the borrower defaults, the lender has no other options. The advantage to the borrower is that none of his or her other assets can be seized (or "repossessed") in the case of default. (Lesson 12)

Usury laws: Price ceilings on interest rates. (Lesson 20)

Utility: A term common in economics textbooks to describe how much value a person gets from a good or service. (Lesson 3)

Zero-sum game: A situation in which the gain of one person (or country) corresponds to an equal loss of another person (or country). In a zero-sum game, mutually advantageous, win-win outcomes are not possible. There are winners and losers. (Lesson 19)

Index